SOWETO TO BEIRUT

JEDIDIAH RAMALAPA

© Jedidiah Lindiwe Ramalapa

Although every precaution has been taken in the preparation of this book, the publisher, editors, and author assume no responsibility for errors or omissions. Neither is any liability assumed for damages resulting from the use of information contained herein.

Cover Design by Tshepo Selaelo Ramalapa
Printed by African Sun Media
Distributed by African Sun Media

No part of this book can be reproduced in any form, or by written, electronic or mechanical, including photocopying, recording, or by any information retrieval system without permission, in writing, from the author.

ISBN: 978-0-620-93181-6 (p/b)

ISBN: 978-0-620-93182-3 (Epub)

Contact Information:
jediramalapa.blog

To

My great-grandparents Mapopane Violet Mtshali and Nyangane Stephen Zulu; their children, grandchildren, and greatgrandchildren and you.

ACKNOWLEDGMENTS

This book was made possible with a generous grant from the Academic and Non-fiction writers of South Africa (ANFASA) through its ANFASA Grant Scheme for Authors (AGSA) program (2016) for the manuscript; *My Journey to Love; A suitcase full of Stories renamed Soweto To Beirut*. Thank you to my editors; Nalisha Adams, Nomsa Mwamuka and Frankie Kartoun for helping me make sense of my words. All errors with regard to facts, language, syntax, structure and tense are entirely my own. Thank you to Prof LB Landau, Dr Zsofia Borsanyi and Jenna Leigh Desfontein for early readings, insightful comments and suggestions. I am also very grateful, humbled and appreciative of the generosity, kindness, empathy and compassion poured over me by numerous friends, colleagues and well wishers inside and outside the world of journalism in South Africa, Senegal, Kenya and South Sudan; Thank you so much for supporting me with shelter, food, rest and friendship in the ten years spent writing this book. A special word of thanks to long time friend, Prof Noah Tamarkin, for never running away from my various states of brokenness. To my siblings; Victoria, Peace, Didi, Sibu and Immanuel you are my constellation. To Mama le Papa, Joy and Samuel Ramalapa, thank you. This book could not exist without you. Ke le rata kudu, kudu.

*NB: Most names in this book have been changed or omitted to protect individual privacy

Chapter 1
QUOVADIS: WHERE ARE YOU GOING?

It's not every day that a contestant in a beauty pageant declares war. But this is exactly what I did when I was an 18-year-old girl competing for the crown of *Miss Pinetown* in 1999. I was the only black person in the line-up that year, though it is worth noting that I was not the first nor the only person of colour to compete. In fact, the reigning *Miss Pinetown* at the time was black. Still, I was surprised to see my picture in our community newspaper, the *Highway Mail*, as one of the contestants selected to compete for the title. I was convinced the girl on the front page of the newspaper could not possibly be me - Jedi Ramalapa.

Yes, I was overwhelmed even though my mom and I had arranged for the photo-shoot, filled in the application form myself and had even gone to the post-office to mail it personally.

Although the prospect of competing with beautiful, thin women for the crown was daunting, I submitted my entry anyway because it was a promise that I had made to myself.

I grew up glued to beauty pageants, particularly *Miss Teen SA* and *Miss South Africa*, which were a big deal in my teenage years. I spent minutes, hours and days gazing longingly into the pages of *Huisgenoot*, *Drum*, *Truelove* and *YOU* magazines wishing to one day become one of the lucky girls pictured in them. I wanted to be that girl: the winner.

I wanted to be in there so much that when I saw a call for contestants for the *Miss Pinetown Competition*, I did not hesitate to apply. I didn't think about my weight - which I obsessed about because I thought I was too fat. I didn't think about my hair, or where I would find the money to put braids in it. I didn't think about the costs. I only thought about wearing the crown on my head and flashing a winning smile for the cameras.

Imagine, I thought to myself, *I could be the next Jacqui Mofokeng - the first black South African to be crowned Miss South Africa in 1993; or Basetsana Kumalo née Makgalemele, the first black South African to compete in the Miss World Pageant in 1994 or, even better, I could follow in the footsteps of India's Aishwarya Rai, who took the crown of Miss Universe in that same year.*

Even though I dreamt of wearing a beautiful gown, holding a large bouquet of fresh-cut flowers in my hands, a glimmering white sash across my chest and a crown on my head declaring me queen for a year, pageantry was never the end game.

What was most desirable were the opportunities that came with the title - opportunities that I perceived to be unavailable to me at the time.

Take for example the prizes. The winners were offered gifts ranging from a fully furnished apartment, a year's supply of groceries, a clothing budget, a new car, and a career as an ambassador of goodwill for causes such as saving the children and campaigning for world peace.

Being an ambassador meant meeting important people in business, politics, and entertainment all over the world. These connections could open new and exciting doors for me. The possibilities were endless.

Beauty pageants were a shortcut to a life that would relieve my parents of the responsibility of taking care of me, at least for a year.

During my final year of high school, when I thought my chances of becoming a beauty queen had faded, I began to consider other options. One of them included joining the *South African Army*, for exactly the same reasons.

By working for the government, I would have access to free accommodation, opportunities to study further, a chance to get a driver's license and earn a small salary on top of it all. This meant that my parents could use the extra money they would have spent on me, on someone or something else instead.

It was a win-win solution, which my mother rejected outright when I suggested the idea to her.

She thought I was crazy, but I was serious.

She told me that going to war was a bad idea. She would never agree to it, even if she knew she could not stop me from joining the army if I made up my mind to do so.

As a countermeasure, she suggested we brainstorm careers that would be less dangerous and yet still suit my personality. We ended up with Journalism. Because I was inquisitive, and always asked people questions, most of which were decidedly inappropriate and often very intrusive, becoming a journalist then gave me the license to ask as many questions as I wished without embarrassing my parents.

Even though I had accepted that Journalism would be my future career from then on, I still had a lingering desire to wear the crown to fulfil a promise to myself.

Joining the pageant was an attempt to manifest a dream I had cherished for a long time. If I succeeded, there would be no blood and gore for me after all, just glitz and glamour.

Once selected, I didn't know how gruelling my schedule would be. By then, I was already enrolled as a first year Journalism student at *Natal Technikon - now The Durban University of Technology* - while also volunteering at a local Christian radio station, *Highway Radio*. At church, I was a member of the worship team and a volunteer Sunday School Assistant Teacher. Then I had to fit in rehearsals, fittings, facials, meetings, and public promotional appearances for the competition.

With this schedule, I hardly had time to watch the news, let alone read the national newspapers - which I could not afford to buy anyway.

As the day of the competition drew nearer, one of the more affluent of our fellow contestants invited us for a cocktail party at her home in *Kloof*, a leafy upper-class suburb in the greater Durban area of KwaZulu-Natal.

I had never been to a cocktail party before, so I had no idea what people do when they are having cocktails.

Once inside the house, I was impressed by its opulence. Everything was large and looked brand new. It resembled a scene from the 90s popular film *Father of The Bride* - when the parents of the bride-to-be pay a visit to their future in-laws for the first time in their exclusive neighbourhood of Beverly Hills.

My parent's house could fit easily into the reception area. I would be lying if I said I was not cowered by it all; it would be an even bigger lie if I said that I was not envious of their good fortune.

Questions began to circle my mind. Why didn't I come from a rich family? Why had my parents not succeeded to such a level in their lives? How does it feel to be this rich? How did they make their money? How much would I have to earn to live in a place like this and call it mine? More importantly, what would I have to do to earn so much money? What was their secret to wealth?

These thoughts occupied my mind as I walked around the house feeling slightly out of place, but also curious about everything. We were all introduced to the other guests who seemed very interested in each of us. The experience was both flattering and intimidating since we were our hostess's competition after all. As people continued to mingle making small talk here and there, someone in the room drifted towards me with a list of questions about my future career goals.

"What do you do?" he asked.

"I'm studying Journalism," I replied.

"Oh!" he cooed with interest. Other people came closer.

"So, what kind of journalist do you want to be?" he continued.

"I want to be a war correspondent." I replied without thinking.

"Really? Where do you want to go?"

Where do I want to go? This question made me freeze because I had never thought about war, much less which war I would like to cover in the future, until that precise moment. In fact, I wasn't even sure it worked like that. Do people get to choose which war they want to go to? Was war supposed to be like a holiday destination? Was there a brochure of popular destinations for war coverage? It seemed odd that I should have an answer for something as unpredictable as war.

"I don't know," I replied flatly.

"Oh!" someone exclaimed with surprise. "You don't know where you want to go to be a war correspondent?"

I realised the trap I had put myself into. But I couldn't think of a single place that was at war at the time.

"Somewhere in the Middle East?" I offered a half-hearted response. I was avoiding the nerves that were pricking my pores open and making my internal organs churn.

"Yes, but where in the Middle East?" they persisted.

Where in the Middle East? "I, I, I..." My mouth ran dry. I had miraculously managed to reach a blank white spot in my hippocampus.

"Oh, you mean Beirut?" someone offered.

Did I say something? I wondered to myself. *I don't remember anything coming out of my mouth.* My cheeks were engulfed in flames of embarrassment and the ground couldn't open fast enough for me to disappear into. I hesitated. I didn't know where Beirut was on the map; I didn't even know whether it was a town or country. It may as well have been somewhere in Timbuktu, which was definitely not in the Middle East. What I did know for sure though, was that the name Beirut was synonymous with war.

"Beirut; that's where I'll go to be a war correspondent," I answered.

Silence enveloped us for a few seconds, only to be broken by soft laughter.

You want to be a war correspondent, but you don't know where war is? What kind of a journalist are you? I imagined them thinking as they promptly turned to each other in conversation. With that, I was dismissed and left alone to survey the damage, with the help of a cocktail in my hand. I had the feeling that it was now a sure thing that I had lost the competition. I had failed to impress. That had been a poor performance indeed, even if I said so myself.

The truth was I never truly wanted to be a war correspondent. I mean I did, but I also didn't. My main preoccupation in life at the time, was to find the fastest way to become financially independent. As to the precise cause of war in the world, I already had an answer for that and it was definitive.

There was no doubt in my mind that all wars in the world were caused by one person, and one person only - the Devil. He was evil; he only came to steal, kill, and destroy and the only way to defeat him was to pray and read the Bible. The question of how to become financially independent on the other hand was tricky. I had no easy answers for that since I never had any money in my pockets to begin with. I was never paid for the work I did for my parents, for the radio station or for the church. I was working hard but I had no income. The money I had was enough to get me to school and back for the month. I never had a penny more than what was absolutely essential. In light of this, where had the idea of becoming a war correspondent come from?

Growing up, my siblings and I did not have carte blanche access to television. Our parents believed that television was generally not good for children, which meant that all the programmes we watched had to be pre-approved by them. However, there was a window period when I was between the ages of 16 and 17 when my parents became more lenient with television viewing.

During that time, we were allowed to watch *Oprah* with my mother in the afternoons when we got back from school if we wanted to, and we could also watch The News. That's when I started to watch *CNN International*, particularly the early morning financial-market reports with business anchor Maggie Lake. She delivered *Market News* as if it contained treasured stories handed down to her by her beloved grandmother and she wanted everyone to not only know about them, but to *understand* them. Of course, she would have been reading from a teleprompter, but I hadn't been aware of this at the time. As far as I was concerned, all this financial information was coming straight out of her head. She was fluent and flawless in her speech. She made speaking to the camera in a cogent, logical sequence seem like her birthright. At times, when I watched her, she ceased to be a human being; she became more like a machine that could process information faster than Bloomberg's black box used for high-frequency trading. She never faltered nor flinched. She made delivering the business economics of financial markets seem as easy as giving the weather report, even though I was still clueless about the NASDAQ and FTSE 100. In all honesty, she suited my character better than the darker, harder, masculine image of Christiane Amanpour, who was famous for her reports on the Persian Gulf and Bosnian Wars in the early 90s. Amanpour was one of a few women I knew of who reported from conflict areas and war zones at the time. I was moved by her deep mellifluous voice. She was bold, direct, and eloquent. She didn't hesitate to share her opinion about matters of life and death. She was compelling and delivered her reports about life in far-flung lands with authority.

I may have only seen her a few times, but she left a lasting impression on me. Not only was she adept at covering war, but she was surviving it and winning awards for her efforts too. Therefore, the idea of going to war, writing about it, and coming out unscathed as Christiane Amanpour had done, had been planted in my subconscious mind.

I reasoned that if I wanted to be a great journalist in the future, Christiane Amanpour would be the best person to emulate. When I found myself under the spotlight, forced to explain the rest of my life plans, all I could see in my mind's eye was the picture of Christiane Amanpour in a flak jacket, somewhere in the Middle East.

I told them I wanted to be a war-correspondent because I thought this would be more impressive than telling them that I was pursuing a career in Business Journalism. There were hierarchies in journalism, and war and conflict reporting were at the top of the food chain. This was the stuff that won major awards, including the much-coveted 'Oscar in journalism' - the *Pulitzer Prize*. I let my ego do the talking because I felt small and insignificant compared to the other contestants who seemed more certain of themselves than I was.

Ultimately, I had signed up to be a journalist regardless of what type of journalism I would end up practising. I should have known where conflict was taking place in the world. I should have known where Beirut was on the map. The competition was not even over and I had already hit rock bottom. In my mind's eye, I had lost all credibility. Who would take me seriously now? Who would listen to me? How could I even hope to represent South Africa in the world?

This is when I declared war.

I promised myself, while standing in a pool of shame, that I would be a war correspondent one day. I was going to be a war correspondent in Beirut no less, even though I could not objectively guarantee that a war would be underway in Beirut for me to report on by the time I completed my studies and got a good enough job that would send me there on assignment. Nonetheless, it was in this moment, at this girl's lavish home, where I made a decision that would change my life in unexpected ways.

So that seven years later, I find myself in a car with three young Lebanese activists - two boys from the *Beirut-American University* and one girl who is visiting family for the holidays from France. We are driving from Central Beirut to the south of Lebanon to deliver humanitarian aid to victims of the war between Hezbollah and Israel.

We are in a convoy of about 47 cars driving from Beirut to Nabatieh, 80 kilometres south of the capital. *The Campaign of Resistance* has organised the convoy to express anger at Israel's forced blockage of South Lebanon. I am here on assignment to report on the war for the *South African Broadcasting Corporation* - SABC Radio News Division.

The convoy carries supplies, including 200 boxes of medication for chronic diseases, 300 loaves of bread, 3,000 incontinence diapers for the elderly, 200 boxes of canned raw food and hygiene bags containing shampoo, toothpaste, and soap. By then, the south of Lebanon had been completely cut off from the rest of the country, resulting in a lack of essential supplies such as medicine and fuel for an estimated 120 thousand people who had not fled bombardment by the *Israeli Defence Forces*.

Inside the car, I ask the students a few questions about the war; what they think of it? If they support any particular side? And why? I want to know if they understand the root of the problem, or if they have any solutions.

I also ask why they've chosen to take part in this civilian convoy to the south. Are they not afraid of dying? Of being hit by aerial bombs? I am not sure what I am going to do with the tape, but I record everything.

I want to tell a different story about the war, compared to the monotonous one I've been reporting on up until this point.

But I am not satisfied with the student's answers. I feel as if I'm missing something - as if there is a fundamental principle about life that I'm simply not understanding. The students tell me that they are tired of the fighting. They take turns sharing stories of growing up as refugees, hiding in bunkers or listening to stories of war told around the dinner table. They tell me stories of how their grandparents endured, how their great-grandparents remained resilient and refused to cower under a series of oppressive regimes. And now, they continue, war is no longer a fairy-tale of a bygone era; it has caught up with them. It is happening in their lifetime and they cannot tolerate it.

They tell me their deepest desire - they want peace. They are willing to die for it. They insist that they are not partisan; they are simply patriots who care about their country. They don't want it destroyed, again, they conclude.

To prove this point, one of the students, who is sitting in the back seat of the car, makes an indentation on his left wrist with a razor. Droplets of thick crimson blood boil out of his skin, which stretches like melted cheddar under the pressure of the blade. The other student, a girl who is sitting next to him, swears at him in French. "*Merde!*" she exclaims. "You are stupid! You know that?" ironically echoing my thoughts at that very moment.

"Yes, I know," says the student. His shoulders are wrapped in the red, white, and green Lebanese flag. "But it's because I care; it's because I care too much about my country, you know?" He continues. "It's not fair what is happening. It's not fair," he says emphatically, while covering the fresh wound with a white section of the flag to stop the bleeding.

From the sound of his voice, I sense that he is fighting back tears. But I can't decide if he is crying because he is truly upset about the war, or if he is crying because the cut hurts. Either way, I tell myself that it does not matter.

We are all on a suicidal mission anyway.

The *Israeli Defence Forces* had warned that any vehicle travelling south of the Litany River, 30 kilometres north of the border with Israel, would be a prime target for airstrikes.

Already 43 people had been killed in civilian and humanitarian convoys carrying supplies to the south. More than 600 roads, 73 bridges, 72 connecting roads including 6,680 settlement units had been bombed and destroyed by the *Israeli Defence Forces* who were targeting what they call "terrorist infrastructure" in Lebanon.

Looking at the student's bleeding hand makes me nauseous, so I turn my attention to the girl next to him. She is gorgeous, with light brown curly hair that frames a delicate symmetrical face, big brown eyes, red pouty lips, and a retroussé nose.

How beautiful can a single human being be? I wonder quietly. She can get anything she wants without ever having to open her mouth or sound vaguely intelligent. Her beauty alone is enough to quench a thirst. I imagine it would be as satisfying as a glass of cold water after a hearty meal. *Oh my God, I mustn't stare at her too much.* Looking at her beauty is *therapeutic*. I watch as she searches her handbag for a tissue to give to the young patriot.

I pry my neck away from her. My eyes rest on the moving landscape, but most of it is a blur.

We fall silent, lulled perhaps by the gravity of the situation, the heat, and the shots of whiskey that we've been taking periodically as libation for our lost souls. No one speaks.

After a while, the driver turns to speak to me.

"You're African; you must know Bob Marley, right?" he asks.

"Yes, I do," I answer. I light a cigarette and drag in the nicotine. My thoughts wander: *I think the students are crazy.*

"I'm going to play some," the driver tells me.

He inserts a *Bob Marley and the Wailers* 1976 CD called *Rastaman Vibrations* in the car's CD player. The beat from their hit single, *War*, infuses the atmosphere.

"Do you know this song?" he asks, penetrating my thoughts.

"Hmm?" I murmur absent-mindedly.

"Do you know this song?" he asks again.

"No," I tell him. "I've never heard it before."

I may be hearing *War* for the first time, but the driver knows the lyrics by heart. Disproving an assumption that I don't vocalise. I'm thinking that he's probably playing Bob Marley just for the benefit of the only African in the car, aka, me. I think he's being *'stereotypical'* but I am wrong.

He starts to sing along with Bob Marley as if he's alone in the car.

His melodic voice surprises me.

I'm feeling uncomfortable, so I pull out my *Marantz* to record the moment in an effort to create emotional distance between us.

The lyrics of the song, I later learn, are not the result of Bob Marley's brilliant mind but are borrowed from a speech delivered by the Emperor of Ethiopia, Haile Selassie 1, during the annual *United Nations General Assembly* session in 1963. In his speech, he declared: *Until the philosophy which holds one race superior and another inferior is finally, and permanently, discredited and abandoned there will be war.*

Everywhere is war! sings Bob Marley. All things being equal, this is a song that I, a South African born in Johannesburg, Soweto, under apartheid's racial segregation laws, should know. I had listened to a few Bob Marley songs before then, but for some reason this one had not been on my playlist.

It occurs to me that there are many things I don't know about my country, the continent, the world and, more specifically, who I am in it.

It seems to me that one is required to go outside of one's borders to understand what South Africa or a South African truly is. In other words, I feel as though I need to find my identity somewhere else, since it is missing at home.

I listen attentively to the lyrics and feel them burn through my soul like an unwanted tattoo. *War!*

After a while on the road, we reach the first checkpoint in Naema, where we find Lebanese police who prevent the convoy from proceeding further. They say they cannot guarantee our safety.

The *Israeli Defence Forces* are targeting cars, particularly minivans and motorbikes, including convoys like ours, because they could be carrying weapons or transporting Hezbollah militants to the south.

I've joined the convoy with the students because I want to document the experience. I also want to get as many diverse opinions about the war in Lebanon as possible. Despite the danger, the drive is like an imaginary holiday for me because I am travelling with peers - students, graduates, and young professionals.

Since the war began, they have been preoccupied with volunteering at various community organisations and youth centres set up to assist internally displaced Lebanese. They provide assistance to children, the elderly, and youth in need of food, medical attention, counselling, and activities to ward off boredom during the day. Joining the convoy allows me to relax a little, to pretend that I'm not in a warzone, but on an adventurous road-trip with friends.

On this '*petit holiday*', I am not speaking to militants, or grieving suspicious women who hide the truth behind their answers and prayers to Allah. This group of Lebanese are "free". They seem unrestricted by religion, politics, customs or tradition.

For days leading up to this trip, I had been following up on the latest Israeli airstrikes, tallying up the body count and the numbers of people injured and displaced in overnight bomb raids in the mostly Shiite-Muslim residential areas in the south of the capital, Beirut. They have been the main target of Israeli airstrikes.

My reports are interspersed with radio sermons and speeches by Hezbollah's Secretary General Hassan Nasrallah, which we listen to on radio and audio tapes in my fixer Wael's car.

Wael, who is a student at a local university, is enthused by Nasrallah's messages which become the soundtrack of our daily drives through Beirut's southern suburbs where we search for fresh news stories and people to interview.

Truthfully, I am in over my head with the Israeli-Hezbollah conflict. This fact often infuriates Wael, who cannot understand why I am in Lebanon covering the war when I don't know anything at all about his beloved country and its complex history of conflict.

He would wake up early in the morning, knock on my hotel door expecting a detailed itinerary for the day.

"What are we doing today?" He would ask eagerly. "You don't know? Oh, just... just make up your mind already!" He would huff in frustration at my ineptness.

Eventually, I let him know that this was why *he* was my fixer; it was because I didn't know anything about his country that I needed him - to teach me, to explain things about the politics, the culture, and to translate the interviews as we did them. I told him that *he* was responsible for educating me about the rich history of Lebanon and its wars, which had begun since before the collapse of the Ottoman Empire in circa 1516.

My capitulation placates him, but I know that there are residues of resentment hidden behind the 100 dollar notes I give him for his services.

You see, the war is a very personal event for Wael and for most Lebanese people for whom Hassan Nasrallah is the equivalent of Nelson Mandela.

Hassan Nasrallah is not only considered a liberation hero for most Lebanese; he is a hero for the Arab world in general, because by then he had achieved something many Arab leaders had failed to accomplish. He had successfully forced the *Israeli Defence Forces* out of Lebanon, thus ending Israel's 18-year occupation of the south.

Even Israeli officials at the time dubbed him the shrewdest leader in the Arab world... and the most dangerous.

For many years, Hassan Nasrallah, and his political party Hezbollah (*God's Party*) straddled a thin line of conventional politics and Islamic extremism.

The party seemed similar to the *African National Congress* - the ANC in South Africa. A former "terrorist" organisation that gained legitimacy in the eyes of the world over time and captured the imagination of millions of South Africans when it won the elections in 1994, by granting the vote to the majority black African population of South Africa. But this is where the parallels ended.

There was a pernicious element in the Israeli-Hezbollah war that was not necessarily a prominent feature of South African politics.

At the heart of the conflict was the very *small* matter of religious faith and doctrine. Religion permeated every aspect of the war in Lebanon.

In a 2006 interview: *Inside the Mind of Hezbollah* with *Washington Post* reporter, Robin Wright, Nasrallah confessed that he had been dreaming of achieving that moment of staging an offensive against Israel since he was a child: "Ever since I was nine years old, I had plans for the day when I would start doing this. When I was 10 or 11 years old, my grandmother had a scarf. It was black. I used to wrap it around my head and say, 'I'm a cleric; you need to pray behind me'."

During the war of 2006, Hassan Nasrallah was a cleric, a spiritual leader and guide to a private army of close to 1000 soldiers who had volunteered their lives to the movement.

In some broad respects in my mind, Hassan Nasrallah and I were two sides of the same coin. In both of our lives, there was hardly any line between religion and politics. Christianity informed every aspect of my life, just as Islam directed Hassan Nasrallah's.

I was a born-again Christian. For a long time in my life, I wore a purple wristband with the acronym, *w.w.j.d*, printed in white, which stood for '*What Would Jesus Do?*' to remind myself to defer to Jesus Christ in every situation. I was an enthusiastic evangelist, taking every opportunity to convince and convert as many people as I could; telling them that Jesus is the only way, the truth, and the light. If they could simply confess their sins and surrender to him, they would have everlasting life.

I fasted and prayed habitually, and read the Bahamian evangelist Myles Munroe's books on leadership and purpose as literature during lunch breaks at school. I referred to the Bible for guidance on almost every problem I encountered. In other words, the Bible was my Google. When I could not pull out my Bible, the wrist band was always there to remind me of the person who had all the answers.

In my final year of high school, I periodically led prayers at our weekly assembly and attended prayer meetings during short breaks with a group of other born-again Christians. I was devoted to my faith. I had a personal relationship with Jesus, and he was my everything. However, during the *Miss Pinetown* pageant my faith in God and his son, Jesus Christ, was severely tested.

The fault lines emerged when I was presented with the dress I was meant to wear for the final part of the competition. My 'dress' consisted of a white, corset-like canvas top that laced-up at the back, paired with a white, transparent-print skirt that revealed the white underwear I wore underneath it. It was concerning for me to observe that I was the only contestant who would be wearing something so revealing in the way of an evening gown. I was terribly conflicted about this, since I had never so much as worn a bikini at a public pool or beachfront.

Having to wear this 'ball-gown' left me feeling exposed. Perhaps out of fear of being kicked out of the competition, I decided not to mention my discomfort to anyone. I told myself that wearing this outfit, which had been specifically chosen for me, was part of my duty as a *Miss Pinetown* contestant. This is what I'd signed up for.

Even though I felt exposed and stripped naked in front of a town hall full of people I didn't know, I tried my best to hide my discomfort and the fact that the outfit did not fully reflect who I was. Those who saw me in it said I looked lovely and so I made a valiant attempt to think of it as a costume.

When my turn came to answer the judge's final question read out to me by the Master of Ceremonies: "What would you do or say to the world if you had five minutes left to live?" I found that I couldn't wait for the competition to be over. The spotlight was blinding and I could not see a single familiar face in the crowd assembled in the town hall. I paused. My eyes darted about.

My heart drummed loudly.

"Are you kidding me?" was the only response I could think of in that moment.

Who in the world comes up with a stupid question like that? I thought in a split second. Of course, this was *not* the answer they were looking for, nor was it the correct response for a potential ambassador to give.

In any case, it was not an answer; it was a question. You can't answer a question with a question in a competition. It's not maths. *What should I do or say?* I wondered to myself. The pressure was constricting my voice box and I wasn't sure that my voice would be heard at all if I opened my mouth.

I am a disciple of Jesus Christ, I thought to myself. *What would Jesus do? What would Jesus say?* Matthew 10:33-34 came loudly into my mind: *Therefore, if everyone confesses me before men, I will also confess them before my father in Heaven. But whoever denies me before men, I will also deny him before my father in Heaven.*

Finally, I had an answer. It was absolutely clear. "I would tell everyone in the world that Jesus Christ loves them," I said, facing the crowd. I looked back at the MC, who was smiling at me. *Did I just say that?* I wondered silently.

But the words were already out and I couldn't take them back even if I wanted to. *What kind of strategy was I employing here?*

This was before the popular game show *Who Wants to be A Millionaire*, came to South Africa. As a result, the MC did not bother to ask if this was my final answer, or if I needed to call a friend or ask the audience. Nada.

My heart sank to my knees as the truth landed like a wet mink coat around my shoulders. If I still held any hope of winning the competition, my answer had just sealed my fate. There was dead silence in the auditorium. One could have heard a pin drop. I don't remember what happened next. I don't think I heard anything after that. I don't know if people clapped or laughed. But whatever their reaction, it didn't matter to me anymore. One way or another, I knew in that moment that I hadn't won!

The judges had asked me a life-and-death question and I'd given them my truth, which was not good enough to win the crown.

In a way, that moment had been equivalent to my laying my life down for Jesus Christ. In a split second, I had given up my dream, the possibility of winning a crown and all its appendages for an intangible, abstract idea - that of a bright future with God in Heaven.

Heather Hamilton, a 23-year-old well-spoken businesswoman, took the crown that night. She also went on to win the crown of *Miss South Africa* later that year - a fact that was bitter-sweet for me. I could not shake the idea that it could have been me. Although in hindsight she was more ready for the role than I was.

My mother said she was proud of me. But what ensued after my public declaration of my love for Jesus, was a crisis of faith. It was as if Jesus Christ had abandoned me, even though I believed in him. I felt betrayed, abandoned and confused. Even perplexed.

I loved Jesus, but he certainly didn't love me because I had been humiliated on his account and he had not defended nor protected me.

I loved peace, but I also wanted to go to war. I wanted to be modest and preserve my *'purity'*, but I had also paraded my near-naked body for the world to see in order to win a prize, to gain access to money and eventually independence.

Perhaps, the only distinction between Hassan Nasrallah and I was that his faith in the greatness of Allah was firm; he never wavered. His actions were justified and reinforced with every defeat and victory. His was a Holy War; I, on the other hand, was a fickle believer.

Even though my faith was shaken after the competition, I chose to keep it a secret. I never told anyone that competing in the *Miss Pinetown Competition* had made me doubt Jesus's love for me. Inversely, having an ambiguous character made it easier for me to report on the war in Lebanon because, even though it was shocking for me to meet with women who wailed without a drop of salty water emerging from their dry eyes, while praising God because their sons who had been martyrs were now in eternal paradise, I understood the concept of sacrifice.

'God is Great' was the other side of the coin to 'Jesus is Love'. Of course, one can never equate losing something that was never promised - a plastic crown in a pageant - to losing a human life, but I understood the precept of sacrifice.

Muslims felt justified in sending their sons and daughters as messengers of death to the 'other side' for the sake of a future paradise in the afterlife.

How could people, whether they were Israeli or Lebanese, be expected to remain compliant, docile and peaceful, to not retaliate, react or revolt, to not defend and attack when they were being constantly bombarded?

How can any prayer protect anyone from bullets, rockets, missiles, and bombs? If there was no way out of misery but death, wouldn't it make sense to think of death as a way to paradise? If a miracle could be performed, *'where the weapons formed against you would not prosper,'* wouldn't it be easier to have a non-violent method of performing such miracles to avoid the onset of war in the first place? If this concept of martyrdom, rooted as it was in the Holy Quranic scripture, was allowed to persist, was it not feeding into an endless cycle of *"an eye for an eye, and a tooth for a tooth"*? If I knew that my death would be rewarded in heaven, why would I choose to continue to live a life full of misery and pain when I could easily become a martyr and die a hero? If life or death no longer mattered, wouldn't war then become a fast-track ticket to heaven or paradise where life would be wonderful? If that was the case, then it meant that the Middle East could remain in conflict and at war with itself forever. If that was truly so, what was I even doing there? Was I there simply for the experience? Was the experience of war, death, and grief really worth it? Or was I also seeking an honourable death - a way out to be with Jesus so that I could ask him why he had abandoned me during the *Miss Pinetown Competition*?

If I took God out of the equation, if I superimposed Nelson Mandela on Hassan Nasrallah's face and the green, black, and yellow of the ANC flag over the green and yellow of Hezbollah, then the reasoning for this war became manageable.

Since God complicated the story for me, the idea of Hassan Nasrallah as a freedom fighter was more comforting. But only for a little while. If I continued with this train of thought and identified the enemy, I would come face-to-face with Israel which would put me in conflict with my faith yet again.

It would put me in conflict with God's "chosen people" - the Jews. That's where I got stuck. If Hassan Nasrallah was considered a freedom fighter, whose liberation was he fighting for?

The Lebanese-Israeli war of 2006 was triggered by Hezbollah fighters who fired rockets into Israeli territory, kidnapping two Israeli soldiers from the south. Nasrallah had employed this tactic before, using kidnapped soldiers as collateral to negotiate the release of captured Hezbollah militants by *Israeli Defence Forces* on the buffer zone between Israel and Lebanon. This time, however, his plan backfired. Instead of negotiating for the safe return of its soldiers, Israel attacked and started the war on the 12th of July 2006.

When Israel declared war, the world stopped to watch. All the major international news networks were there: *CNN, Reuters, The Washington Post, Al Jazeera, The New York Times, The BBC, Associated Press, CBC, RFI,* and *France 24*. All the top journalists had already taken up their rooms at the 5-Star *Le Commodore Hotel*, which had by then a half-century long tradition of housing all the major news networks and journalists covering the civil war in Lebanon from 1975 to 1990, including the various wars waged by the *Palestinian Liberation Organisation* - PLO against *Israeli Defence Forces* in the south of Lebanon.

In addition to my ambiguous faith, I was faced with a professional crisis. I wasn't so sure that I could be the '*voice for the voiceless*' because '*the voiceless*' in this context had a voice. It was rockets.

What difference would my presence make? What kind of unique story could I tell that all those famous and more experienced journalists - such as CNN's

Jim Clancy, who were armed with producers, fixers, lights, camera, and make-up crews - could not tell even better?

How could I compete with the news wires, which broadcast the news seconds after it happened? How could I even attempt to compete with *Al Jazeera*, or Hezbollah's own television network *Al-Manar News Agency*, which enjoyed support from most Lebanese? These networks for whom hospital doors and emergency rooms were opened as if they were celebrities, with red carpets of blood rolled out for them to take a full record of what Israeli weapons were doing to the bodies of their brave martyrs and innocent civilians.

Television screens reflected real life ghost-like men and women covered with white dust, their mouths wide with wails, screams, shouts and public vows to avenge their country and relatives by giving their lives to the Holy War. Because, God is great. God is great; God is great! The price of 'freedom' was paid with human blood, bones, and flesh. Each death became a celebration, a victory on earth and in paradise. Who was I kidding?

Wael was right. I had no right to be in Lebanon reporting on a conflict I did not understand. What unique viewpoint could I add to a story which had been told for decades from multiple angles, with no viable solution in sight?

Slowly, it dawned on me that the only person who was new to war, was me, Jedi Ramalapa. Everyone else around me seemed to be old hands, including Wael who was a fervent supporter, if not, devoted member of Hezbollah. I was simply a naïve African girl, who had no comprehension of what was going on, a girl who was hopelessly following a promise made secretly to her 18-year-old self in the hope that covering the war could make her a household name, just like CNN's Christiane Amanpour or the SABC's star war reporter at the time, Renee Horn.

Yet, since I was there, I needed to report *something*. I had to file. If I followed only the major news events or peace negotiations taking place at the *United Nations* in New York, my voice would be drowned by the louder, older, and more established ones.

Because I could not escape my dream, I had to find a way to kick the other voices out of my head and report the story as if I were the only person witnessing the war in Lebanon.

Yet how could anyone be sure of anything in this environment?

At some stage during the assignment I resolved that no matter the outcome, I had to tell this story in my own voice, with my own eyes and through my own mind. I couldn't ask someone else to be there for me, to see for me, to hear for me, to write and speak for me. I was the one who had chosen to come to Lebanon, precisely because I wanted to use my own perspective to tell this story.

Yet I was afraid. I was afraid of failing. I was afraid of getting it wrong. I was afraid of being vilified and ex-communicated, of being on the wrong side of the fence. I was afraid of being hounded by the Jewish Board of Deputies just like South Africa born journalist Paula Slier had been trolled for "negative" reports on Israel. I was afraid of being stripped naked yet again, of providing false proof, of being caught in the middle of a political and religious war I had nothing to do with. I was afraid of being forced to choose sides. Because what was there to choose if peace was not an option, what choice did I have?

Storms were forming in my eyes and I needed to see clearly. It was time to make peace with death; death of my innocence, death of my career, the death of myself, or at least who I knew myself to be back then. I thought I had made peace with it when I signed the indemnity form the SABC had given me before I set off. But the gravity of going to war had been overshadowed by a certain level of hubris - the excitement I had felt at the prospect of fulfilling my desire to become a war correspondent and the fact that my 'dream' was finally coming true. I did not consider all the costs associated with the assignment.

My eagerness induced a level of self-confidence I had never before experienced in my life. It gave my life a new hue. The colours were brighter, clearer, sharper. I was floating high, with so much expectation, I could burst.

I was surprised by how easy it had been for me to go on this trip. My assignment editor had come into our daily morning editorial meeting one day and after having gone through the diary, he'd casually asked: "Who wants to cover the war in Beirut, Lebanon?" My hand had shot up the second I'd heard the word 'Beirut'. No one in the office stood a chance. "Me!" I shouted. I had not asked any questions, nor had I even looked around to see if any of my colleagues had raised their hands too.

"Alright," my editor had said in resignation. In hindsight, I don't think I was the person he'd had in mind for the job. However, because of the nature of the assignment I suppose it was better to have people volunteer instead of being asked to go. They would have a duty to protect, which they would not necessarily have if someone had volunteered. That was why I'd had to sign the indemnity form, as proof that I had gone to war willingly. It was a legal document, absolving the SABC of any responsibility should anything happen to me while I was on assignment.

My family would not be able to claim any damages of any kind if anything happened to me while there. Whatever the SABC chose to pay would be out of goodwill and not an obligation or duty. The trip had been organised by the *Gift of the Givers*, a Johannesburg-based Islamic aid organisation which was going there to deliver 80 tonnes of much needed aid and medical supplies to internally displaced Shiite Muslims in Lebanon. The *Gift of the Givers* often invited local journalists on missions to conflict, disaster, and drought-stricken areas to publicise and inform South Africans about their work. It was a win-win situation. The media houses would get original stories from the field and the *Gift of the Givers* would get media coverage for their humanitarian work. Thus, the SABC decided to send two radio journalists and a television crew. I didn't understand why two radio journalists had to go on the same trip, but there was no point in complaining. I went about excitedly buying clothes and a new backpack for the trip. I packed very lightly, mostly white shirts, loose cargo pants and running shoes. That, and my equipment which included; a satellite transmitter, laptop, recording equipment, batteries, plugs, memory cards, notebooks, pens, a cell phone, money, my passport, and press card - was all that I took with me. I never once thought that it was possible that I could get hurt or not return whole from the trip. It was just another adventure for me.

One evening, after some time out with Wael in the more upmarket part of Beirut, I had to face reality.

As I was getting ready to go to bed in a room I was renting from Wael's uncle - because *Le Commodore Hotel* had become too expensive for me and I needed to save money - I felt the earth move beneath my feet. The building was shaking. It was the aftershock of an airstrike.

The bombing was very near to where I was. I had to face the truth. It was very possible that I would not see tomorrow.

In order to be able to first go to bed and sleep and to fully do my job the next day without trembling, I had to accept that death, in this situation, was not just a far-off idea, or something that happened only to other people. It was a real and very possible eventuality for me too. The more I thought of it, death was preferable to living a life without limbs or sight, or with severe physical injuries.

I decided that I would rather die than live half a life. I took a picture of myself, smiling. I picked up the phone, stood out on the balcony and called my father. I told him that the bombing was coming nearer and nearer to where I was, that I could think of nowhere else to be in that very moment. In case I didn't make it out of the trip alive, he must know that I loved them all and that I had enjoyed my life with them, and the one I had lived without them as a journalist.

This was one of the two times I remember tasting my own fear as it seeped through my teeth. My father listened and wished me all the best.

From then on, I remained fully present in the now. I did not live in the future or in the past. My focus was on each and every moment. Soon, I even forgot that there were other people, other journalists who were telling the same story I was. I just did what I thought was the best in each situation. Some moments were good, some were not so good. But because I was no longer fighting the possibility of death, I was free. Once the certainty of my eventual death was confirmed in my mind, all I was left to do was to live. Because of this epiphany, covering the war in Lebanon was paradoxically the first time I experienced what being alive truly felt like as an adult. It forced me to pay attention to what was going on in ways that I never had before... and I am generally very observant. I was obligated to face the world as it was to me in that moment, not what it should be, used to be or what I wanted or hoped it would be. Because even though the past affected my present and the present would affect my future, in a moment of certain death none of it actually mattered. Only the moment mattered. To be true to the story as it unfolded, I never actually reflected on any of this; it was a subconscious decision. In fact, I was not analysing anything in particular. I only thought of what I needed to do at that moment: conduct the interview, write the story, file it, call the traffic desk, do the Q&A, go where I needed to go. Do it now - this moment - as I thought of it.

The next morning we learned that a civilian woman and a Lebanese soldier had sustained injuries from overnight Israeli airstrikes in Central Beirut. Residents said they'd heard at least four airstrikes in an area of the city that had always been considered to be safe or off-limits. The Israeli missiles had struck a 40-year-old lighthouse, built by the French, a few metres from Beirut's western beachfront. This particular airstrike rattled many people because it did not target the mostly Shia-Muslim communities where Hezbollah soldiers and headquarters were known to operate. The airstrikes were seen as an affront to Lebanon as a whole; and a sign that Israel was prepared to go the extra mile to defend her territory. As the fear mounted in the streets, the coffee tasted sharper; the heat penetrated my skin, drawing water out of its pores like raindrops in summer; the scent of the sea salt from the shore, which rested on my near-invisible nose hairs, was crystal clear, brimming as it was with oil from an earlier spill caused by Israeli raids on a Lebanese power plant. Reports from the *United Nations' Headquarters* in Nairobi on the 9th of August 2006 estimated that the oil spill could rival that of the 1989 *Exxon Valdez Disaster* which had despoiled the Alaskan coast. By day, Israeli airplanes hovered overhead, throwing death threats like confetti on a wedding day. By night, it was fireworks. Despite the grief of the mornings, and deaths by night, days were as normal as they could be during a time of war - too normal, in fact.

Somehow, I had expected to be camping outside in deserted lands, seeped in muddy trenches, or hiding under shelters, or in jungles in the style of *Rambo*. But in this war, I had started off sleeping in a hotel room under sparkling clean white sheets, with a flat screen television giving me access to the world's leading news networks. I had hot and cold water, fresh towels every day and the hotel ran a routine laundry service as one would expect any 5-Star Hotel to do. I had my own chauffeur and a translator, a continental breakfast with no ingredient missing. What kind of war was this? It was easy to forget that people were dying as I went about the daily business of keeping clean, taking my clothes to the laundry and dusting sand off my running shoes after a day in the field. Apart from the bombs that shook the ground every so often, life seemed normal. I could have been on holiday. One night, Wael and I shared a soft drink at a nightclub which was otherwise empty. The price of Coca-Cola was through the roof. In the morning we paid visits to hospitals, where we met victims like Ali Lathiya who had survived Israeli attacks in the suburb of Chiah. Lathiya had suffered injuries to his head and body after two Israeli bombs reduced his home to rubble. When we met him, he was sitting on the chair in his hospital room talking to friends who had come to see him. He didn't know then that he had lost three of his four children. He also didn't know that the Israeli attacks had killed his brothers, their wives and five children. He was aware only of the great pain that coursed through his body, a pain made worse by the knowledge that his mother was also dead; she had been killed in the same explosion in which he'd been injured. Lathiya and his family lived in the predominantly Shia-Muslim neighbourhood in the south of Beirut, which was under fire. His family had refused to leave and he couldn't leave them behind on their own. He had been standing on his balcony when the airstrikes began.

He would soon find out the whole truth about the previous night's fatalities. Perhaps the only saving grace would be that he still had a wife and one son who had miraculously survived the attacks. We met a lot of people like Lathiya in Lebanon. People who went to bed whole and woke up with gaping, vacant spaces in their hearts, with parts of themselves missing, either physically or metaphorically, amputated forever. Born-again into the reality of life without balance.

We visited most of Beirut's 72 schools, 16 of which provided shelter for close to 10 000 people every day, something which the head of the *Chiyah Municipality* and executive member of Hezbollah, Mohammed Khansa, said at the time, was unprecedented. We conducted interviews in *Karm El Laytoon* - a secondary public school in Beirut that housed 350 people from about 70 families, each occupying 12 classrooms in the basement. Internally displaced people occupied two floors in the three-storey school building. Food was provided by donors and most families survived on one meal a day. We paid visits to bereaved families, to crumbled homes, to abandoned relatives, to schools and shelters - any place where internally displaced people could be housed. I was happy to break free of the daily routine of blood and gore, sweat and tears. I was glad to be free of Wael and his judgemental eyes. I thought I could do an individual report and form an independent opinion.

As I let the voice of Bob Marley and that of the driver cool me down in the car. It occurs to me that my black South African-ness comes with a moral responsibility I do not fully fathom. The world, particularly the oppressed world it seems, has been invested in my freedom, in my growth and development in ways that surprise me. Despite my own personal growth and development plans, the world also expects me to be above reproach. It expects me to always be on the side of the weak, of the suffering, of the disadvantaged, disenfranchised, marginalised and oppressed people of the world; those who are not yet free, or those who have just stepped into a life of bondage just as the world had stood up for me and my black countrymen during Apartheid. My support for the Palestinian/Lebanese cause is a foregone conclusion. I do not have to say anything. I am expected to stand for what everybody agrees is right. I cannot be indifferent in the face of injustice. The name Nelson Mandela opens doors for me. It softens people's hearts because in him, in the person of Nelson Mandela whom I represent by my presence here, they find a sympathiser, someone who understands their struggle and their pain. Someone who can speak-up for those who cannot speak for themselves.

I hadn't known this until I was in that car listening to Bob Marley with a Lebanese man who knew the lyrics of that song by heart. In this fight, in this war, whether I liked it or not, I was a comrade.

My history made me a comrade. This reality was exacerbated by the fact that I had chosen to wear a T-shirt depicting a black-and-white graffiti-print image of Bob Marley - a sign of allegiance to a particular way of thinking. But the fact that I was wearing a Bob Marley T-shirt did not mean that I personally understood the war in Lebanon, or that I agreed with everything that Bob Marley stood for as an individual and artist. I empathize with the Lebanese and Palestinians on a visceral level - on the physical experience of pain and anguish that I bore witness to. But intellectually, I did not understand it. Somehow, the rationale behind the war itself on a larger scale eluded me. I did not understand, nor was I privy to the unshakable knowledge that everyone there seemed to have, of who was right. I knew that my reports were obviously biased because they were stories reflecting only the lived experiences of Lebanese and Palestinians who were dying under Israeli missiles and bombs. It was not a figment of their imagination. My own eyes were not showing me things. It was not an illusion. But I found that somewhere, deep inside of me, I also pledged allegiance to Israel. I empathize with their plight simply because I was a born-again Christian. I considered Israel to be God's country, a place where God's chosen people, the Jews, would end up.

While the facts of how the State of Israel was created revealed the identity of the true imposter, my view was clouded by my belief in the Bible which, in my mind, was the final Word of God. The rules and regulations set out in the Bible were higher than any authority on earth. So by virtue of my faith, I was behind enemy lines, so to speak. This was despite the fact that the Jews had rejected the person of Jesus Christ as their Messiah. They claimed Jesus Christ had not fulfilled the Messianic promises that included, among other things, building a third temple, gathering all Jews to the land of Israel, ushering in an era of peace, and ending all hatred, oppression, suffering and disease by spreading the universal knowledge of the God of Israel, which ultimately would unite humanity as one. Christians responded by saying Jesus Christ would fulfil these requirements in the Second Coming. But in the Jewish faith, the concept of the second coming of Jesus Christ does not exist. Jews believe that Jesus Christ did not embody the personal qualifications of a Messiah; that he was not a prophet. Further, he was not a descendent of David, because he was born of a virgin. The Christian idea of a virgin birth is derived from Isaiah 7:14 describing an 'alma' - a young woman in Hebrew - as giving birth. Early Christian theologians translated this as 'virgin'. In contrast, Jews believed the Messiah would be born of human parents and possess normal physical attributes like other people. They believed that Jesus did not observe the Torah; he contradicted it. Further, the Roman Catholic idea of the trinity which breaks God into three separate beings, the father, the son, and the Holy Ghost, contradicted the *shema* - a prayer derived from a verse in the Torah that declares that God is one, indivisible and there is no other, which forms the core basis of the Jewish faith. So, not only did I believe in Israel as God's country and homeland, I supported Jews on this basis, even if they did not believe in the validity of my Christian faith. I think there was no human being who was more diametrically opposed within themselves than I was in that moment.

My presence in Lebanon to witness flying rockets, missiles, and bombs, seemed to me an exercise in futility. I was neither in nor out. The idea of *'losing my religion'* was not far from my mind; it echoed in a song by the American rock band R.E.M of the same name. Like the singer, I felt like I was *'in the corner, in the spotlight, losing my religion'*. Now that I was at war, I discovered that losing one's religion is one thing, but losing one's faith, one's core beliefs, was quite another. I was beginning to unravel in ways that were not immediately detectable to me at the time. My small mind couldn't deal with the implications of the war in Lebanon and all the other wars that Israel had waged since the country was created on the 14th of May in 1948. Each successive bomb Israel threw into Lebanon rattled me. It shook me up like a saltshaker, emptying everything that I had put inside it. I was no longer the salt of the earth, but the salt on the earth. To question the legitimacy of the State of Israel as it was then constructed, would be to question the Word of God. As it is, Jewish belief is based solely on *national revelation* - which is the creation of the State of Israel. The Jews claim that of the 15,000 religions in human history, only Judaism bases its belief on the national revelation that God will speak to the entire nation.

Even though Christian crusaders tortured and killed Jews in the 11th century in the name of Jesus, today you would be hard-pressed to find any born-again Christian who is against the legitimacy of the State of Israel.

There are divisions in the interpretation of Holy Scriptures everywhere, within all the three major Abrahamic religions, and even within Islam, between the Shia, Sunnis, Sufis, and other sects. At the very core of it all, regardless of who started it, the Hezbollah-Israeli war is fundamentally about this: the right of the State of Israel to exist, regardless of how many people have to die, be maimed, and rendered homeless. Despite the human rights abuses they commit; they still have a right to exist because they are God's chosen nation through which God will reveal himself through the Messiah.

Yet, God will not reveal himself until all his children have returned to Jerusalem. Because of this, born-again Christians believe that they have to support the State of Israel, even if Jews have openly rejected Jesus Christ as their Messiah. The immigration of Jews to Palestine, which began in the 13th century and increased in 1889 with the expulsion of Jews in England, France, Austria, and Spain, is proof of this. Born-again Christians, in particular, see this gathering of Jews from around the world in Jerusalem as a sign that the Second Coming of Jesus Christ is near. Many of them view it as a sign of the prophetic Word of God coming true. It is God's Will.

I tried hard to block the issue of God in the story I was covering. Not only was I trapped in the physical world, I was also trapped in my mind and could not resolve the issue for myself in any meaningful way. The only way of coping was to focus on the facts at hand, the information that was at my disposal. A huge part of who I was had to die for the second time. The first time had been as a *Miss Pinetown* contestant because Jesus had abandoned me, and the second time now as a reporter in Lebanon. Because if I truly believed in God, in His existence, I would also have to accept that this war, the war that I was covering, was also part of His Divine Will. It was also part of His Plan. I was not ready to accept that my God could be such a violent, callous, and ruthless being.

***

At the *Naema Checkpoint*, the leaders of the convoy try fruitlessly to protest.

Others attempt to force their bodies through a police barricade. Others sit in the shade, away from the blaring sun. It is a protest against war, perhaps not as dramatic as the organisers had hoped, but still it let everyone know that most Lebanese people desire peace.

The main buildings in town still bear the scars of years of civil war. I can understand their fatigue with continuous wars; anyone would be tired. After a few hours of waiting, the convoy is forced to return to the city.
We are all exhausted and demoralised. The entire exercise has been a failed mission. For me, this means that I don't have a strong story to tell. I also have a splitting headache the size of Mars, which is probably yet again a result of the whiskey, cigarettes, the sun, and a lack of water and food. I am dizzy and nauseous. I can barely make it to my hotel room, as the very act of walking

itself is painful. I shower and sleep for the rest of the day, without filing a single story for the first time since my arrival in Lebanon.

The following week, the SABC television crew and I decided to head down to the south of Lebanon to report on conditions there. Everyone we tell about our intention to travel down south tries to dissuade us, saying it is too dangerous. There is no guarantee that we will be safe from Israeli airstrikes. We are going too close to the fire, for real this time. We were courting danger, they say, courting death.

But we had already heard that some of our colleagues had braved the unofficial no-go-zone-warning and were now filing stories from the south, where most of the heavy fighting is taking place. They are still alive - so we take it as a green light for us to follow. The evening before we leave, Wael invites us for supper with his family - his parents and his uncle. We take pictures of all of us together, sitting on the family's golden couch. We all look very happy. The next day, we drape a South African flag on the roof of our beige circa 1970 Mercedes Benz and head down to the town of Saida, which is also known as Sidon, 40 kilometres south of Beirut, on the Mediterranean coast. It is as close to the south as we can get without going into the town of Tyre, since the Israeli military have destroyed all access to roads leading in and out of it. The Israeli Prime Minister at this time, Ehud Olmert, and his security cabinet authorised more troops into southern Lebanon, about 20 kilometres from the border with Israel to the Litani River. This development is a disaster for hundreds of people waiting for relief aid and the humanitarian aid agencies that are waiting to reach them.

When we arrive, we find the town of Saida with its residents still reeling from the shock of the previous night's bombs in which at least four people were reportedly killed. We see a few men sitting outside a restaurant smoking the *hookah* - a tobacco water pipe - and drinking coffee with expressionless faces, a routine they have not interrupted despite the war. In a chilling way, their faces give me an impression of a town that is normal, a town in which nothing extraordinary is happening. It is incongruous to me - the images and the information I have do not match. *Is there a war going on here or not?* I wonder to myself. *How could these men sit outside so casually, smoking tobacco when bombs are falling? Then again, what more can they do? Doesn't life always go on?*

As we conduct our reconnaissance, we meet a journalist working for the *Agence France Presse* (AFP). He tells us that the previous night was the worst he's ever had. He couldn't sleep because of the constant low banging sounds of bombs dropping incessantly. He feels lucky to be alive. He came to Saida, he tells us, to cover a funeral for 15 people who had been killed in recent airstrikes. Despite the town being so close to the Israeli border, no one there had imagined that ordinary civilians would become victims of the Israeli offensive. Many of them say they do not support Hezbollah.

But it is becoming clearer as the days go by, that Israel is determined to teach Hezbollah a lesson. Keeping an accurate count of people being killed on a daily basis is difficult. In that respect, war reporting is extremely localised. I am only able to report on and or verify incidents where I am and not in the rest of the country. At this point, the *Israel Defence Forces* are said to be targeting the north and south of Lebanon simultaneously, so it is impossible to know what is going on elsewhere. It was only Hezbollah and the Israeli army that seem to have a clear record of how many people have been killed. The final report by Gift of the Givers says the war killed between 1191-1300 Lebanese people and 165 Israelis.

Before we move into the interior of Saida, I do a live interview with the afternoon current affairs show on *SAfm* on SABC. The anchor of the show is Tshepiso Makwetla, who is notorious for asking difficult questions.

I was always nervous during live interviews on the radio regardless of who I was speaking to. Each time I had to go on air, it petrified me. It was as if I were someone who had never done it before. Being interviewed by Tshepiso often added more pressure to my strained nervous system. I could never understand why I was so petrified of going on air, as live interviews were the backbone of radio journalism.

Normally, I would try to forget every interview the second it was over, vowing not to talk about it. I always felt a keen sense of embarrassment and shame. I felt like I had failed someone. This feeling often made me hesitant to seek out any feedback because I reasoned that in the event that the interview had been very good, I would appear like a pompous narcissist; and in the event that it had been very bad, it would confirm my lack of ability as a broadcaster and, more importantly, a journalist.

In this interview however, I am not nervous at all. There is a peculiar absence of fear. I have found a way to ignore the doubter in me, who frequently bombards my mind with annoying questions such as: Are you sure he said that? Are you certain that's what he meant? Are you sure you saw, read, or heard right? How can you speak with such certainty? Do you have proof? Evidence? Are you sure your facts check out? And many others like that, making it difficult for me to focus on the *actual* Q&As.

But this time the doubter is absent. I update the listeners, telling them what I know of what is happening and where we are going next, without questioning if I'm choosing the correct word or using it in the right sequence or context.

It is only when Tshepiso Makwetla says: "Stay safe" to conclude the interview that I'm struck with a feeling of remorse and sadness.

The way she says those words, with such weight and solemnity behind them, feels as if she's saying goodbye to *me* specifically. I put the phone down and look back at the men sitting outside the restaurant still smoking their colourful pipes. If I had a camera, this scene would make for a memorable holiday picture. It is the kind of souvenir image tourists collect to show people back home how locals live. I look at them as they calmly inhale and exhale, blowing smoke into the ether. I think to myself that if they can somehow live this war, if they can wake up and smoke the *hookah* as if there is no war going on, if they can survive it, I can too. I accept that Tshepiso's outro was simply a '*See you later*' and not a goodbye forever.

We move from the coast into the interior of Saida in search of stories, people to interview and voices to record. The town is mostly deserted. Those who did not leave for safer areas are either going to, coming from, or preparing to attend the funeral of a close relative, friend or neighbour. In this environment, I begin to feel like an intruder. A vulture coming in to feed on other people's grief.

As our feet sink into the hot sand that makes up the streets of Saida, our eyes dart around beckoning passers-by to speak to us, people close their shutters and disappear behind heavy curtains. A sense of desolation pulls me in. But I am also relieved that those we encounter do not want to be interviewed. I am relieved because I honestly don't want to disturb their lives any more than they already are. I don't think my presence, or our presence here will improve the situation in any way. We are not here to help anyone; we are here to get a news story. Ideally, it has to be a juicy one because we've travelled far to get it.

It has to be dripping with blood to make it into the news bulletins; not just one but hundreds and thousands of people have to die for it to become a top story. So far, my stories are probably going to be light pieces the recounting of which news readers will say: *"and further afield..."* - that is if it they even make it into the national bulletins ahead of any other reports from news agencies such as the now defunct *SAPA*, *Reuters* or *AFP*.

As it is, I have no idea if the stories I'm filing are being broadcast at all, or how many times. In many ways, these details that often preoccupy radio journalists, do not matter to me now as the fire from above penetrates the threshold between life and death.

As we walk on, we come across a man walking aimlessly up the street. By then, we had decided to take a break from walking and are resting under the shade of a large tree next to the road. The man walks as if he is searching for something, but somehow can't remember exactly what that something is. My television colleague asks Wael to stop and ask the man if he'd be willing to do an interview with us about what he's seen or heard regarding the latest bombings in the area. To our surprise, he agrees to do the interview. He is our first interviewee of the day. Although it is great to have someone agree to an interview, I am still not convinced by him. I am sceptical about what he has to say. He doesn't appear to me like someone who has a compelling story to tell. I'm fearing he's one of those dead-end witnesses who know nothing but insist on being interviewed simply because they want to see themselves on television. But as it often happens, it is his story, innocuous as it is, compared to what we have already seen and heard during the war, which finally breaks me.

"My name is Omar Merishar," he tells us. "I used to live not too far from here, just down the road. Two days ago, I was sitting with my family, my wife, daughter, and grandson. I was drinking afternoon tea as usual with my son-in-law when our house was struck by a missile. It crashed and collapsed. I spent the rest of the next day searching for my wife and children through the rubble. We found them, but they are all dead now. My entire family is gone. I don't know how I survived, how I am standing here talking to you. I don't understand why I am here now. Because now I have nothing. Why did they strike us? We have nothing to do with the war. We have nothing to do with Hezbollah. In fact, I am against what Hezbollah is doing. But this does not matter anymore. The Israelis don't care about us. Nobody cares about us. Right now, I have nothing to live for. I think I will join Hezbollah and become a martyr. Because that's what they want, isn't it? That's what they want. They want to turn us into animals, into savages, people who will kill without a second thought. I'm ready to kill. I have nothing else to live for. Everything I cared for is gone. Gone!"

While listening to him talk, I don't realise that I'm crying. Tears are streaming down my cheeks for the first time since I arrived in Lebanon.

"Where are you coming from now?" I hear Wael ask. He has taken over the interview.

"I am from where my house used to be," he replies.

"Where are you going now?"

"I don't know!" he says, his voice cracking. "I don't know where I'm going now. I don't know. Where should I go? This is my home. That's why I'm saying that if I can find any Hezbollah recruiter looking for soldiers, I will join them. Let them come and I'll join the war. There's nothing left for me right now."

The interview is over. What more could we ask of this man who has lost everything and has nothing left? There is nothing to say. I look at my television colleague and see that her blue eyes are also bloodshot. We are all crying. Thankfully, we are all still human. We remain silent for a while, allowing Omar's words to seep into the ground to become one with his own flesh, the flesh he has just freshly buried. I feel heavy. The sun doesn't help. But there is no time to wallow in the misery of Omar's new life situation. We have to move on. There is a funeral about to be held for two more people killed in last night's strikes at a Palestinian refugee camp, south east of

Saida. I have never been to a refugee camp before. I don't know what to expect when I get there.

I am speechless when we get there. I have seen and been to some of the worst places to live, both in my home country and in other countries on the continent. Such as Kibera, in Kenya. Kibera is said to be the largest urban slum in Africa, a place that is not only infused with heaps of pollution in the form of human and animal faeces, garbage and other waste, it is also a place that could be, according to a lyrical 2012 feature by *The Economist*, quite possibly the most entrepreneurial place on the planet. The refugee camp has all the hallmarks of a township or urban slum, with an edge. This place, though, is different. In it I feel trapped, like a mouse or a rabbit. Like prey. I feel completely vulnerable, naked, open, hollow, empty, and stuffed full of hot air that is suffocating me. The clothes I am wearing are not nearly enough to cover me. The air is dusty and humid, sticky, and dry. Cold and hot. I need to breathe. As it happens, I am already outside, so practically there is nowhere else to go. I do the next best thing and look up, hoping that a clear blue sky may offer my senses much-needed relief, but there is none.

Instead of birds flying freely over fluffy clouds, I am met with a mesh of wires, electrical cords and cables crisscrossing the street above us. The cords are so dense they seem to enclose the camp with snake-like wires as thick as a wriggle of worms. I've seen illegal electrical connections before, but this mesh is exquisitely complicated; it hovers over me like a net.

I can't move.

"We need to get you a scarf. It's a funeral. The dress code is very strict here," says my TV colleague, breaking the spell I'm under. She tells me to move closer to her.

Wael is busy negotiating with Hezbollah security. The driver of our car has disappeared to purchase a scarf for me in one of the many shops along the main street. We are two women surrounded by a multitude of young men who are chanting with militant passion down the narrow street. I can barely see the ground they are walking on. The crowd is hyped up to a frenzy, buzzing around like flies. Gunshots are fired at will as the funeral procession gets closer to where we are, which makes being there extremely dangerous. Not only is the refugee camp a prime target for Israeli airstrikes, but there is also the possibility of being injured or killed by stray bullets. The camp is one of 12 refugee camps in the country, which hosts approximately 400 000 Palestinians who are descendants of refugees who had been present at the creation of Israel in 1948. Under a long-standing agreement, Lebanese security forces are barred from entering the camps, where armed Palestinian groups regularly clash with each other.

"Here," says my television colleague, handing me the scarf that I proceed to put around my head, covering my dreadlocks. "We have to follow the funeral procession. Come."

Allahu Akbar! Allahu Akbar! Allahu Akbar! a throng of voices chants together. In my ears, they sound like a swarm of bees buzzing around a honeycomb.

I have seen scenes like this before on television; young boys and men chanting about the greatness of God, while holding up the cadavers of their beloved martyrs. It is one thing to watch this type of funeral procession on television and quite another to be there in person, within reach of the limp bodies that were fully alive mere hours ago, but which are now covered in white sheets with the black, red, green, and white Palestinian flag and being paraded victoriously through town in order to be promptly discarded beneath the earth.

I stop breathing.

After the funeral, we move on to other parts of Saida that have been bombed. We visit a hospital and drive around the city, until the locals advise us to take shelter. Israeli drones are hovering overhead and we are now in danger of being a target or getting in the way of one. Their whines form a backdrop of the town's soundscape; nothing else moves.

There are no other cars moving on the street.

We are under surveillance and any suspicious manoeuvre could result in the end of our lives. At some point we are compelled to wait at a local police station until the drones disappear and it is relatively safe for us to drive around.

When the drone sound recedes into the distance, we go out quickly so as not to arouse any suspicions. Internally, I am reluctant to leave the relative safety of the police station. I don't want to be a target of Israeli missiles, yet at the same time I signed up for this. This is what brought me to Lebanon. I have to do it. Our driver drives as if we are on a high-speed chase. My television colleagues need to get fresh footage of the devastation. I need to collect emotions of what it feels like to walk through a town that has been abandoned by residents fleeing death.

We stop at what was once a thriving business district and active marketplace. The driver parks the car so that it is out of sight.

I can hear all my bodily functions, especially my heart as it pumps blood through each and every one of my veins. As the pulsating sound intensifies, it sounds like tidal waves at sea. I am aware of every breath I take. Time slows down.

We walk into a partly bombed clothing shop, where clothes still hanging on their rails are covered with thick layers of dust. With each step I become braver, but the sound of the shards of glass crunching underfoot is frightening. The sound is so loud I fear it'll alert the drones that we are in here, trespassing.

The shop's roof has concaved, but all the merchandise in the shop remains perfectly in place. I look with wonder. I am hypnotised by the garments. These clothes were once so valuable to someone. They were worth something. They were going to make the wearer feel good, attractive, help them land that job, or get that man to notice. These clothes were going to make someone feel secure, safe, covered, special, loved, valued and maybe even sensual and beautiful. These clothes were going to make someone rich and provide jobs for people. But now they are worthless, or definitely way too expensive. No one is willing to sell them, no one is willing to buy them. No one is crazy enough to come here and steal them. There is nobody to wear them. The cash register is still there, half-open; even money has lost its value. Just then, an absurd thought crosses my mind.

What if I take an item of clothing as a souvenir? It's not such a bad idea, or is it? I wouldn't exactly be stealing since the shop has been abandoned. Besides, who would even know? Or care? It wouldn't be an out-of-place thing to do. Journalists are prone to that type of twisted sentimentality. I once read an account of one such incident in journalist and author Michela Wrong's book: *In the Footsteps of Mr. Kurtz: Living on the Brink of Disaster in the Congo*; published in 2001, where she tells the story of how she took a piece of cutlery, a silver spoon or fork, from the deserted palace of the deposed former President of Zaire now the Democratic Republic Congo, Mobutu Sese Seko. Somewhere, in her collection of things, there is a piece of silver retrieved from Mobutu Sese Seko's private home. I mean, wouldn't that be something? Wouldn't that make for lively dinner table talk if I were one day to tell my dinner guests that the scarf or dress that I was wearing came from a shelled-out fashion store in the south of Lebanon?

It would be quite a tale to tell, except that I would have to make up most of it, given that I don't know who the owners of the shop are, where they are or even if they are still alive. I know nothing of the conditions under which they had to escape, or how hard they had worked to build their business. I have no information about them and there is no one around to ask. I don't even have the name of the clothing shop, to say the least. But I can't act on my thoughts. I can't even get myself to touch the clothes or browse, looking to find the perfect souvenir.

As my feet step over fragments of glass on the shop floor, they make a sound which gives the place a sacred aura. As if it were a gravesite, or a place of worship. There is a quietness here that I cannot disturb. This silence interrupts an irrational need to shop right there on the spot, because I could literally shop 'till I died.' Also, there is something eerily familiar about this stillness, about the sound of broken glass crunching under my feet. I know the sound.

I have been here before.

I had been in a Mosque, gingerly following in the footsteps of another reporter, a radio reporter who was narrating to the mic what he was seeing, as if he were doing a live report for television. He was recording his voice-over, and the sound of broken glass as he stepped over it.

I was learning something new, a technique on how to use natural sound as a compelling way to tell a story for radio - how to take the listener there with you. I had been milling about the bomb site wondering what story I could tell about something so obvious. The Mosque had been bombed; what more could I say? What more was there to say about rubble? It had never occurred to me to do that; to compose a report on the spot as if it were live. To take a detailed itinerary of broken dreams, lost hopes, shattered lives, and loss of faith. I had observed that reporter keenly. I had lurked behind him, listening to what he was doing, instead of filing my own report.

Focused, the reporter, who worked for an international news organisation, didn't see me, and if he did, he didn't allow my presence to distract him from what he was doing. We were at one of eight locations in which terrorists working for the Afrikaner terrorist group the *Boeremag* had planted bombs which had killed one woman and left her husband injured in Soweto, on the 30th of October 2002.

I, along with many of our colleagues from the SABC Radio newsroom in Johannesburg, had been assigned to cover the aftermath. Following the attacks, the country had been on high alert. The string of bombs had caused consternation throughout the country, raising fresh fears that a civil war could erupt between the Afrikaners and the new majority black government seven years after the first democratic elections had been held. I had been frightened by this particular assignment, in part because I was still new to working alone as a radio journalist, and also because those were bombs, not guns. What if there was another one which had not yet been discovered?

I was used to working with a team, having been a bi-media reporter before. I often travelled with at least one other person when on assignment. So, in the absence of a colleague from work, I used this foreign correspondent as a replacement for an imaginary team-mate. In the beginning of my work as a radio journalist, I had been completely overwhelmed by the job. Like an investigator, I had to study the scene, describe the events that had taken place to the listener as if I myself had been there when the events happened. I'd had to piece together fragments of information from various sources, authorities, witnesses, and passers-by in order to tell a coherent, accurate, and unbiased story within a few minutes of arriving at any scene.

This was perhaps one of the largest contributing factors to my anxiety and nervousness, which never left me when I reported news live.

Still, there was something about being there at the Mosque, carrying my *Marantz*, wearing headphones, and holding a directional mic, that excited me.

I was finally doing it! I was a journalist!

One day I was sitting outside at the Bronkhorstspruit Taxi Rank, 50 kilometres east of Pretoria, staring at the black and gold hair clips, hair pins, rows of different coloured nail-polish, lipstick, and hair products we had to sell. My parents had dropped my grandmother, my little sister and me off at the informal market one Saturday morning, to sell the products at a small stall. Being at the stall in the informal market in town was an improvement from having to walk door to door in our neighbourhood of Ekangala - selling to our neighbours *o makhelwane*. This time we didn't have to move around, but I still hated it.

"Go and sell those products," my father instructed. "The money you make will pay for your school shoes." I needed school shoes then, since the ones I'd been wearing to school were light-brown leather strap-ups and they stood out from the black *Buccaneers* and *Toughees* shoe brands that other children wore. I had an incentive to sell because I didn't want to be singled out at assembly and punished yet again for wearing the wrong-colour shoes to school, but for some reason - instead of being motivated - I had performance anxiety.

The truth is I was not a shy person; introducing myself to people and talking to them was not the problem. It's the selling that got me stuck. I hated having to convince people to buy something they didn't need, want, or desire. I enjoyed conversations and felt that people responded better when they were not being sold something. One time I was sent to sell at the local factory area a few kilometres from our home, in a place called *Ekandustria Industrial Park*. Going there was an adventure for me. I enjoyed getting into a taxi and landing in a place whose landscape was not like anything that I had seen before. But Ekandustria was not as remarkable as I had imagined. The factories were lined up next to each other in long, grey, horizontal rows. Not quite the colourful *Charlie and The Chocolate Factory*. There was an open field somewhere in the middle where taxis, buses, vans, trucks and bakkies, which ferried workers to and from home and the workplace, waited. It is also there that hawkers and informal traders of food and other merchandise gathered to sell.

In the morning, midday and afternoon, this little dusty patch of land would become a hive of activity. We arrived in time for the afternoon traffic, but I was a little more than reticent to start selling. It dawned on me that I would much rather sit somewhere in a corner and watch people as they got in and out of buses and taxis, searched their pockets for match boxes, and lit cigarettes. I would rather watch women laughing as they cupped their ample bosoms searching for money folded in handkerchiefs, clear plastic or tissue, to buy spinach, tomatoes, or onions. I would rather watch other people selling their stuff, trying to figure out how much change to give to this or that person. I didn't know how to approach people and tell them about what I was selling without worrying about how they would react.

I was afraid of rejection, even the most minimal kind. Selling was an art and I was bad at it. Fortunately, on this occasion, I had gone with one of my aunts, my mother's youngest sister who was a year older than me. She turned out to be a brilliant salesperson. I saw a side to her I had never seen before in our life together. She was a natural.

"But you're not selling," she said after a while of me meandering nervously without approaching anyone.

Hunger gripped my stomach, as whiffs of *amagwinya* with *achar* and *Mangola* drifted up to my nostrils.

I ignored my aunt and focused instead on factory workers who whizzed past each other, some rushing to go home in time to cook supper while others were rushing to clock in for the night shift. Everyone knew where they were going and what they were doing and I was overwhelmed by the activity.

"You must sell!" my aunt urged, pushing me forward. "Bring this bag here, let me show you," she said. She got into one of the buses and greeted the passengers waiting inside. She told the women sitting there about the benefits of wearing nail polish: "It moisturises your nails, it protects them from water and soap. Wearing nail polish makes your nails grow faster. It also makes them stronger." I was impressed by her performance. As soon as she finished, one of the women in the bus asked: "How much is one?" My aunt told her. The woman bought two and asked to see what else we were selling: "Velvet, black and gold hair-clips, hair products; *Soft' n Free*, gel and spray, great for S-curls, you can try *Black Like Me* hair food, it's great for hair growth... These hair clips, you'll never find them anywhere else; they will look nice on you see?, especially if you have long beautiful hair like yours," she said to one woman, who blushed at her compliment.

I was spellbound by her salesmanship. She sold the goods. I couldn't wait to get off the bus and ask, "Is it true?" and then, with surprise, "Does nail polish really make your nails grow long and white?"

"Yes," she said smiling.

"Really?" I was sceptical. "How do you know?" I asked.

"I know because I wear nail polish myself. Each time I paint my nails, they grow faster and come out white. Besides," she continued, "you want to sell, don't you? You've got to tell people something they want to hear. Let's go. It's your turn."

When we got home that evening, we had sold more than I had expected. My mother was impressed, but it was all her little sister's doing. I knew that I didn't want to sell any more beauty products.

Still, my days as a salesgirl were far from over. As I sat next to my grandmother in Bronkhorstspruit watching the white tablecloth flap under the weight of hairpins and ribbons, rows of nail-polish, combs, lipstick, and hair products, I knew that I still didn't like selling. People often came with a lot of enthusiasm asking the prices for our products; *Malini le?* and then *lena? Le yona?* My grandmother would answer patiently, unaffected by their disinterest. They would say, *Okay, Ngiyabonga* and walk away. Others would ask: *Yini le? Yenzani? Oooh...* then still walk away. It made me so furious. I had no patience for it. I just couldn't bear it.

On that particular Saturday, as we sat waiting for customers, we learnt that a policeman had been killed and another injured at the Indian-owned shopping complex across the road from us, after one of them had accidentally detonated a bomb. The police had received an anonymous tip-off that someone had planted a bomb there. One of the officers had gone out to inspect the package and had kicked the parcel in question, thinking it was fake. The parcel had exploded, killing him, and injuring his partner. Everyone was talking about the bombs, which had been planted by a right-wing Afrikaner group called the *Boere Weerstandsbeweging* or BWB. It was the morning of 17 September 1993.

"*Izo phuma ezindabeni,*" was one of my grandmother Makhosazana answers to the endless stream of questions I threw at her. Gogo loved the news and always had stories to tell. *Bathi uthi, Bathi uthe.* She was the first news junkie I ever met. Most of the time I didn't know how she knew or where she got her information from because she didn't move around as much as I did, but she always had news. *Iya, angithi bathi bekune bomb lapha emakuleni. Awuboni ukuthi kunjani. Bheka nje ukuthi kumoshakele kangakanani. Bhekukhona abantu bezindaba, iya, bathi iyophuma na ku TV, namhlanje ebusuku.*

I couldn't believe my ears, but instead of being scared I was curiously excited by it all. I wanted to know more and I couldn't rely on hearsay, so I told my grandmother that my little sister and I desperately needed to use the toilet. The public toilets were in the shopping complex where the explosion had taken place. We walked past the rubble just to see it all for ourselves. I couldn't believe that a bomb had exploded so close to where we were. A bomb! *"Bathi bebafuna ukubulala abantu abamnyama,"* Gogo continued explaining that the group had been targeting black customers, as if to herself. The incident was so big that SABC reporters were sent to Bronkhorstspruit to cover the story. I had missed the action. Yet somehow, Gogo, who was sitting right there next to me, knew all about it. When they came to ask people questions, she said: *"Kube bekuyimi beng'zothi angibonanga nix! Bengizothi angazi lutho, ngiz'thulele nje ngithi du-toe ngomlomo."* She lamented. *"Ngiz'valele umlomo wam nje. Abantu baz'thanda kabi izindaba, bazok'khulumisa bese bak'shiye lapho uyi one, Hmm, Uzoz'mela lezindaba zakho? Ngeke mina ngikhulume!* Never!" she said, clapping her hands together once. *"Ngeke ngitshele abantu niks, nomangazi. Bazo suka bajikele wena futhi."* I was amazed.

If reporters had come and asked me questions about something, even if I was ignorant about the matter I would still answer. I would say that I didn't know what had happened of course, just so that I could be on television.

I couldn't imagine why Gogo would not have wanted to say anything, even if she'd known what had happened. I couldn't believe my bad luck. I had missed out on an opportunity to see journalists doing their work, and I'd missed an opportunity to be on television.

A few months earlier, before the bombs in Bronkhorstspruit, something else had happened in the news which had gripped everyone's attention. That morning, I had just woken up from a nightmare, which involved our newly installed black gate. Something horrible had happened on our driveway or somewhere near there, but there'd been no sign of the incident on the red, unpaved earth. It was just a feeling. All I could see in the dream were the streetlamps, whose yellow light cast shadows of young men walking parallel to the thin steel rods that made up our gold and black gate. These shadows were menacing and provocative; they hovered around our gate in the still of the night, spelling some kind of danger. I could not shake the bad feeling when I walked into the lounge that morning, searching for my parents. I found them glued to the television screen. It was so unusual to have the news on, on a Saturday morning, but I found them watching it. Someone important had been killed. His name was Chris Hani. It was the first time I had heard of him. The famous newsreader at the time, Noxolo Grootboom, was being interviewed. A crowd had gathered around her. She must have just woken up. She wore a yellow *doek* and her hands tried to speak words that could not come out of her mouth. She was saying something I could not understand. Then the camera followed the crimson trail leading to someone lying face down, head and body barely covered with a red blanket. The cameraman must have been equally stunned by the smell of fresh human blood that seemed to still flow from Chris Hani's motionless body. There was Chris Hani - the leader of the South African Communist Party - with half of his face pressed against the paved driveway. Chris Hani, wearing a tracksuit and white sports shoes, had gone out to buy a newspaper when someone called his name. Chris! He turned around and was met with two bullets to his chest and two to his head. Fellow activist Tokyo Sexwale's grief-stricken screams reverberated on multiple television screens in South Africa and other parts of the world. But they were even louder in my head. I couldn't turn them off: *Chris Hani is dead*. Everyone in the country was mourning him. I didn't even know who he was or why everyone was so shattered by his death. I didn't know why he - of all people who had died in the world - was so important. I even forgot to tell my mother about my dream. It had become all too real. Perhaps, it was then in 1993, somewhere between the death of Chris Hani and the terrorist bomb blast in Bronkhorstspruit - that I decided I wanted to be a journalist. My reasons for wishing this were simple: Curiosity. As far as I could see then, journalists, like the police, were given permission to go anywhere, and ask questions as long as there was a story...

"Come! We've got to run. Let's get out of here!" yelled my television colleague, pulling me out of my stupor. She tells me that they've gotten all the footage they need, but we need to move before something bad happens.

At the police station, we had learnt that there were families still around who refused to leave their homes. They were intent on staying put in Saida, despite increased bombings.

We wanted to meet them.

So, despite the threat of being hit by airstrikes, we insisted on meeting at least one more family. We were determined to do one last interview.

In an absurd way, there was not a lot of difference between Hassan Nasrallah and me. We were both living out our childhood dreams. His, to one day become a cleric and lead a group of followers to war; mine to one day become a war correspondent. We were indispensable to each other. He started the war, and I was telling everyone about it.

Chapter 2
TAKE YOUR TIME

I am alone, sitting on a bed in a room that smells like wet rotting wood. It's humid. The small old-school television mounted in the corner, above the main door, is silent. A colourless screen stares back at me, mute. I try pressing the power button over and over again to turn it on - nothing. I've checked the back to ensure the cables are connected. The plug is in. It is on. But the television won't switch on. I am exhausted by my efforts. In fact, I am as blank as the TV. I have no clue what to do with myself since my dreams became plans, which turned into actions that led me here to Saint-Louis.

It's been about a week since I arrived in Senegal. I am meant to be in Dakar right now; house-sitting Aisha's apartment while she visits with her family in her hometown, just as we'd agreed.

But I'm not. I've ended up here, alone in this room.

Positively.

Losing.

My.

Mind.

I am scared.

It's unclear to me why exactly, but the fact that this television won't come on is not helping. I need a distraction. The B&B does not have WIFI and I don't quite know what to do with myself.

The silence is driving me nuts. There is absolutely no-one to talk to. What am I doing here? My heart rate is speeding up.

The first time this happened, I was sure I was dying. After experiencing it a couple of times without telling anyone, a friend finally told me that it was a panic attack. "It will pass," she'd said. "Just breathe and you'll be fine. You're not going to die. Eventually yes, but not right this minute."

It was a strange experience. I thought it would never happen again, but now it has and there is no one to talk to, no one to calm me down. I have to find a way of doing it myself. I am crying now and hyperventilating. It was so stupid of me have come here; what was I thinking? *What were you expecting to find Jedi? What possessed you to spend Christmas holidays in a foreign country on your own?*

As my heart rate increases, I begin to imagine the worst.

I am about to die and no-one will know it. The fear of dying eventually grips my entire body. I am short of breath. At this moment, I feel as if death will win.

I am not strong enough to fight it. I try to pray, while writhing on the bed as if I am being eaten by something inside; the sheets are the only thing I can hold onto. I am holding onto them to prevent myself from rushing out of my room, screaming like a mad person. It takes all my willpower for me to stay in the room. Then in the midst of my panic attack I realise that if I do die, nobody will know what had led to my death.

An idea occurs to me just in this moment: I have to write about this experience, so that in the event of my death those who love me will know what happened. I have to leave something behind, an explanation of sorts to let my family or whoever would eventually find me know the reasons behind my journey to Senegal, to explain to them why I'd decided to do this.

I need to write down what happened, what led me to this place.

Alone, fearing death. I pick out a notebook and start to put words on paper.

I can barely hold the pen straight between my fingers; my handwriting is illegible and squiggly, but it gives me something to focus on besides the palpable reality of my imminent mortality.

I write and write, alternating between the notebook and laptop.

I write until the orange glow of the rising sun finally puts me to sleep for two or three hours. In one of my emails arranging the terms of my visit with Aisha, I told her that I wanted to write. I had no idea then that this writing, which I had romanticised, idealised and fantasised about since the day I could read, would happen so violently, so roughly and painfully. I didn't know that instead of it being one of many things I could do, it would become the *only* thing between me, death, and insanity. Before she left, Aisha's neighbours invited me to dinner with some of their French expatriate friends. They asked what I planned to do during the Christmas and New Year holidays. I told them I had no plans. They suggested I visit the historic town of Saint-Louis: *"C'est très tranquille."*

Seduced by words and descriptions of fantastic views, the town's historic and architectural beauty, along with breath-taking landscapes of crystal blue beaches, I came here.

I reasoned that it was better for me to be on the move among people than to be alone behind four walls. So naturally, when I arrived, I expected to be in heaven. I had imagined myself taking long solitary walks on the beachfront and later retiring to sit and write at an antique wooden table in a cool corner café, where I would step right into my novel, my moving fingers creating the scenes and characters I wanted to bring to life on paper. My aim had been to live the stories my daydreams were made of. Not this.

As she was busy putting the last of her clothes into a large black suitcase, I hinted to Aisha that I might travel to Saint-Louis. She glanced up at me through her eye-glasses and continued to pack. It had been a long time since I'd been completely alone. I didn't want her to leave me, but I also didn't want to burden her with my anxiety, which seemed to be taking over my life lately.

Fortunately, I had plans to meet Mathews, a South African diplomat who had been living and working in Senegal for three years. At this point in my life, I was ready to do just about anything - within reason - to avoid being alone. I confided in Lesego, a friend and colleague, via Skype, that I already regretted coming to Senegal and that I was practically on the brink of despair. She gave me Mathews's number. "Call him," she said.

Aisha looked at me quizzically, as if I were a reckless child, when I told her of my plan to visit Mathews that same evening. "You're going to be alone with a stranger? With a man you don't know, in a foreign country while I'm away?" she asked.

Her words and tone caused my metaphoric balls to shrink to the size of raisins.

"Yes," I replied, looking around for something steady to lean on. There was no furniture nearby, so I remained standing upright.

"Lesego referred me to him," I added. Aisha continued to pack, filling her bags with T-shirts and jeans, while I filled the air with explanations.

"He's a South African diplomat. I trust that," I said.

She zipped the two large black bags on the floor, straightened her sweater and answered her ringing phone as she stepped outside to open the gate. Her ride had arrived. After we said our goodbyes, I didn't waste any more time in her apartment. I had to go out, immediately. I headed to the upmarket suburb of *Mermoz* to meet Mathews, who was expecting me.

Mathews lived in a mansion large enough to impress a presidential candidate. The house came with 24-hour security in the form of a man stationed at the small wooden guardhouse at the entrance. His house had high beige walls and a solid gate, which made it impossible for anyone to see anything beyond it. I was taken aback by the security; in my mind, even just one guard at the gate seemed like a *cordon sanitaire* around him. The security was exaggerated and made me feel both safe and vulnerable.

As I waited for the guard to confirm that I was, in fact, an invited guest, I began to realise just how foreign Senegal was to me. I was a foreigner in a foreign country, whose heart and mind I did not know nor understand.

After the guard confirmed that I was indeed expected, he moved to unlock the gate and motioned for me to go in. The garden was overrun with large green trees, which made it look like a house on a tropical island.

My mind immediately began racing, searching for any images of Africa from my mind's archives; scenes from film clips and books I'd read came rushing in front of my irises, so that I was already a spy or someone whom local soldiers and rebels were chasing after as I made my way up a very modern but precarious spiral staircase into the living-cum-bedroom suite of a man I had never met.

My entrance took him by surprise, which surprised me too because I thought he was expecting me.

"Hi, Mathews, right?" I heard myself saying loudly, in a voice I thought resembled that of a calm but shrewd spy.

"Yes, hi," he said, looking at me and smiling broadly.

"I'm Jedi. Nice to meet you."

"Nice to meet you too," he said, taking my hand in his.

After we shook hands, he began to fidget with an assortment of papers, ashtrays, cups, glasses, bottles, and several remote controls strewn across the glass coffee table in the middle of the room.

"*Howzit?*" he shouted, using South African slang for 'how's it going?' This woke me up to the reality that I was not in a movie. This was real life, my life. The room was cool and richly furnished, with dark brown sofas and heavy curtains. The buzz from the air conditioner competed with a large flat screen TV that blasted music.

His hands eventually found the correct remote and he lowered the music, then changed the channel. He had satellite television - South Africa's DStv which broadcasts, amongst other international content, locally produced programmes from South Africa. Wow, I thought to myself, he hasn't left the country yet! Which meant that I too was still in South Africa.

This was comforting for me. Here I had a chance to dive into the familiar before going deep into the mysterious landscape of Senegal. I was also grateful for a brief respite from biting my tongue in my attempts to speak broken French, interspersed with English. With Mathews, I could finally speak my mother tongue, isiZulu, or Sesotho. Mathews was fluent in both. We could understand each other, even though my particular brand of Sesotho was a combination of different languages from the Sotho language group.

I mixed Sesotho, Setswana, Sepedi with a few Afrikaans and English words thrown in here and there. My father spoke Sepedi, but since I had not been raised in my father's rural Limpopo home, I spoke a kind of slang. At school, I was taught first in Setswana, but later changed to isiZulu, then English and Afrikaans. At home, I spoke Sepedi with my father, isiZulu with my mother and Setswana with my cousins and siblings. I was used to having conversations in multiple languages, a common trait among people who lived in Soweto and greater Johannesburg.

From his accent, I deduced that Mathews was from the black townships of Pretoria, the capital city of South Africa, which included Soshanguve, Mamelodi and Garankuwa, amongst other places.

Even so, we could still have conversations in multiple languages simultaneously and we could both understand not only what the other was saying, but also what the other meant. He could understand me. He wouldn't miss a beat in what I said, with all its implied meanings, contexts, symbols, euphemisms, ironies, idioms, histories, metaphors, emotions, and jokes told over generations until this point.

We spoke in English. "Who was singing just now?" I asked, trying my hand at small talk.

"What? You don't know Zahara?" He paused from what he was doing and ran his eyes over me from top to bottom, as if he were seeing a ghost. As if I was someone who couldn't be real, except that in this case I was. "You don't know Zahara? And you say you're from South Africa!" he asked, astonished.

Not knowing how to respond, I laughed.

"Yes, I do come from South Africa, but I don't know Zahara. I suppose I'm not plugged in," I concluded weakly. He shook his head from side to side and offered me a drink, which I declined.

He looked at me curiously and said: "You guys must tell us when you are coming.'

"I'm here, aren't I?" I responded.

"We need to know when you're coming and what you're doing here," he said, taking a gulp of his whiskey and coke, and then proceeded to light a cigarette of his own.

"I'm a freelance journalist," I told him. "I'm here on holiday. In fact, I'm going to Saint-Louis tomorrow to relax at the beach. No one sent me here, so I didn't think it would be necessary to report to you until Lesego suggested I come see you since I don't know anyone else in this country, except for my friend who just left town tonight... which brings me to why I'm here," I continued. "I was hoping you could tell me more about Dakar. Show me around a bit you know; places to go and things to do. Give me some tips on how to navigate this city, nothing too serious," I said.

I was still wondering what he'd meant by his earlier statement: "You guys must tell us when you come here." *Who are you guys?*

"I'm also leaving tomorrow," he said, interrupting my thoughts, "so you're lucky to find me here. I'm going home for the holidays, which means there's not much time to show you around. Besides, there's not much to see here, not much to do or to say about this place." He laughed, shaking his head from side to side. "I don't really like it here myself," he continued. "It's hot and dry and the cab drivers are always trying to scam you. This is the last place I'd think to come for a holiday; seriously, you must be mad to come here. You should have stayed home. There must be something you can do there. I am here because of work, but seriously I don't like Dakar."

His honesty disarmed me.

"Really?" I asked incredulously.

At that moment, we both started laughing, unexpectedly. The laughter seemed to break down our walls. It was a hearty laughter, tinged with the early onset of absurdity, a lingering madness behind delirious smiles. We were meeting again without the smokescreens of our meticulously crafted personas. It was as if we were saying to each other: "Hi, it's you!"

We started talking as if we were old friends, continuing a conversation we had begun many years ago. He'd studied journalism, he told me, in Pretoria and had been one of the best writers in his class when he was head-hunted and offered a lucrative career at what was then the *Department of Foreign Affairs*.

His induction had been gruelling.

"You have to be honest," he said. "You have to come clean about your habits and everything you've done in the past, including smoking weed." He opened a newspaper full of weed, which he crushed, preparing to roll a joint. "You can't admit to it, naturally, as it could be cause for dismissal or suspension. After attending diplomatic school, I was posted here. But I've been depressed ever since. Being here has made me so lonely."

"Aren't you married?" I asked, wondering why he was not yet hitched.

"No," he answered.

"But you have children," I interjected.

"Yes," he said, "I have two. But their mother and I have not been able to get it together. You know, I want to marry. I built a huge house back home, almost like this one for my family. A mansion, which I'm worried about now."

He licked the rolling paper and folded the joint, which hung between his index, thumb, and middle fingers. His hands were shaking, making him look like a beginner or a raging alcoholic.

"I've had to hire 24 hour security to guard the house. It's costing me, but you know how it is. I want to move there with my family. I love South Africa *tjo!* Life is so much easier, better, and more fun there. Here, I'm in no man's land," he said, inspecting the rolled joint and lighting it.

"How about Senegalese girls?" I ventured. "Haven't you found someone here you can marry?"

"*Eish*," he said, rubbing his thigh with one hand. "Those girls? Those girls, most of them are only after money. I want a real wife you know, someone to cook for me, look after me and be my partner, someone I can take to work functions with me, my plus one. Besides, most women here are Muslim, so even if we could date for a while it wouldn't last. Muslim women are not allowed to date, let alone marry someone outside their faith. They'd be disowned by their family and community if they did, so it's a bit difficult for me to find someone. I did meet someone here once, someone I truly loved and hoped to marry, but things didn't work out for us because she was Muslim. I have to find someone from home and bring them here, like you. Don't you want to get married?"

His question took me by surprise.

"Do I want to get married?" I repeated, incredulously. "No, no, I've just arrived here and, in any case, I am a lesbian. I don't date men."

He looked at me and laughed. "You don't look like a lesbian to me," he said.

"What do lesbians look like?" I asked. "Why don't you just ask to be transferred or to be moved somewhere else, if this place is making you so miserable?" I asked, changing the subject, but just as soon as I'd asked the question, I realised it was rhetorical.

"The money is good," he replied. "The government takes care of everything for me and I have enough to build something back home. This is the worst assignment. I wouldn't wish it on anybody, but, like I said, the money is good enough for me to stay. I had a complete breakdown once. I told my superiors that I was not coping. The isolation and loneliness were breaking me at times. I wasn't sure I would make it out of here alive. I thought I would die here, seriously. They asked me to hang in there. I have one more year to go and then I'm going back to South Africa. It's hard, but it's worth the sacrifice."

He shook his head as if waking up from a dream and looked at his watch, then suddenly said, "Let's go!" as if he'd just had an epiphany. "I'll take you to *Les Almadies*! Have you been to *Les Almadies*?"

"No," I said.

"It's a popular space to go out to party and potentially meet people in Dakar."

"Now?" I asked, looking at the time. "It's way past midnight!" I exclaimed, suddenly feeling too tired to go out.

"That's when the partying starts in Dakar, don't you know? Dakar is the city that never sleeps. Let's go."

He stood up and disappeared into his bedroom adjacent to where we'd been sitting. He came out wearing a pair of long, smart pants and a black jacket. I was surprised and relieved by his youth. He was in his early thirties, a few years older than me. I had been expecting to meet someone much older, which would have meant that my visit would have been cut short. Fortunately, he was not an old man, nor was he stiff and staid. *He* was ready to party and I was the one who wanted to stay home and chat like an old woman.

On our way out of the house we rushed past his security guard, while Mathews shouted inaudible instructions to him. We walked a little way to the main street, where he hailed a taxi while I tried to catch up. I was still getting used to walking on sand. I had never considered just how hard it is to walk on sand when one is not strolling on the beach, barefoot or wearing flip-flops on holiday. It is a skill to master and I was still clumsy, sinking with each step since not all the roads in Dakar were paved. Once inside the taxi, I was introduced to another side of Mathews.

In this car he was a changed man, one who shouted orders to the cab driver, fighting with him over directions and taxi fare. I nudged him at some point during the ride, asking if it was necessary for him to be so rude.

"They won't understand unless you shout and scream at them," he said. "That's how it is here."

He looked back at me like a professional showing a novice how it's done, but it was not my first cab ride in Dakar. I had observed how Aisha and other locals interacted with taxi drivers. It was civil, cordial, polite. The process was simple: They hailed down a taxi, negotiated a price with the driver before getting inside the car and if they didn't agree on a price the taxi driver would drive off and another would come. The procedure would be repeated until they found a cab driver who agreed to the price they were willing to pay.

Taxis were aplenty, so there was never a risk of being stranded. Locals didn't just hop in and negotiate while on the road like Mathews did.

This gave me the impression that, at least on the surface, most things were negotiable in Dakar, although cab drivers had the advantage at night because there were fewer of them. However, one could still negotiate without causing such a scene or being so unpleasant.

"No! no! Mon ami! Les Almadies. I'm going to Almadies!!! Yes, the discotheque, no, no, no Mon ami. Trop Cher! No, you're crazy! I'm not paying that! No, no, Talala Drive! Tout droit, Tout droit. No, it's okay, it's fine!"

Mathews' loud voice interrupted my thoughts.

"I thought you knew French," I said, trying to divert his attention from the driver.

"Yeah, I do, but I don't like to speak it. I prefer to speak English here," he said.

The ride to *Les Almadies* was unpleasant for me and I couldn't wait for us to arrive at the destination. It seemed to me that Mathews got a kick out of arguing and fighting with cab drivers, which made me extremely uncomfortable and for the first time that night I didn't feel safe around him. I didn't want to be embroiled in a fist fight in a foreign country, even if it was just for show and even if that show was just for me.

When we arrived, we stepped out onto a strip of road illuminated with bright lights. The pavements on *Route de Ngor*, the main street in *Les Almadies*, were lined with fancy cars and cabs. It was the trendy part of Dakar: *where money came out to play*. Well-dressed partygoers littered the sidewalk, making me feel sorely under-dressed. The women wore tight-fitting dresses that were only long enough to cover their underwear... that is, if they wore any. Many of them were tall and thin and, with their long arms and legs, they looked like models to me. In comparison, I felt like a stub of an old woman in black jeans, pumps, and a black headscarf.

Les Almadies at night could not have been a greater contrast to daytime Dakar. During the day, most women were fully clothed in long flowing dresses, scarves, and *hijabs,* with every part of their body completely covered. Now, I couldn't tell if we had just walked into an upmarket brothel where all the beautifully dressed women there were working, or if they were like me, regular people out to have a good time. The discotheque, which is what most nightclubs are called in Senegal, was dimly lit, but respectable.

The dance floor was already populated with gyrating bodies dancing in front of life-size mirrors. Each person danced with the reflection of themselves in the mirror, as if it were completely normal. I had experienced this phenomenon before. The first time I'd seen it had been in Accra, Ghana, but the establishment we'd visited had been an actual strip-club, not a regular bar like this one. That made this current reality all the more confusing for me. I hadn't realised that this was becoming a prominent feature in mainstream clubs. The only thing missing here though, was a dancing pole.

Mathews led me through the front bar and dance hall to the back of the club, where there was an open terrace and separate bar with plush chairs and tables for patrons who wanted to have a full meal, or converse in a quieter atmosphere. Mathews was a regular at the restaurant and was on friendly terms with the staff and resident disc jockeys. We ordered drinks: Indian tonic for me and whiskey for him.

"This place is generally overpriced," he warned. "In fact, most clubs and restaurants here are overpriced. It's like they are punishing you for going out at night and drinking. Senegal is a Muslim country and drinking alcohol is forbidden to Muslims and generally frowned upon in society."

With that, he reverted to his usual charm.

"I'm glad that you're here with me," he said. "At least I don't have to fight off the many girls who work here. They can be very persistent."

His eyes smiled at me.

"Please," I said, taking a sip of my tonic water, "don't let me get in your way."

We laughed. We had been laughing and talking for what seemed like two minutes when we realised, hours later, that it was already morning. We had bar-hopped to several clubs until the sun had come up, with the city's early risers already piercing through the morning fog and getting on with the day's activities.

We shuffled back to his house, where we made some food and then he asked me to accompany him to the *Sandaga Market* downtown to shop, before he'd be flying back to South Africa later that evening. He had promised his relatives, chief amongst them his mother, some fabric. It was a little over a week before Christmas, so he was under pressure to buy all his relatives something. I was apprehensive about being his shopping assistant, hoping he didn't expect me to give him advice on what he should buy, which print was attractive, or which colour he should choose. I was hopeless when choosing for people I knew, much less for those I didn't know. I only agreed to go with him because I didn't want to be alone, and it was an opportunity for me to learn more about the city. I was excited by the prospect of wading through stalls, shops, peddlers, buyers, sellers, and hangers-on.

Once there, it was impossible for me to figure out how anyone found their way around the market, because not only was it densely populated, it was as if the ground itself was constantly shifting, being continuously rearranged by the wind which changed the atmosphere with every passing second. Everything from the ground to the structures was in perpetual motion; everything was nebulous. To me, it felt as if the very ground we walked on was porous.

Despite it being so unpredictable, this kind of environment woke me up; it forced me to stay alert and listen to all the sounds and inhale all the scents. It called me into the present moment, and when I focused in the present moment, no matter what was going on around me I became infused with such energy it was addictive.

A motorbike could come speeding past on cramped walkways; someone could jump hurriedly out of a taxi into a puddle of water and spray showers of muddy liquid on your feet or clothes; a donkey-cart could squeeze through and force everyone into tight corners within breathing distance from each other.

Once we were done shopping, we made it out of the maze unscathed and still relatively clean. Instead of parting ways, something I was more than ready to do after spending nearly 24 hours awake, Mathews suggested we stop for lunch at a restaurant adjacent to a filling station not far from his house. It was one of a few places that sold alcohol outside of the night clubs in *Les Almadies*. Mathews knew all the spots.

"You can't get alcohol in most places here," he said. "But there are some places like this one where you can get it. I also don't like Senegalese food," he confessed as he inspected the menu. "They drown everything in oil; all their food is very oily."

"I haven't tasted Senegalese food yet," I told him. "I was looking forward to it actually. I heard it was good," I said.

"No, no, no, the food here is not great at all. It's just rice, fish or rice and chicken. Whoever said it was great food lied to you. It's oily, everything is marinated in oil; if the food is not swimming in oil, it's drenched in onions. These people put onions in everything; it's like a national vegetable!"

He told the waiter that he'd like some pizza.

I ordered chicken with chips, a meal I thought was substantial enough to last me for the next 24 hours. Though I generally enjoyed chicken and there's not very much one can do to spoil a potato, I was still not a big fan of fast food. I secretly yearned for a delicious home-cooked meal.

"I was thinking of becoming a diplomat too," I told him, changing the subject to something more appetising for me. "Before I came here, I had seriously considered it as an option. In fact, I'd applied for a job at the *Department of International Relations and Cooperation*. I was weighing up my options, trying to figure out what else I could do besides Public Relations, if journalism did not work out for me. I thought becoming a diplomat would be a great alternative because then I'd be compelled to learn new languages, which I love. I also yearned for the experience of living in a different country. I thought I would end up in a foreign country at some point in my career, having travelled to several countries on assignment, but things didn't work out that way. Even at the SABC, by the time I left they were shutting down most of their bureaus around the world and with that my hope of one day landing a foreign post as a correspondent. I tried to move horizontally by joining the investigative reporting team within the SABC *Special Assignment* unit, but I was blocked. Regardless of how hard I tried, there were restrictions; I couldn't access a car, a cameraman, tapes, or even a video editor. Everything that was necessary to put a story together was off-limits." I went on:

"While there, I applied for this job as a Multimedia Editor for an online developmental news organisation. The job advertisement promised travel opportunities to different African countries, which I was excited about. But even there, the reality was different to what was advertised. I was drowning in administrative duties, having to constantly follow up on more than 14 freelance journalists, editing scripts, commissioning pieces, and writing features, while making sure that the work commissioned and approved filled the month's quotas for each line project. I also needed to ensure that all the freelance invoices were up to date, in addition to producing a weekly podcast on news affecting women on the continent.

My private-family life was crumbling. I was not coping and as a result my contract was not renewed. I was so deeply depressed by this, I wanted to die. It felt as if all my dreams came crashing down."

"I started doing bits and pieces, freelancing here and there until I landed a job as a media consultant for the *Municipal Demarcation Board* doing media relations and reputation management. While I was doing that, I missed being a journalist. I missed being in the field, speaking to people, learning new things, telling stories on the radio. But after my disastrous tenure at the development organisation, I feared I had lost my ability to be a journalist. I didn't have faith in my ability to write, to construct a sentence, let alone be a fairly good journalist." I sighed at the memory.

"After working for a little over six months, I decided to take a leap of faith and do something drastically different. I came here on holiday to clear my head and figure out what was going on with me, to ask myself the cardinal questions in our profession: Who? What? Where? When? How? Why and so what? I wanted to come to a place that didn't resemble my past or anything I knew. I wanted to dive into my own mind so to speak, to figure out what was missing. What am I doing wrong that it has turned my life upside down like this?"

"I mean, I've travelled a bit, but my travels have all been rather short; a week or two at the most - you know how it is, it's an in and out job. I wanted a bit more time, I guess. My knowledge of certain places expanded only to the conference halls and hotel rooms. My scope of what the countries I was visiting were about was limited to whatever was presented at the conference. It felt very much like a curated experience, similar to attending an art exhibition at a gallery. Because of this, I longed for the freedom to explore a country more fully than the work trips at the SABC would allow. When I saw the International Relations job being advertised, I was excited at the prospect of accomplishing all these things without spending my own money. I thought to myself, 'It's not journalism, but it's something, something even better maybe.' I thought I would study for three or four years and then become a career diplomat, but I've heard nothing from them since I sent in my application," I concluded.

Our food arrived. My chicken looked very different to what I was used to; it was big, tough, and dry, and the bones were too hard for me to crush so that I could suck out the marrow. I bit a piece off from the drumstick to taste and it was bland, but I continued to eat since I didn't know how to ask for salt in French or Wolof. Frustrated, I decided to forgo the salt, recalling my sister's complaints that I put too much salt in my food anyway. We focused on eating for a few moments, letting my story sink in with every bite.

"But what I want most," I admitted between bites, "is love. Since I can't force anyone to love me, I thought focusing on my purpose in this life, finding out why I'm here, is probably the best thing to do."

Mathews seemed surprised.

"Really? Look," he said, wiping his mouth with a serviette, "they usually take a while to vet people at the department, sometimes even three years, but this job is so boring, I don't know why you would even consider doing it. You know there's so much information one acquires in the process, but it's all for internal uses. I can't disclose it to anyone. Even if I did, it would be so easy for them to trace the leak back to me. We call it intelligence. It's above board. I file hundreds of reports on different subjects that never see the light of day. At times, I find myself wishing I could write a story when I have something very juicy, but I can't. I miss being a journalist; there's much more freedom in it. I wouldn't change careers if I were you. I'm sure you can find work somewhere back home. There's nothing here, I promise you," he concluded.

My heart began to ache.

The conversation moved on to other topics and we continued talking until it was time for him to catch his flight home. It was an hour before his ride to the airport would pick him up from his house, but he had already packed.

"You don't get that feeling…?" he asked while we were in a taxi driving me back to where I lived.

"What feeling?" I asked, almost afraid to hear his answer because it would confirm what I was thinking at that very moment.

"You don't get the feeling that you should come back home with me?" he replied, looking at me with such longing. My heart was ready to burst open.

"Come back with you?" I laughed, trying to lighten the mood a bit.

"Yes. Don't you get the feeling that you should come back to South Africa with me, tonight? Right now, come back; just go in, fetch your bags and let's go!"

I looked down, not wanting to meet his eyes because my God, I was tempted. "You know you want to, hmm?" He looked at me with pleading eyes, taking advantage of my uncertainty. I swallowed the urge to say what we both wanted to hear.

"It's tempting, but I think I will be very disappointed in myself if I went back with you now. I mean, I haven't even seen Senegal properly yet," I said, hoping this rationale would be a convincing one more for myself than for him.

"Okay," he said, in a voice that thickened the smell of defeat wafting in the car.

It was becoming difficult for me to breathe. I wished we had more time.

"Take care of yourself. Be safe and enjoy," he said, as I slid out the back seat.

"Ciao! Enjoy your holiday and see you when you get back," I said, holding back tears.

I was suppressing an overwhelming need to shout: "No! Don't leave me, I don't want to be alone… Wait, I've changed my mind. I'll go back home with you!" but his taxi was already disappearing into the darkness and I was back inside the bleak, quiet, empty house. Alone. I expected fear to give me a warm embrace, but it was not in the room that night.

The next day, the sun glowed that honey-coloured hue which is bright, warm, and full of promise. It was as if the world was giving me a warm cuddle. I set out in the beautiful morning light, flagged down a taxi on the main street and when one stopped, I asked the driver to take me to *Le Garage Pompier-Sept-Places-Saint-Louis*. My French expatriate friends had instructed me to say these exact words to the taxi driver, so that he'd know precisely where to take me - to a place where people boarded seven-seater taxis to Saint-Louis.

In Senegal, most of the population spoke French mixed with Wolof, which made it difficult for me to comprehend anything that was being said.

I became a child who was learning everything from scratch, except I was not as cute doing it.

No sound was familiar to me except for the word *waaw*, which means *yes* in Wolof. When I first arrived, before learning what the word actually meant, I thought Senegalese people must live such amazing lives because they said 'wow!' all the time, which is how the word *waaw* is pronounced.

"Saint-Louis, *waaw!*" The taxi driver responded. He knew where it was. I hopped in, relieved that I didn't have to engage in verbal gymnastics with him the way I'd once had to with a taxi driver in Barcelona, Spain, who'd helped me find a place to stay when I'd first arrived in the city. For him, I'd had to draw a house and money in my reporter's notebook to communicate that I needed a cheap place to stay.

Le Garage Pompier, one of the busiest bus and taxi terminals in the city (which has since been closed) is not nearly as glamorous as it sounds. In actual fact, the English translation of *Le Garage Pompier* is a sobering fire-station. Most of the vehicles at *Le Garage Pompier* did not look roadworthy at all, so that the terminal itself resembled a scrapyard for cars in need of repair, rather than a thriving transport hub. Everyone was on the move; people were everywhere, arriving, leaving, waiting, negotiating, and loading mountains of bags, suitcases, and luggage on top of bonnets and car boots. Some people arrived by foot, others were met or brought in by Dakar's black and yellow taxis - which are ubiquitous to the city's landscape.

"So, how do you find Dakar?" Aisha asked shortly after my arrival from a cab ride to one of the city's private beaches at the *Radisson Blu Hotel*.

I thought about her question for a moment, since I was not sure how to answer it. At that point, I hadn't seen much of the city to have formulated a real, informed opinion of it. Since my arrival, I'd spent most of my time cooped up in her apartment. Although I sometimes took walks in the early mornings to alleviate heavy bouts of insomnia, they were not enough to help me form an impression. I was often lost in my own head; those walks were less about orienting myself within the Senegalese landscape and more about finding my own soul.

I played a game by setting little tests for myself each day by going down different routes, marking shops and anything that I found significant or peculiar to help me find my way back home. Those small uneventful walks were also terrifying for me. After walking a little over a kilometre, I would be overcome with such fear that I'd completely lost my way that I would panic.

Looking this way and that while trying not to appear like a lost foreigner to onlookers, it would take all my energy to suppress the anxiety until, as if by a miracle, I would recognise a shop or house and then be able to find my way home.

After processing all of this I settled on my final answer, which I hoped would make sense to her. "It reminds me of every city I've been to and none that I've been to at the same time," I said.

She nodded.

I wanted to continue and tell her that each street took me back to a location somewhere in Barcelona or New York. Sometimes, I'd find myself in Egypt or Kenya and I'd get completely lost, then I have to come back to the present and remember that I was in Dakar and that it was a whole different place. It was as if my mind was playing tricks on me. It had nothing to do with the landscape or geography but was just a feeling of being somewhere else, in all those places and all at once.

But I decided against it, fearing that she would think me the craziest woman in the world and expel me from her apartment with immediate effect. I already felt a little unhinged. A bit out of control internally, like someone who hasn't been home for decades and is searching for traces of herself in places she no longer recognises.

At *Le Garage Pompier,* it didn't take too long before I was squashed between three men at the back of an old Peugeot station wagon. All of us tried to find comfortable positions to sit in for a journey I was told would take about four hours. As I didn't know what time it was when I'd arrived in Senegal, I had no idea what four hours actually meant. Time means different things in a new country.

The trip seemed to get off to an interesting start when, after stuffing my backpack in the boot of the car, the marshal asked me for the fare. I gave him the required 5,000 CFAs for the trip, but the guy kept asking for more: "*Sengsa, sengsa, sengsa?"* he demanded. I had no idea what *sengsa* meant, but it was clear that he was asking for more money. I was holding a 10,000 CFA note in my other hand. The marshal was looking straight at it, bypassing my perplexed expression. If I gave him the 10,000 CFA note in exchange for the 5,000 note I had already given him, that would be double the fare!

He simply can't be charging me more, I thought to myself.

I decided to protest, because that's what we clever blacks do.

Some of the passengers tried to explain what the marshal was trying to say, but they all tried in different versions of French and Wolof, which made the entire situation more confusing. Each person who tried to intervene was pointing to the 10,000 CFA note in my hand. I thought to myself, *oh my God, it's worse than I thought, they are all in on it! They all want me to pay double the fare. I'm being robbed in broad daylight.* Seeing that I was outnumbered, I gave the marshal the 10,000 in exchange for the 5,000 CFA note I initially gave him. I was delaying the trip and everyone wanted to get on the road. Despite all my protestations, I didn't want to wait for another *sept-places* where I would go through the same thing. So, I gave in. Maybe the prices had increased, or maybe there was a special price for people like me who could not communicate in Wolof or French or count. I had almost forgotten about the money as we drove out of the populous city when the driver gave me 4,500 CFA back. I worked out that the trip cost 5,500 CFAs, not 5,000 as I had been told. The additional 500 was for extra baggage. What I heard as *sengsa* was actually *cinq cents,* French for 500. I could have kicked myself. I felt more stupid than before, but reasoned that I could never have guessed it even if I had carried a French phrase book with me. Realising that the driver was not trying to rob me took a load off my shoulders. I allowed myself to finally relax.

Feeling comfortable, I started to drift in and out of sleep even though I had promised myself that I would keep my eyes open all the way to Saint-Louis, which was located north-west of Senegal near the mouth of the Senegal River. I wanted to take in everything on the trip.

As I looked out the window into the distant, low, rolling plains, the rhythm of the car's engine became a soothing romantic ballad by one of my father's favourite artists.

I am in a car driving from Jordan to Lebanon through Syria.

I look to the left at my colleague sitting next to me. Her brown hair is blowing in the wind, sticking thin, featherlike strands onto her eyelids and bottom lip. My eyes start to fill up, a lump is growing in my throat and I feel a sharp pain piercing through my heart, so I decide to make light conversation.

"That's one of my father's favourite artists," I say to the taxi-driver.

He nods and turns the volume up a bit.

"I must say, I'm surprised that you like him," I continue. "For some reason I didn't expect that to be the case here in Jordan."

"We also like Julio Iglesias; he's a great man," he responds in highly accented English. He is driving very fast, as we need to get to our destination before sunset. We are on a dangerous mission and our driver is one of a few taxi operators willing to take us there. I think about where I'm going and decide then and there to call my father.

"Hi Dad, how are you?" I say. "I'm on the road travelling to Lebanon. The cab driver is playing one of your favourite songs by Julio Iglesias. Yes, it made me think of you. I'm going for a story, on assignment. Yes. We are in Jordan right now. There is a war in Lebanon and I'm going to cover it. Yes. I just wanted you to know. Yes. I also wanted to say thank you for the music. Okay, thank you Dad. Me too."

I put the phone down, hoping that the call hadn't cost too much money. I need to file as much copy as possible when I get there, so the last thing I need is to have my phone blocked. I look out the window again, feeling a little calmer and less panicked after making the call to my dad, until the music stops.

And then I am at the back of a Peugeot 404 family car, with my older sister sitting next to me. There is a lot of space in the car and my feet can barely reach the floor. I am twisting and turning, restless, my heart pounding. I am beginning to regret my decision to take a ride in Uncle David's car. I am missing my dad. I keep looking behind me and ask my sister: "Where are they? When will I see the car? When will they come? How long until we get there?"

"Relax," she says, "you'll see them just now."

I settle in and face forward, looking ahead at the dashboard, and hoping that I wasn't making Uncle David feel bad about giving us a ride in his new car.

But I missed my parents already.

Then suddenly my sister was falling on top of me and screaming. The car was flying and gas cylinders were tumbling off a long truck that had been driving alongside us, forcing Uncle David to veer off the road onto a gravel pavement, as one of the large cylinders missed the car by merely a few inches. There was also a large pothole on the side of the road, which Uncle David managed to avoid. He did his best to maintain control of the car, which seemed to have momentarily developed a life of its own.

And then time stood still.

We were alive.

"Are you both okay?" he asked, looking back at us.

We nodded our heads yes, even though we were scared out of our minds.

My heart sank; Uncle David's new car had been damaged by the falling cylinder, but hopefully he could still drive it.

My parents, who were driving a few kilometres behind us in a Toyota Pick-up truck, stopped when they saw us parked on the side of the road.

"Are you okay?" my mother asked.

"What happened?" my father asked Uncle David.

"One of the cylinders from this truck fell straight into our lane, and look, *Daai man* just kept on driving. He has no idea what damage he almost caused."

My father knew about cars. He could fix anything. He started working on the car with Uncle David.

In the car on the way to Lebanon, Julio's soulful voice kept calling me back from my family: '*I bless the day I found you, I want to stay around you and so, I beg you let it be me, don't take this heaven from us, if you must cling to someone now and forever let it be me...*'

I was fast asleep by the time we arrived in Saint-Louis. A fellow passenger beside me was pushing me: "Madame, Madame!" I opened my eyes to a deserted space, where our seven-seater vehicle was parked.

"Is this Saint-Louis?" I asked.

"This is where this car stops. If you want to go into town, you will have to get one of the local taxis," replied the driver, pointing to the empty streets as he handed me my backpack.

Saint-Louis was nothing compared to what I'd read in my brief research online. I wished people would write about their *feelings* and *impressions*; facts can be so misleading. It felt as though I had just been parachuted from space into a foreign land, without any further instructions on what to do.

I pushed away my dread, telling myself that there must be more people in the centre of town where I was headed. I didn't believe the cab driver when he said we had arrived at the B&B I had booked into, even though I saw the name written quite clearly outside.

"Are you sure it's here?" I asked the driver an obvious question, hoping he'd say he made a mistake and that it was in fact somewhere else, where it would look similar to the descriptions of the place that I had read about.

My heart sank on entering the B&B, because there was no one in sight. After about 10 minutes of waiting, a manager came out and showed me to my room without a word.

I showered, changed into fresh clothes, then took my laptop and went outside in search of food. I was hungry. The B&B was not serving food until much later in the evening, but I couldn't wait until then. The street was quiet. There were no restaurants for a least a kilometre - and worse still, there was not a single person in sight. It felt as if the town had been evacuated just for me. It was eerie.

Eventually, I found my way to the main road, where I saw an elaborately decorated restaurant, so I went in. I was hoping to find more people inside, but there was nobody - no patrons. All the tables and chairs were empty. The only person inside was a woman whom, since the place was decorated with pictures and artefacts of a South Asian country, maybe Thailand, I took to be the restaurateur. She was preoccupied with something while I sat looking at the menu, searching for something familiar.

Where are the people? I wondered to myself. I was thinking about leaving when she walked over to my table and asked what I wanted.

I told her I was hungry and she responded in French with something that sounded like chicken and chips. Okay, I told her and said that I'd also like some tea to drink. While she went to the kitchen to place my order, I pulled out my laptop and discovered to my pleasure that they had functioning WIFI, which was as good as a plate of food.

The food eventually arrived, after about an hour or more, even though I was the only person in the entire restaurant. I wondered why it had taken so long, especially as the food was cold and the chicken tough and tasteless; however, I polished it off because I was starving. The tea was a flavour I had never tasted before; it was made with fragrant white flowers, yet it was bitter and cold, no sugar.

I ordered some coffee. When it arrived, the coffee was also cold. My first meal in Saint-Louis was an unmitigated disappointment and after paying 8,000 CFAs for the meal, I felt thoroughly cheated. I had paid almost double the amount of money I had spent coming to Saint-Louis, to eat cold, hard chicken and chips and drink cold, flowery tea and coffee. I wanted to leave without being noticed, because I wasn't planning on leaving a tip and I didn't have enough vocabulary to say why. When the waiter, who was also the cook and concierge, came and took my cheque I told him that their food was very expensive. I did not leave a tip... which is how I ended up here alone in this room at a B&B in Saint-Louis.

After my night of writing, I wake up at midday, parched. But the canteen is empty, and there is no coffee or tea available. I decide to go to town to find an ATM to withdraw some cash. My choice of clothing does not help me on my walk to town; I wear tight-fitting jeans with black Doc Martens, a black-hoodie, a jacket and a heavy handbag. As I walk, I sink into the sand, and struggle to maintain my balance with every step. I am surprised I don't collapse from the sheer weight of my clothes.

On my return, I continue to write and write, until my fingers cannot hold a pen or type any longer, just to avoid the onset of another anxiety attack.

I wake up very early the next day, after less than two hours of sleep, and find that my heart is racing again. The fear and panic are back. I start to sob. The sadness turns to anger. I am annoyed with myself. I get out of bed, take a shower, and wear the lightest clothes I can find, promising myself that I am going to have a good time even if it kills me. I am not going to die in a B&B on my own; this is not how my story will end.

I tell myself that there has to be life in this place and I will go to town and find it. Instead of rushing down like I had the previous day, I take my time now, strolling and taking in the buildings and homes that I pass along the way.

I look around me at the shops lining the side of the tarred road. Traders and artists sit in little dark holes, which are filled to the brim with all sorts of arts, crafts, and paintings. I feel too foreign to even venture inside and do some browsing.

I let the images of men sitting outside drinking tea, school children walking listlessly while going to or from school, goats bleating and tourists constantly looking up and around them in case they're missing something, rush past in the corners of my eyes like a motion picture. I am in a historic town, one of the very first slave ports used to transfer African slaves across the Atlantic

Ocean to serve new masters in strange lands. Saint-Louis is also famous for its original French colonial architecture. Though it is dilapidated, some parts have been preserved. It is picturesque, but to me it isn't warm or welcoming. Eventually, I found a quaint coffee shop on a busy corner street.

It is quintessentially French; a *pâtisserie* that serves coffee, sandwiches, and pastries galore. There is even something I recognise on the menu - *omelette du fromage*.

I ordered some coffee and a cheese omelette. It's a good find. I sit by the window that is lined with blue-grey French shutters, which rest open against the pastel-pink outer walls of the building. I look over at a woman sitting on the pavement selling fruits and vegetables. It is a beautiful, colourful scene, fit for a postcard. At this moment I wish I had a camera, because this scene would make a perfect picture... if it weren't for the legion of flies. The flies make it difficult to execute the *'cute girl typing at a French coffee shop, chewing on some delicious petit cake or smoking a cigarette in-between coffee sips, while engrossed deeply in her computer'* look.

Nevertheless, it is a welcome change from the previous day.

The coffee shop is busy; it has a steady flow of people coming in for coffee or quick sandwiches. It at least tells me something about the place: the clientèle consists of tourists like me. However, most of them are white, and none of the locals who live in Saint-Louis or Ndar, as the locals call it, frequent the place.

It occurs to me that I don't want to get trapped on the tourist map; I want to meet locals who can give my stay here some life.

I have been in Senegal for almost two weeks and still have not eaten any of the local dishes. I'm hungry, but I stay at the coffee shop until sunset, catching up with friends on Facebook.

One of them is Lilly, a friend I met months earlier, with whom I have become fast friends. Lilly was vehemently opposed to this trip. She thought I was making a mistake by being here. She reiterates her feelings to me as we chat, telling me that there's still time for me to change my mind and come back home, to her. Our relationship is interesting. She wants more, but I want less.

We talk about feelings, about love, all the while skirting around our true feelings. I tell her of my hellish two days in Saint-Louis. I am comforted by our conversation and it is good for me to speak to someone familiar; she reminds me of home. But more importantly, she confirms that I am still alive and not a ghost floating around on an empty island, like the young unidentified protagonist in Ben Okri's 1995 short novel; *Astonishing the Gods*, who leaves his home country on a quest and arrives on a fantastical island, where he is met by three enigmatic guides and undergoes some abstract and allegorical trials. I had read and finished the book on my flight to Senegal. It is short, yet magical. I hoped to God that it did not portend to my visit in Senegal, even though a part of me was intrigued by the prospect of a challenge.

Speaking to Lilly is proof that I am not yet dead, not yet invisible. I am still me and not someone else. I tell her about my stark loneliness, my inability to sleep, my constant fear of death, my strange and quiet relationship with Aisha, whose friendship I am beginning to doubt.

Everything I tell Lilly, affirms what she believes to be true - I have made a mistake. I can still cut the trip short and spend the rest of the holidays ensconced in the bush with her, she says. Her suggestion sounds inviting, familiar and warm. After the two days of hell on earth I experienced in Saint-Louis, I am strongly considering returning home, but I don't let her know just how much I want to do as she suggests. I tell her that I have yet to experience Senegal.

I haven't done the most basic touristic things, such as having a local meal or visiting at least one of the many tourist attractions in the country. I have not listened to the Mbalax music the country is so famous for. I have not visited the Grammy award-winning singer, composer, and businessman Youssou N'Dour's music club, which he owns and performs at on Fridays - when he is in the country.

According to Aisha, N'Dour's club is not far from her house in Dakar. However, because clubs open late, at midnight, and N'Dour normally performs at 2 a.m., Aisha can't go with me because of babysitting logistics.

There is still so much of the country I need to see and experience.

After all the talking and the money I spent buying a plane ticket out of South Africa, I have to stay and experience something beyond my own thoughts and frustrations. I had missed the funeral of my grandmother, who passed away two weeks before my travels, due to my choice to come here. Lilly and I agree to disagree.

By the time I look up from the computer it's already dark, although it's still early evening, and I have two choices: either to go back to the B&B or to find a livelier hang-out where I can get something to eat before calling it a night.

I leave the little coffee shop and walk down the main road, which is littered with different types of restaurants, many of them empty. I hear loud music coming from a large restaurant, but like the others it is also almost empty. There are about four patrons inside, who cheer the singer on. He is a rotund, grey-haired, Santa-Claus-like Frenchman, who sings loudly and jubilantly. I decide to go in - despite my aversion to the singer - because the restaurant has more people in it and the noise is welcome after two days of silence. The music feels rough against my skin. I most certainly did not fly all the way to Senegal, to listen to off-key ballads from a French restaurateur who loves the sound of his own voice.

But I have no alternative.

I sit down, order some Indian tonic water and a plate of food, and start to write.

Then, another musician joins the keyboard player and the guitarist who have been graciously supporting Santa as he hums and haws. The new musician starts playing several *djembe drums* at once, and offers backing vocals, which brings some much-needed soul into the music. The drums transport me further into my writing, until a tall, dark, frail-looking man comes to my table and introduces himself. He asks me where I am from, and tells me that I should wait for him after his performance; there is another place he wants to show me.

I agree absent-mindedly, because I want to return to my writing.

He has interrupted my train of thought.

Later, while eating my first plate of Senegalese food, a dish called *yassa-poulet* - which is indeed drenched in oily onion rings - I watch him as he saunters to the small corner where the musicians are playing and starts singing. His voice forces me to look up. It echoes the smoky poetic tune of the late Cape Verdean songstress Cesária Évora. I stop writing. I need to make sure that Évora's ghost is not in the restaurant.

He dedicates his next song to: "the lady from South Africa," pointing in my direction. I feel shy, warm all over. My eyes immediately begin searching for places to hide, even though there is hardly anyone to hide from. The four enthusiastic patrons have already left. I smile and bow imperceptibly in acknowledgement. It is a sweet gesture; for him to sing as if the room is full of people and I am the honoured guest.

At the next restaurant we go to, he tells me that he is 60 years old and has been a French, Portuguese, Spanish singer for 30 years - my entire lifetime, at this point. He tells me that he will be performing with a group of young musicians, whom he promises to introduce to me later. I am still unsure about Senegalese music. My introduction to it is harsh, as far as I am concerned. It is loud - to be mild. It is different to anything I've heard before, especially the traditional *djembe drums*, which fill the entire music score, making it hard for me to find a rhythm I can swing to. What I hear is a multitude of drums that are loud and lack any harmony. The drums seem to compete with even louder wails from the main vocalist - it sounds to me like African techno. There is also the more popular religious *khassida* music, which are songs based on writings by the revered Mouride founder Cheikh Ahmadou Bamba or Serigne Touba. This music, which is played by almost everyone in the country as supplications to Allah, sounds like a series of monotonous chants to me. I am annoyed by the music; it's as if drones are buzzing endlessly in my ears, day, and night, with breaks between the five daily calls to prayer that everyone observes religiously.

In Senegal, Islam is not just a religion; it is a way of life.

All these sounds make me feel as if I am in some kind of sonic torture chamber, caught between extremes. I can either have loud silences or deafening noise. I am curious to find out if the music the bands play tonight is going to be any different to what I have heard so far.

I define good music by its ability to evoke tears of joy in me, or move me to dance. If a piece of music can make me do both at the same time, then it is sublime in my book because it allows me to dance with God. When music is that good, I enter into a *tarab* - a state of bliss. In that state no one else exists, just me and the music.

I sit at the bar on my own, drinking tonic water and smoking. The bar is not yet full. My anxiety begins to fill the vacuum, but before it takes over, I let it spill out on the page as I take out my notebook and start writing. As I sit at the bar, I reflect on the history of Saint-Louis.

As one of the very first slave ports in West Africa, I reason with myself that it is natural for it to be an intense space for me to be in. My body seems alive to the emotions in this town. Walking through the streets earlier, I became furious at the continued slavery of Africans. Who still live in small little holes, produce arts and crafts for tourists who are mostly white and, in this region, mostly from mainland France. The tourists still ship talent and human capital, resources, and anything they can trade, except the sun, back to their home countries.

I find it ironic that the very slave masters who colonised and brutalised Africans can be the same people who return as tourists to marvel at what they have done.

While slavery was 'abolished', it still continues legally under capitalism.

I am alert and sensitive to the tiniest injustice around me.

Saint-Louis makes me angry. Yet, I am on a journey to love, and in love there are always solutions; there have to be alternatives. I write a poem about being an activist of love and think it lame, ridiculous. *Don't quit your day job Jedi; oh wait, you just did!* I laugh at myself.

It is pretty ironic to be fighting for love.

The tall singer and I have established, on our walk to the bar, that we both don't speak enough French or English to understand each other. His English is as bad as my French, which restricts our conversation to monosyllabic *non* for no and *oui* for yes.

A band walks in and starts to do its sound check.

Even though the bar lady can speak more English than my 60-year-old companion, she is busy. Whenever she has a spare moment, we ask her to translate our conversation so that we can understand each other.

I am already feeling tired of being out at bars with music and people I don't understand. My mind is tired, yet I cannot bear being alone for one more night in the quiet empty room at the B&B. Images of my crazed, panicked, self, grabbing onto the sheets for comfort send shivers up my spine.

No, I can't.

I decide to wait and see what, if anything, the night will reveal about the famed city of Saint-Louis. Tranquil, is how locals describe Saint-Louis to me, yet since my arrival it has been anything but. I have not yet found a place where I can breathe, relax, and let go of my anxiety. Because conversation between me and the tall one is strained, I write in-between as he talks about his life in Saint-Louis. His real home is not far outside the main town, but because of his late-night performances he rents a room in Saint-Louis and goes home every so often. He enjoys singing, he tells me, and drinking *Flag* - a local beer - while chatting to young, pretty South African women like me.

"*Je t'aime,*" he says, between unsuccessful attempts at a conversation.

"*Ce n'est pas vrai* - it's not true," I reply.

"*Si, oui, je t'aime.*"

"No," I say, "how can you love me when we have just met?"

"*Je t'aime*" he repeats, nodding his head emphatically, as if I am denying a fundamental truth about life.

"*Okay, merci. Je ne veux pas vous embrasser ou avoir des relations sexuelles avec vous.*"

"*Oui,*" he says. "You can kiss me, and marry me. I am single and my love is real."

The conversation continues like this, back and forth, until I am forced to relent.

"Yes, I believe you," I say. "Thank you, I love you too, but I cannot marry you."

Later, he introduces me to several men and some of his friends and fellow singers, who are gracious in their greetings. However, the fact that I am not fluent in either French or Wolof discourages further conversation, until he finally introduces me to Ali - his "son" he says. Ali is my age. Handsome, with an attractive smile, a full beard, and shoulder-length dreadlocks. He is simply gorgeous. It is towards the end of the evening and we move to yet another venue, this time a discotheque, where we dance.

Ali tells me, as we drive to the next venue, that he can see I am not Senegalese or West African by the way that I dance. He is from French Guinea known today as Guinea-Conakry and makes a living playing music. He plays the *djembe drums* and also teaches travelling tourists how to play. That's how he makes his money.

Music makes him happy he tells me.

I can see he is already attracted to me. At the club, after dancing with abandon, I start telling him about love, universal love, and women's emancipation.

After listening to me for a while he begins to cry, which surprises me. I don't know what I've said, but I am moved by his vulnerability and immediately want to protect him. He tells me I remind him of his mother, whom he has not seen for many years.

I drag him to the dance floor to change the heavy atmosphere. We dance and talk for a while, until the tall one leaves to go home to sleep.

Ali says I should come with him to their campsite and sleep there, as it's by the beach and will be relaxing. I want to go with him for the experience, but I am also afraid because he is a man and I am a woman.

I am alone in this country; I know no one.

Although I have no intention of starting anything physical with him, I can't be sure that he will not force himself on me as men are known to do. Being trapped under a man's strong masculine arms is one of my greatest fears. The thought of it makes me feel powerless. He can rob me, hurt me, kill me, or torture me.

I am going through a list of things he can do to me in my mind when he says: "Relax, don't worry, I won't do anything to you."

I decide to trust him. The fear of the unknown becomes more appealing than a night alone in my room.

He is beaming at me. I look up at the sky. It is so dark it is almost navy. The stars glitter like a trillion diamond pieces on a length of blue velvet cloth. It is simply brilliant. It is so captivating that it diverts my attention from this human being walking next to me.

"Look," I say. "Look at the sky. Isn't it magical?"

"Yeah," he says, looking down at the sand and laughing. He thinks I'm crazy. He's seen this sky a million times already.

We arrive at the campsite and he suggests a swim.

I don't want to swim, I tell him. It is almost 5 in the morning by now and I am cold, tired, and really want to sleep. In the tent, I am disappointed to find a very thin sheet for cover.

Ah, so this is what being a bohemian is like, I think to myself.

Being there reminds me of Virginia Nicholson's book: *Among the Bohemians: Experiments in Living 1900-1939* first published in 2002. It was a gift I had received from my mentor, because I had expressed a fascination with the bohemian lifestyle. Faced with the reality of this lifestyle now, though, it doesn't look too attractive. The campsite is cold. I want to be warm. Ali hugs me and tells me I am not alone. I thank him and tell him I have no intention of "sleeping" with him. He laughs and promptly falls asleep.

I try with all my might to fall asleep, but sleep doesn't come.

The next morning, Ali and I walk along the beach. As we stroll, my eyes are met with the vastness of the blue ocean. Ali suggests I move in with him, to save money, he says. He has a room in town, which he shares with his friend, who is more like his brother.

Since I want to save money, I think leaving the B&B would be better as I won't be alone and I won't have to pay the rate there either. But the thoughts are still there, thoughts of: *What are you doing? You don't know this guy, what if he ... what if this or that happens? What would you do? Who would know? What if he robs you? Are you crazy?*

But I ignore them and decide that since I don't want to be alone, I have to trust that things will work out. I decide to move in with him and his friend welcomes me like a long-lost sister.

On Christmas Eve, Ali and I go to *Lodge Océan et Savane*, a small, secluded resort in Ndiébène, where the river Senegal and the Atlantic Ocean meet. This place is the paradise I have been dreaming of. The weather is perfect - crisp and warm. After getting on the ferry and going over to the resort on the other side, I discover that Ali and I are the only black people on the island. Everyone else, with the exception of the staff, is white. Everywhere we go, the staff ask if they can help us, wanting to make sure that we are not lost. I tell them: "No, we are fine. We do not need any help."

It has taken me so long to get to paradise, to feel some level of contentment, which hinges on happiness, that I don't want anyone to taint my time here; we only have a few hours. After having a drink, we go out to the back of the resort where we are enthralled by a spectacularly pristine beachfront. We decide to swim in the clear water, which is full of crabs. We alternate between swimming and lying on the beach, which only has the two of us on it for kilometres on end. Ali is fantastic and swims like a dolphin. After another round of swimming in the water, Ali falls asleep. As I watch him sleep, the words of the Sufi poet, Rumi, *"What you seek, is seeking you,"* keep circling my mind.

But this is not true of Ali and me. I am not seeking him. This makes me feel bad, because he is such a special human being. When he wakes up, I tell him that I am gay, and that nothing can ever happen between us. He will be my brother and I will always love him like one, but I cannot be his girlfriend or wife. He had already started to speak of us as a couple.

A few days later, we leave Saint-Louis for Saly, another coastal town about an hour and a half from Dakar. Ali tells me that his friend from Guinea lives there. They haven't seen each other for close to five years, so we can stop by and see them on our way to Dakar, we can stay with them free of charge, he says. After a few wrong turns in the taxi, we eventually find the place.

Saly's streets, except for the main roads which are tarred, have more sand than Dakar and Saint-Louis put together. I am far from graceful walking on them.

Ali's friend beams with joy upon seeing him. I have never seen two people more happy to see each other. The sight of them being so happy makes the trip worthwhile, even though I'd been reluctant to take this detour.

Ali's friend and his girlfriend rent a room behind a restaurant. It's a small space. They have a mattress, in a small part of it that serves as the bedroom with a mosquito net as partitioning. At the foot of the bed there is a table and two chairs, which serves as the lounge area. They have a small television set, from which Bob Marley videos beam.

The walls are decorated with Bob Marley posters - the words *One Love* are everywhere. The place closely resembles a shrine. After they make sure we are comfortable and have something to drink, the friend rolls a joint while his girlfriend, a Gambian, named Mbali - which means flower in isiZulu - prepares a meal. She lights a fire outside, and another on a small gas stove inside the room in an area that serves as a kitchen and a bathroom. This I can't believe; I hadn't been aware that the toilet served as a kitchen too. *How can they pee and wash their dishes in the same room?* I think. Their place is so small that I start to worry about our sleeping arrangements. *Where will they sleep and where will I sleep?* I wonder.

Ali tells me later that they have another room in the area where they will sleep, so I shouldn't worry; they are giving up their room for us. I feel bad for putting them out of their room, but they are so chilled about it that it's pointless and impolite for me to argue against it. Besides, it's not like we have alternatives at this point. As soon as they leave, I immediately begin to worry about spending the night alone with Ali. But he doesn't try anything, which makes me grateful.

In the morning, I immediately begin to write to avoid the onset of anxiety. Now that we have arrived, Ali looks so comfortable and relaxed he doesn't want to leave. So instead of asking him when he thinks we can get going, I sit at my computer writing all day and all night, only taking breaks to smoke, eat and take walks in the evening at Ali's insistence. After about three to four days of doing this Ali, shouts at me out of frustration: "You are not on holiday. You are working!"

What I've been doing hasn't been work, though; I've been on a race to finish my story before death arrives at my door saying my time is up. Writing serves an important role in my life; it has helped to stave off the anxiety and panic attacks, and will explain, in the event of my death, what had happened to me. I have no choice. But there is nothing I can do about Ali. If he values peace, he just has to let me write.

Ali's friend and girlfriend are both dancers and earn their living performing at exclusive hotels and the homes of white clients. We spend our New Year's Eve at a private home along the beachfront, watching as his friends perform traditional Gambian and Senegalese songs for white people. I thought I'd left this behind me, but here I can see the racial and class distinctions that exist. I am still thinking that since it is New Year's Eve and since it is close to midnight, we can hang back a little and enjoy the party with the hosts, as would be the custom in South Africa from my own experience. But the roles here are clear and well-defined. We are the servants; they are the bosses. We have to leave immediately after our friends' performance. We only realise halfway through our walk to catch a taxi back home that it is past midnight. We wish one another Happy New Year.

It is a full moon and I know it is time to move on. On New Year's Day, we go to the beach for the first time since our arrival in Saly. I have been so cooped up in the room writing on my laptop and in my notebook that I've forgotten to sightsee, but I don't care. I have developed a close friendship with Mbali and Ali's friend. After a trip to town, they gave me a teddy bear. I tell them I will name my first child Mbali, if it is a girl. I also give Mbali the bridesmaid dress that I'd worn for my younger sister's wedding just a few weeks before, because the two tell us that they plan on getting married later in the new year. The next day, I tell Ali that I must go back to Dakar, with or without him. He wanted us to stay in Saly for longer. He is quite resistant to leaving: "Why are you so adamant about going back to Dakar? Dakar is noisy, polluted and overpopulated." In fact, he hates it. He says. I tell him that it doesn't matter what he thinks of it, I will be returning to Dakar. We take a picture together, but both Mbali and Ali's friend say they can see it in my eyes that I don't *love* Ali. I wish Ali could hear them, but he refuses.

We set out for Dakar in the afternoon. I feel apprehensive already about being back in Aisha's apartment and being alone. In town, however, we are told there are no taxis going to Dakar because the taxi and bus drivers are protesting there over high fuel prices. People are being advised not to travel to Dakar. "*C'est très grave,*" Ali says to me. "We can't go back to Dakar today," he says. He looks elated at the unexpected delay. But I am not happy. I don't want to be in Saly anymore. I am determined to find a way to return to Dakar somehow.

As a South African journalist, I am, admittedly, used to protests. I am also aware that protests can sometimes turn violent, but I have no idea what a protest in Dakar means. I am beginning to fear travelling back, because I do not know what I will be confronted with once there, but I also don't want to be trapped in Saly for an indefinite amount of time either. After a while, a *sept-place* taxi with two seats to Dakar becomes available; I jump in. Ali follows behind me, reluctantly.

On arrival at Aisha's house in Dakar, I tell Ali that he cannot stay with me, not even for one night since it's not my house. He must leave. We exchange gifts. I give him a picture of clouds in the shape of hearts. He gives me a batik fabric drawing of a mother and child. He doesn't want to go back to Saint-Louis without me.

"Have you been to Ngor Island?" he asks. This is a neighbourhood island just off Dakar's north shore but close to the city centre.

"No, I haven't," I say half-heartedly, because I'm not interested in another island. I'm more interested in visiting Casamance, a region, famous for its exceptionally beautiful vegetation and landscape. Sadly, there has been unrest and guerrilla fighting, which makes it very risky for tourists travelling there. I am a little unsure of going there with Ali, who has not been to Casamance in years himself. Moreover, I don't have enough money to pay for transportation, accommodation, and food for both of us.

Before we part ways, he declares: "I am going to visit my friends in Ngor. You must come."

After he leaves, I am glad to finally be alone. I still have a lingering fear that the panic attacks or fear-induced anxiety will return, but it is also comforting to be on my own after two weeks of negotiating life with complete strangers.

I am so relaxed I don't even venture outside for two days. On the third day, Ali sends me a text saying he is returning to Saint-Louis and I should visit him in Ngor Island before he leaves. I agree to visit him.

The next day, I get dressed and set out for Ngor. It takes two hours before we can find each other on the island. The beach is not as spectacular as the one in Saint-Louis. It is very rocky and the tides are turbulent. We talk and I watch the sea water as it ebbs and flows in and out of shore, crashing on the immovable rocks. The following day, at Ali's insistence, I returned to Ngor Island to hang out with him and his friends, who are craftsmen and musicians.... we end up sleeping on the open beach. The next day I tell Ali that nothing he can say will change my mind about him or leaving Dakar. He had been asking me to consider moving to Saint-Louis with him to start a new life there. I wish him all the best and tell him that he is not the one I want.

In between, I have been entertained listening to him and his friends jam on *djembe drums* in a small tourist shop, where they sell paintings, musical instruments, traditional shoes, and miscellaneous items.

They show me how they live, and share their hopes and dreams with me. I sleep with them in their home - an abandoned, half-cracked building near the airport. It is a brutal form of existence - loud and open to all the elements. They talk of how they used to sing together when they first arrived in Senegal as immigrants from neighbouring Guinea-Conakry, living precarious lives, facing frequent arrests, harassment, and discrimination from the general public. They tell me of how they used to be a band playing gigs together in Saint-Louis. They were very good, they tell me, their eyes glistening with nostalgia.

I know a producer who needs new sound. I tell Ali that I can connect them with him if they decide to work together. But by the time I am ready to leave, I realise that it was all just talk. They were reminiscing about old times and never had any intention of recording anything together again. They are too busy trying to survive.

I go back to Aisha's apartment, which feels more like home compared to all the places I have been sleeping in lately. A day or so later, Aisha and her daughter Nala arrive. After a couple of days cooking and being a playmate to Nala, I tell them I am going on a pilgrimage to Senegal's Holy City of Touba. I am too restless to stay in one place.

Chapter 03
WHAT DO YOU BELIEVE?

"You want to go to Touba?" Amadou asks, as if to make sure he's heard me right. We are sitting at Dakar's French Institute, on a bench under a large baobab tree. His big brown eyes make slits to the side in my direction. He is not convinced. Amadou is one of two guides that Shaka, a friend back in Johannesburg, recommended I contact while in Dakar. He told me they would be perfect guides to the city, especially Amadou who makes a living as a tourist guide and trader downtown. We didn't get off to a great start though, so his scepticism is well-founded. I was late for our first appointment the previous day, a fact that he didn't appreciate. He gave me a stern reprimand over the phone, telling me that he would not be willing to meet with me again. If I wanted to see him, I should come on time. I said I would. I therefore made sure that I was on time the next day; I was even a little early. He found me waiting for him.

"Yes, I do," I answer, lighting a cigarette to calm my nerves. He is silent for a while, as if waiting for me to say something more - maybe to convince him or give him a reason why he should trust someone like me. "Are you going to the Grand Magal?" I ask, changing my tactics.

"Yes," he answers.

"Can I come with you then? I mean, I would not like to make you do something you don't want to do. But, if you are already planning to go there and I am not taking you out of your way, can I come with you?" I ask, my uncertainty increasing.

He doesn't seem to be interested in what I'm saying. He doesn't seem to be listening to me either. He is, from my perspective, very far away from me. I'm hoping that he will agree to take me because, well, I just have to go.

After what seems like forever, he replies.

"There's no smoking in Touba. Will you be able to go for three days without smoking?" he asks, holding onto a customary chewing stick, his sothiou, which many West Africans use to clean their teeth as an alternative to the standard toothbrush and toothpaste.

I let my eyes rest on his face in a vain effort to read his mind, but his eyes are impenetrable. The only parts of his body that betray his emotions are his hands. Amadou has a thick mane of neat dreadlocks, which he twists himself. He tells me he doesn't drink alcohol, smoke tobacco, or have sex. He lives a clean, highly-regimented life. He runs for an hour three days a week, sells Senegalese art and other merchandise for six days a week, goes to prayers on Fridays, and relaxes on Sundays by drinking tea with friends and family in the afternoon. He prays five times every day of the week without fail. His body is athletic and rippled with muscles. He never smiles, at least not at me. His routine frightens me. He was born in the same month and year as I was, with just a few days apart.

I write in my notebook after our lunch meeting that I am in love with him - this just 60 minutes after we first met!

I need to love him. Perhaps, more accurately, I need him to love me. Or at the very least, I need him to love me enough to take me to Touba with him. The Grand Magal of Touba is the largest pilgrimage of its kind in West Africa and attracts over 3 million pilgrims each year from the region. It is on my list of things to do for the holiday. It is also the last big adventure I can go on before returning home to South Africa.

I simply have to go.

There are so many reasons why it is not a good idea for me to go to the Grand Magal, the biggest one being that I am not a believer in the truest sense. I am not a Muslim and have no desire or intentions of converting to Islam or

Mouridism. All I desire is to go through the motions of being a devotee, without the responsibilities of actually being one. I want to immerse myself in their world, deliberately lose sight of who I am, in the hope that the experience of everything I am not, will in the end reveal the one thing that I am - my true self. I have not yet worked out how this feat can be executed. It doesn't occur to me that I am in fact manifesting a desire that is so deep within me that I had completely forgotten its origins by the time I am pleading my case with Amadou under a tree in Dakar. Basically, I am following a script I wrote decades ago as a child. Amadou's hesitation threatens to delay my role in this particular act. I have waited for too long to be a pilgrim. After some consideration, Amadou agrees to take me with him. We arrange to meet early the next day, so that I have enough time to purchase everything I need for the trip.

We spend hours at the Sandaga Market, negotiating a fair price for a used camera. Amadou is a skilled negotiator, which means that finding the right camera at a fair price will likely take all day. I wish I could just walk into a shop and pick one I can afford, instead of having to go through all this haggling that seems to make up the very essence of life in the marketplace. Each time I try to pull him into what I consider a 'proper' electronics shop, he insists that he can get me something better, at a cheaper price, someplace else.

I also need appropriate clothing for the trip. My clothes are either too revealing by Islamic standards, or completely forbidden for women: for example, my jeans and trousers. In Touba, and particularly during the Grand Magal, everyone has to adhere to the strictest dress and behavioural code of utter and complete modesty. We search for pieces of clothing to buy, but I cannot find anything suitable to wear at a reasonable price. In the end, Amadou says the pants I am wearing, which are loose and resemble those worn by the Baye Fall and Yaye fall of the Sufi-Mouride sect of Islam, will be just fine for this trip. I ask him if he is sure.

"Yes," he says, "It's allowed."

I am relieved that I don't have to spend extra money on clothes I do not need.

Even though we have planned to spend two nights in Touba, I choose to carry as little extra baggage as possible which means, I do not pack a change of clothes.

We leave later that evening.

Buses to Touba, Senegal's second largest city after Dakar, are filled to the brim with men, women, and children all squeezing through every opening and crevice to take their rightful seats on the trip to the Holy Land. It is a frenzy of activity. It is not unlike what I had imagined going on a pilgrimage would be when I was just five years old watching my cousins and other relatives going up and down the house packing lunches that consisted of steamed bread, cooked chicken, apples, bananas, oranges, bottles of juice and flasks of sweet, milky tea or coffee. Usually, as with my pilgrimage to Touba, these trips would take place at night and for some time while the packing was happening, excitement would perfume the air, intoxicating me from head to toe. In my drunken state I would plead repetitively, asking in different tones: "Please, please, please may I come with you?"

I would do this while pulling on my cousin Nana's freshly-pressed, long-sleeved, royal blue tunic that she wore with sheer black stockings and black Buccaneer brand school shoes. On her head, she wore a green beret with a silver star of David on it and a black and green lapel badge pinned just above her breasts. That was the uniform for young women at the church and my cousin looked amazing in it. "You're too young to go, sisi!" she'd respond. My cousin was just a teenager then too, so she had no authority to decide whether or not I could go. "Please, I want to go with you! I want to go with you!" At this point, I would be holding onto the edges of her dress and she would be helplessly trying to extricate herself from me. But I would not let up: I wanted to go to Moria; I wanted to wear the uniform; I wanted to be in the bus when they ate the steam bread and fruit, and drank the sweet, milky tea.

"Okay, okay we'll go next year, okay? Next year you must remind me and I'll go with you, okay?" she would finally respond, exasperated.

My pilgrimage to the Magal of Touba, was to be my Moria. The Moria I never went to, despite numerous promises to the contrary.

Moria, in the Limpopo Province of South Africa, is the birthplace of Joseph Lekganyane, the founder of the Zionist Christian Church the ZCC. The ZCC is the largest African-founded church in Southern Africa. The church is known for mixing African and Christian beliefs, so was often labelled a cult by the Apartheid government. An estimated 3 million members of the church would join the pilgrimage and congregate in Moria City at Easter every year.

The ZCC was my father's church. He grew up in the faith and wore his badge until his married life, which is when things changed. My parents took my sister and I to a few services when we were both children. The church service usually began outside with singing. Before the congregants could enter the church, they would have holy water sprinkled on their faces, hands, and the soles of their feet, a ritual I enjoyed. Married women wore yellow shirts with green skirts, head scarves and belts, and men wore khaki military uniforms with white boots and policeman-like hats. Others wore green suits, with yellow trimming down the sides. Modesty was required amongst its members, which meant that women could not leave their shoulders bare or wear clothing that would reveal their bosoms... and forget about trousers. Their heads had to be covered at all times, but most importantly at church. However, I did not recall any of this as I climbed into the bus to the Magal of Touba.

When pilgrims embark on a spiritual journey, they do so in part to fulfil a desire, a wish. Generally, there is something in their lives that needs to change. Whether it is a cure for an illness, success at work, in business, marriage, and children, or they go on pilgrimages simply to give thanks for blessings already received, everyone has something they want. Everyone is praying for something. I start to think about what it is that I want. Is my life an aimless search for adventure, a passing thrill? Or am I searching for something more meaningful? What can it be? Is it peace?

I am harbouring a kind of restlessness that has gotten me involved in situations that have complicated my life in such a way that I've literally had to run from it. Perhaps I am looking for love, for that proverbial once-in-a-lifetime romance. Maybe I am yearning to be someone's wife? Maybe I want one day to become someone's mother? Or perhaps what I really want is success in my chosen career, in journalism. Maybe I want to break a huge story, be at the right place at the right time and tell a story that will change the course of history, or of politics as we know it, a story that will cement my name in the history of the world. It may also be that I want power and influence. Maybe I want to be able to change things. Perhaps I want my voice to matter, maybe I want people to stop and listen to what I have to say, instead of ignoring me or telling me to shut up all the time. Maybe wanting or desiring something is what causes people to become vulnerable to manipulation and abuse. Perhaps it is not good to want any one thing too much. Maybe I don't want any of it. Perhaps what I actually want is some level of detachment, a desire not to desire or even need these things in the first place. Perhaps this is where true power lies.

While I am not exactly sure about what I want for my life right now, I am sure about one thing: I want to go to Touba and experience being a pilgrim on a pilgrimage. I turn to Amadou, who is quietly facing ahead in the bus.

"What do you want?" I ask him. "What will you be praying for on this pilgrimage?"

His answer is simple, straightforward: "I want to find love," he says, "get married and have a family of my own." I quietly reflect on his answer. That's what I want too, I think to myself.

Even though my heart's desires are not clear to me at this moment, there was a time in my life when I was crystal clear about what it was that I wanted.

I wanted precisely three things.

It was towards the end of 2010, a year before my trip to Senegal. After a fun night out with friends, I took all the pills I could find in my friend's bathroom cabinet and drank them all before going to bed. I was distraught. I couldn't find my brother Peace, who had disappeared from my grandmother's house in Meadowlands Township after she'd kicked him out one night. She told me she didn't know where he was when I asked about his whereabouts. Thoughts of him being mauled by evil forces around Johannesburg sent shivers down my spine. I didn't know where or how to begin to search for him. I didn't have the strength to search. But more importantly I was, above all, tired of living. I was exhausted with life. The year had been such a rough roller-coaster ride that I was emotionally spent. I thought I could make some kind of bargain with God. His life for mine. I was willing to die in his place.

At least then, I thought, my life and death would mean something; there would finally be a purpose to my existence. After I had taken these pills, I fell into a deep sleep. However, I was woken up in the middle of the night by searing fear. I was scared out of my mind. It was a strange fear because I was still alive, yet I felt completely different.

My friend, who was in a room next to mine, was still awake as her lights were on. I went into her bedroom and asked if I could join her. I didn't tell her that I was afraid of being alone. I didn't tell her why I was afraid, or that I had taken sleeping pills to kill myself. To distract myself from my thoughts I asked her to tell me a story, to describe to me her dream home and what it would look like, what it would feel like, or sound like to be inside it. Who would be in it? What would they be doing? After some time, I desperately needed to go to the bathroom. As I stood up to go, thinking at this point that the pills I had taken had not been effective, I looked ahead and saw a door in a wall I knew for sure did not have one.

The door opened to a cloud of white mist which hovered over the passage to the bathroom. I froze, stuck at the door. I couldn't leave the room. It occurred to me then that if I stepped towards the bathroom, I would never come back; I would die. I rushed back to bed screaming: "I don't want to die! I don't want to die!"

My friend, who had been having a wonderful time telling me stories, could not understand my sudden hysteria.

"What are you talking about? What happened?" she asked. "I thought you were going to the bathroom. What's going on?"

I could not explain it to her. I felt I was running out of time and my refusal to go to the bathroom was just a way to delay the inevitable.

"I don't want to die, oh my God, I don't want to die! I don't know where I'm going!"

My screams became louder and more desperate.

I wanted to fight death and yet I knew that I was powerless against it. I was regretting having taken the pills, because now that I was dying I realised that I didn't know where I was going. I didn't know where my spirit or soul would end up. The reality that once I actually died, I could never return, I could never come back inside my body, made me completely delirious. Suddenly, there was so much I needed to do, so much I needed to say. I thought of my mom and how devastated she would be to learn of my suicide... and what about my father, my sisters, and brothers...

I was in agony, but I was also growing tired of fighting, crying, and screaming. I wanted to run out of the house, just so that I could stay awake for long enough to say one more thing, see one more person. I needed more time to tell this person that I was sorry, or that person that I loved them.

"Please forgive me!" I asked my friend, acknowledging even then that I had put her in an impossible situation. I was a mental, emotional, and physical mess. There was nothing peaceful about death and I was wild with fear. Deranged.

At some point my friend remembered that my youngest sister, who was visiting, was in the house, asleep in another room at the far end. She asked me to calm down and said that she was going to fetch my sister. Somewhere during my hysteria, I had managed to tell her that I had taken all her sleeping pills. I had wanted to die, but now that it was actually happening, I didn't want to die anymore. When I saw my sister and the concern in her big brown eyes, I knew that I was dying. I told her that I was sorry. I had taken some sleeping pills, thinking I would die in my sleep but, alas, it was happening now. I was dying. Could she please tell everyone at home that I was sorry and that I loved them?

"Oh Dad!" I screamed. "I don't want to die!" I cried over and over and over again. "Noooo!!!"

At that point, it felt like a strange force was pulling my soul from the tips of my toenails through to the back of my neck. I kept seeing myself lying lifeless on the bed and with no way of being able to get back into my body. My sister kept asking me to calm down. Fear flowed through her eyes, even as she asked me to breathe slowly and keep my eyes focused on hers. I was battling to keep my eyes open. There was this strong force pulling me, drawing the very breath out of me. Each time the pull became stronger, I would scream even louder.

"I don't want to die!" At this point, my hysteria was mixed with fatigue. The sun was coming up, but I felt I could no longer hold onto life. My sister, who is a born-again Christian, decided to lead me through The Sinner's Prayer. By then, I had accepted that I was going to die, but my fear came from not knowing where my soul would go. She asked me to repeat the words after her. I was familiar with them, having said them a thousand times as a child at church and when I was witnessing to friends and strangers. I repeated the prayer and accepted Jesus Christ as my personal saviour.

But the pull did not abate. It came in waves, as if I was drunk but was trying with all my might to remain sober, except I didn't think I could recover. My sister suggested that we go to the bathroom, so that I could pee. I was still hysterical. I was petrified of standing up, because I thought falling would mean the end of me. I thought I could delay everything by shouting and screaming. I was holding on with every iota of human strength I could muster, but I was growing weaker and weaker.

I crawled on all fours to go to the bathroom, with my sister's assistance. My friend ordered me to calm down: "You are not going to die. Drink this water and milk. Everything will be fine," but I was not convinced. It was as if a portal had been opened on the nape of my neck and an energy more powerful than me was sucking my spirit out of me, like a vacuum cleaner pulling dirt from a heavy thick carpet. Each time that happened, I made kicking motions with my feet. I had to fight off the heavy pull. At that moment, the English phrase of someone having "kicked the bucket" held new meaning for me. But more viscerally, the story of how my grandmother Mamani had died came sharply into focus.

My cousin Bonang, who had been with her at her time of death, told me the story: Mamani had been sitting near the door of the old silver and cream coal stove in the kitchen in Meadowlands. She had been sick for a while and her condition had deteriorated to such an extent that she had become incontinent. They had ordered a car to take her to Baragwanath Hospital. When the car arrived to pick her up, she didn't want to get into it. She kept on saying: "Ang'fun' ukuhamba, Angiyilapho, Haayi, Angifuni. Angifuni uk'hamba! Kuphi? Es'bhedlela? Bazongenzani lapho? Haayi! Angifuni uk'hamba! Hhheyi!" They kept reassuring her that they were taking her to the hospital for treatment, where she would get better. But Mamani didn't want to hear any of it.

As they tried to pick her up to put her into the back of the van that had been parked close to the kitchen door, she refused to get in, and continued to fight them. The more they tried to pick her up, the heavier and heavier she became until they couldn't lift her up anymore. They put her back on the chair, so that she could rest for a bit. But then, her eyes rolled back and she began foaming at the mouth, blood dripped out her nose and tears rolled out of her eyes. "Mamani! Mamani!" My cousin had screamed, but Mamani was gone. "Mamani! Ungenzi so, Mamani, Mamani vuka! Mamani!" But she was already dead. At the time, my cousin told me, she'd thought that Mamani hadn't wanted to go to the hospital, but at this moment as I heard the words, Angifuni Uk'hamba - I don't want to go! - coming out of my own mouth, I understood then what she'd meant. She'd been saying that she didn't want to die. She, like me, didn't know where she was going. And now it was happening to me! It was my turn.

As we were walking slowly towards the car to take me to the emergency room, I became more and more frantic and inconsolable. "I want to live! I want to live!" My feet were growing heavy; I imagined them turning navy blue. My sister and friend assured me that I was fine; their colour was normal. That's when I became clear about what I wanted to live for: "I want to get married, have two children and write books! I want to live!" I carried on like this until we got into the car.

In the car, I became more hysterical. I wanted my friend to drive faster, because I was not sure I would make it to the hospital alive. By the time we got there, my sister and friend were as panicked as I was, but the hospital staff were calm. They had seen too many cases of attempted suicide. All my vitals were fine. The blood tests came back clear of poisoning of any kind. I was overwhelmed with shame. After all this drama, I wasn't about to die or in any danger of dying.

They kept me in the emergency room for two hours to monitor any changes.

The doctor came to tell me that I was fine to go home, but before letting me go he gave me a card with a number for a psychologist. He asked: "Why do you want to kill yourself?" but I couldn't give him an answer. This was my third suicide attempt.

The first time I'd tried had been after a work trip to Spain, which had turned into a disaster. Upon my return, my assignment editor told me simply that I had "fucked-up". It had been my first solo, international assignment. I drank sleeping pills then, which put me to sleep for a day and a half. The second time had been a month after we'd buried my grandmother, Mamani. I had gone to my cousin Bonang's house, where they had given me a suitcase full of my grandmother's clothes, several of which were my favourites of hers. I'd also gotten a plastic bag full of toys which my sister and I had played with as children. My grandmother had brought them for us from work, and she had kept them for over two decades. In the suitcase, there was also a photo album that had belonged to her, which I also remembered from childhood. In it, were newspaper and magazine cut-outs of her favourite recipes, pictures of herself and all of us in them. When I got home that evening, alone and overcome with grief, I had opened the suitcase and put on one of her dresses. The smell of her perfume had driven me absolutely insane. I cried until I decided the only way to end the pain was to join her wherever she was. I didn't know how to live without her. I couldn't say goodbye.

When I first heard of her death, it was as if something snapped in my mind. It was as if an umbilical cord that I never knew existed between us had been severed. It was a permanent loss of a connection to someone I truly loved and whom I believed truly loved me.

I went to the mortuary to see her - just to make sure that it was not a case of mistaken identity. I didn't believe she was capable of dying. I told my mother over the phone that I was going. She warned me that I shouldn't do it. I shouldn't go and see her, but I didn't listen and now it's an image that I can never erase.

I went to the mortuary with Mamani's older sister Gogo and Aunt Beso. Everything felt like a dream I would wake up from.

I walked through the small corridor leading to the fridges behind Gogo. But as soon as I caught a glimpse of Mamani's head, I got the shock of my life. I let out a small scream and turned back to the waiting area to compose myself. Then I went back in again. Her greyish body lay like a mound of defrosting flesh on a silver tray. The face was double its size - but it was her. The nose was hers. Her lips, which were my favourite part of her, small, well-defined, and pert, were now flat and lopsided. Her nose was dripping with blood. Her breasts had flattened to her sides, with the nipples facing up close to her chest, frozen - they looked like deflated balloons. Her stomach was distended and looked rock hard. Parts of her looked like the inflated orange mascot on the popular Oros concentrated juice brand. I looked at her hands, which were hanging off the silver table. I looked at her fingers - they were definitely hers. I touched them and for a moment thought she would wake up. I wanted to say: "Wake up Mamani - it's me. I'm here, wake up!" But she was still. I looked at her face for a second time and it looked like she would smile and say "Hooo, beng'dla ngawe!" For a moment it felt as if I was alone in a room with her until Aunt Beso and Gogo, who had stood by watching me go through these motions, said that it was time to dress her. I tried to help them lift her, but her body was too heavy for the three of us. The two men who worked at the mortuary came to assist. Dressed in blue overalls, they were like construction workers lifting a slab of concrete. They were rough, but quick. I wanted to shout at them. Be gentle! I screamed in my head, but they were done dressing her before I could compose the words. They were clearly used to handling stiffs. The green shirt that they had put on her body did not have buttons on it, so it would not close over her breasts which were now protruding through the delicate slip she wore underneath it. "Why are there no buttons on this shirt? Where are the buttons on this shirt?" I asked. "Why is this shirt without buttons?" I asked again in an accusatory tone.

"That's how it's done," Aunt Beso and Gogo replied.

"How what is done?" I asked.

"It's tradition. You can't bury someone with clothes that have buttons on them," Gogo replied.

"Was there nothing else she could wear? A dress?" I inquired.

"No," they said. "She wanted to be buried in her church uniform and this is it."

"What kind of tradition is this?" I asked angrily. "What would happen if she were to be buried with a shirt with buttons? Look, it doesn't close. Her breasts are out in the open. Do you want her to go like this? What is this? I don't understand."

I was livid.

Gogo was now wiping Mamani's face with her old face cloth, while the workers stuffed cotton wool in her nose to stop the bleeding. I was furious. Yet there was nothing I could do about it. My grandmother Mamani would have to be buried this way, with her breast sticking out. If they opened the coffin for people to see her, they would see her face and two nipples. There was no one who could explain this nonsensical tradition. Why do people do things they don't understand? I wondered to myself.

Back in my bedroom, wearing the navy dress with white polka-dots that could have covered Mamani's body, including her nipples, I drank whatever sleeping pills I had from my trips abroad in an attempt to join her, but they were not enough. I lived. I was so ashamed. My friend, who had taken me to the emergency room at the hospital, was also a colleague. As a result, everyone from the office came to my bedroom that afternoon - an event that counts as one of the most embarrassing moments in my life. My house was dirty; I hadn't cleaned, washed the dishes, or made my bed. I hadn't taken a bath since that incident and there they were, standing around my bed in front of me - all my editors and colleagues from work, there in my messy house, in my bedroom surrounding me, while I squirmed under my duvet. I wanted to die right then. How do I answer their questions? How do you tell someone who doesn't want to live, that they must live? Not only did I feel like a complete and utter failure, I was humiliated and utterly ashamed of my physical and mental condition. One of my editors said: "You must relax a bit. Go and watch a movie sometime."

It was the only time I laughed during their visit.

Thinking back to numerous failed attempts at suicide, I made a pact with myself right then on the hospital bed that no matter what else might go wrong in my life from then onwards, death was not an option. I would not attempt to kill myself again. I would try and figure things out, get to the bottom of what was wrong with me. Why did I behave this way? Why was death my only solution to emotional pain? How did other people solve their problems? I was in free falling mode and there was nothing to hold on to. I had no faith.

The only thing that got me through the emotional turbulence was the thought of writing. I consoled myself with this idea: That if I could get through this moment, if I could land somewhere on solid ground, I would write about it. What I regretted the most, though, was exposing my younger sister and friend to my insanity and for traumatising them. I was full of remorse, but I didn't know how to apologise. Sorry was such a hollow word. Sorry for what?

I was ashamed of myself. I was mortified by my apparent "immortality." I was now ashamed of being alive. How long would I continue to live like this?

On the bus, I do not tell Amadou any of this. Instead, I say he must invite me to his wedding when he finds his love, as I would like to meet the woman who would eventually win his heart.

The motion in the bus pulls me in and out of sleep. My head rests on Amadou's shoulder every once in a while, creating a false sense of intimacy between us throughout the trip. Four hours later, we arrive at the Holy City and it is like nothing I have seen before.

The Holy City of Touba, for all I had heard about it, does not feel holy to me. I am confronted by a sea of bodies streaming in and chanting up and down the main street. The cars trying to drive through the multitudes seem like they are wading through a river of human mud. Though we are out in the open, it is like we have just stepped into a house made of dust and sand drummed up by hundreds of pacing feet. As we proceed further into the crowd, it feels as if we are moving deeper and deeper into a hot steam room. It is humid, sweaty, with dust whose flakes act as an adhesive between our bodies that are crammed together like a school of sardines in motion. It's as if we are all slipping in and out of each other.

You have to keep moving or you risk being pushed over by other pilgrims, an incident which could, judging by the mass of people around, certainly cause a stampede. Amadou falls easily into step with the rhythm of the city and its determined multitudes. Here, he and I are forced to hold hands because it would be easy for us to lose sight of each other in the tide. Everybody looks like the next person.

All I can hear at that point is the pattering buzz of footsteps, surpassed only by the shrill and continuous prayer emanating from the Mosque's resident Muezzin. I am doing my best to keep up with Amadou's frantic pace, which moves like a bolt of energy, pulling me this way and that. After a while of this twisting and turning, I realise that we've been walking around in circles.

"I can't remember where the place is, or where we are supposed to go," Amadou says, looking distraught and frustrated for the first time since I met him.

"I know that it used to be here somewhere." He is referring to his Marabout or spiritual leader's compound, where we are meant to spend the night.

He takes his phone out and calls his 'brothers' to ask them for directions, but each call seems to get us even more lost. We are getting nowhere. We have been walking around in circles for close to an hour, when I start to think that maybe I am in hell.

Hell, according to Christian scripture, is a place of eternal damnation. It is a place where people who did not accept Jesus Christ as their personal saviour are banished. A place of fire and brimstone, where sinners are engulfed in flames to burn without ceasing for all eternity; to infinity and beyond. In this place, there is no death, no rest. The sinners live to burn, day in and day out forever and ever - Amen.

Perhaps this, then, is the truth I have been seeking. I have died and gone to hell, and this street in the Holy City of Touba is the reception area. I am like everyone else here - a ghost. One of those unfortunate souls who'd refused to be saved, who'd refused to accept salvation when it had been so freely offered. Now, I am banished to an eternity of walking endlessly in a hot dusty, loud street, with no place to rest, no water, no food, and no relief.

As he walks, Amadou glances back at me with exasperation. I have no idea how to calm him down. First of all, I don't know where we are, or what he is looking for. I start to wonder what he expects me to do. What advice can I offer him? He is the one who goes to Touba every year; I thought he was familiar with the terrain. By this time, I'm also beginning to feel the onset of fatigue; I'm so tired it's now making me dizzy. My legs are growing weak, but I cannot afford to slow down. I tell myself that I have to see this episode through to its logical or illogical conclusion. I will walk for as long as I need to walk. To gain strength, I begin to pray silently with each step, making sure that I remind myself of who I am and why I am there. My name is love, I come from love. I am here to love and I am going to love. I am happy to be here. I focus on this prayer, which I repeat over and over in my mind, until Amadou exclaims that he has found the place. When we arrive, the compound is quiet and most of its inhabitants have already gone to sleep in the different rooms. Our place to rest is a thin plastic mat outside in the open yard.

Amadou's Marabout comes out to greet us and joins us on the mat to pray. I do not know what is being said in prayer. We sit cross-legged on the mat and the Marabout asks us to cup our hands, with our palms facing up to receive a blessing. It is the same hand gesture that was used in Mamani's church when the congregants sang and prayed. By the time she died, she had convinced her older sister, Koko Norain, to join the church. When Koko Norain died two weeks before my trip to Senegal, I went to Meadowlands to pray with the family on the day of my departure. I remember thinking then, that I would never pray that way again. Now, here I was, thousands of kilometres away, in a foreign country, praying with open, cupped hands. I was surprised but relieved that there was, even in this remote and hellish place, something familiar I could hold onto, even if it was in Islam.

After the prayer, the Marabout retires to his place of rest while Amadou makes himself comfortable on the mat. He uses his small bag as a pillow and promptly falls asleep. I stay wide awake, listening to the sounds of the compound until the early birds start chirping and the roosters begin to crow, signalling that the sun has risen. This is when my eyelids, heavy with sleep, collapse into each other. Soon enough, everyone in the compound is awake. The flurry of activity all around me makes sleeping impossible. I have to wake up. I am relieved to see that there are other women in the compound, even though most of them keep their distance. I am dreading going to the bathroom area, because I do not know what I will find. Most things in the compound are communal; there is little privacy.

I am ill-prepared for this camp-like set up, which is much more rural than I anticipated. I crave a private flush toilet, with ceramic white seats, a clean shower with hot water, and a mirror - all the amenities of modern life which are absent in our compound. I have to find a way to quickly adjust to this new environment, before I become a nuisance to myself and others. The toilet and shower area are behind a block of rooms that face the open space where Amadou and I have spent the night. It is muddy. I can't stop my mind from wondering what else could be down there. It is too late to ask myself why I came here.

I am already here, in too deep, and I have to see this experience - which I had so fervently desired with so much enthusiasm two days ago - through to the very end. Most of the showers and toilets are vacant by the time I gather enough courage to face the music. On entering, I discover that the lavatories are all drop toilets, a fact which brings back childhood anxieties linked to going to the loo in Botlokwa, Limpopo, and in Meadowlands. I have to remind myself that I am no longer the three, four, or five-year-old girl who is scared. There are no dogs barking at me, threatening to bite me, and it is humanly impossible for me to fall into the manhole unless someone is forcing me into it. No one here is doing that.

After I finish washing up, I join Amadou on our mat where bread and tea is being rationed. By mid-morning, Amadou says we should get ready to walk towards the Mosque.

As we set out in the sun, the streets are already teeming with people. It is difficult to estimate just how many of us are walking down the main road leading to the Mosque, near where the founder of the Mouride Brotherhood Cheikh Amadou Bamba is buried. I have heard many stories about this man, who is idolised in most of Senegal. The only picture of him, taken by French imperialists, shows him wearing a flowing white robe and a headscarf that covers his face. This image can be seen everywhere in Senegal. The first story I heard about him and his significance in Senegalese culture, politics and spiritual history, is pretty fantastic. The story goes like this:

Cheikh Amadou Bamba was a freedom fighter, born in 1853. He was an anti-colonial pacifist, who campaigned for the liberation of black people. He also refused to bow to French pressure to convert to Christianity. One day he was arrested and brought to the court for his refusal to renounce his beliefs, as he was one of the more influential spiritual Islamic leaders at the time. During a trip when he was being deported to a place where the French Privy Council sat in Saint-Louis, he was mocked: "Your fanatic preaching will not have any effect." While aboard the boat Bamba took out his prayer mat to pray. One of the guards stopped him from praying on board the ship, saying that it was not a Mosque. Cheikh Amadou Bamba insisted that he would pray, even if doing so would cost him his life. He told the guard that he would be subjected only to God. The guard told him that he could say his prayers, but not on the boat. So, Cheikh Amadou Bamba put his prayer mat out over the Atlantic Ocean and went out to pray on a floating mat. He didn't sink. After finishing his prayers, he got back onto the ship. This feat earned him the respect of the guards. The legend was born. However, the story that is recorded in history books states that after he was arrested by French authorities, before appearing before the French Privy Council in Saint-Louis, Senegal, Cheikh Amadou Bamba prayed two rakats - with their specifically prescribed movements and words - in the governor's office, before addressing the Council. Through this symbolic prayer and his bold stance in front of these deniers of Islam, Bamba came to embody a new form of non-violent resistance against the aims of colonial evangelists. He was exiled to Gabon and then Mauritania for seven years and nine months, after which he was kept under house arrest in the Diourbel Region outside Dakar, for 15 years. His crime was his insistence on practising and teaching his faith openly. The French colonial policy then, was to 'Christianise and assimilate to the cultural values of France in Senegal. Their mission: to systematically eliminate Muslim spiritual guides. Despite this, Cheikh Amadou Bamba did not cease to defend the message of Islam until his death in 1927.

As we walk amongst throngs of his disciples, I am keenly aware that I do not share the passion which propels their limbs forward in the scorching heat. I try to keep my eyes on Amadou, while also keeping my eyes on the road. Doing both at the same time is impossible. Eventually, Amadou and I lose sight of each other. I am unable to see past the sweat and humidity, which is making thick films of steam on my eye-glasses. Looking back and around me proves fruitless. If I take my glasses off, I won't be able to see where I am going at all and I risk losing them.

It is already difficult to keep my eyes fully open against the glare of the sun. I have to squint just to see through them. I have been taken by the wind and Amadou has disappeared into the vast ocean of pilgrims making their way to the Mosque. As we inch closer to the main entrance, I wait. I hope I will be able to spot Amadou from here. While waiting I try to recall the way back to the compound, just in case we don't find each other here.

I am already a lost soul - how can I find another?

After some time, I hear a man's voice shouting my name: "Jedi!" I look up and spot Amadou waving at me from the crowd. I wave back to discover that a miracle has happened. Amadou is smiling for the first time since we met. He must have been very worried. We proceed through the black iron gates and inside to the Mosque, on whose marble floors we have to walk barefoot. It is like walking on hot coals.

This adventure of mine gives new meaning to the idiom: "out of the frying pan into the fire." My experience, though, is the opposite - I had come out of the fire, right into the frying pan.

The Mosque is beautiful. If it weren't for the multitudes of people, the scorching heat, and my own lack of faith, this would be heaven.

Still, I am happy that we have accomplished our mission. We take some time to walk around, taking in the atmosphere and posing together for photos for the first time, pretending to be husband and wife.

Having arrived though, I have no idea what to do. What do you do when you get to heaven? Pray. I find a cool spot with lots of shade, where I sit and wait for Amadou while he does his salah. Here, there are many women, but I do not think of finding a place where I can observe women pray. I am astonished by the sheer activity here. How everyone manages to keep going and work in this heat is beyond me. I am so hot I want to peel my skin-off, like the aliens in the 1980s science fiction television series, 'V'.

I sit and watch as workers walk across the Mosque, carrying large plastic dishes full of rice, meat, vegetables, and water. Others sweep and polish the marble floors with machine-like precision, all the while moving at great speed. They are dressed in blue and white, regal-looking uniforms, which resemble aristocratic costumes from Shakespeare's Romeo and Juliet, making them look more like actors than custodians of the Mosque. There are all kinds of people of all ages, and colours who arrive on the marble floors looking just as elated and clueless, as I am.

After Amadou finishes his prayers he asks: "What would you like to see next?"

"I'd like to go to the library," I say.

At the entrance of the library, there is a jam. There are too many people, particularly women squeezing in and out, clamouring to go in. I can't even manage to get close to the door of the main library. I am becoming quite light-headed. I suggest we take a break, instead of fighting to go inside.

We buy some water and sit in the shade on the library grounds. I gaze at the sights and sounds. I sit back, let my eyes follow people's movements. It is putting me into a semi-meditative state and I can feel myself being drawn to sleep. Other pilgrims have already succumbed to the nocturnal calls at midday, a few people are splayed on sponge mattresses strewn around the library grounds and walkways. We take a few pictures of the Mosque and its surroundings.

After resting, Amadou suggests we go and visit another Marabout in a different compound which he says will be less crowded.

At the compound, we find women dressed in brightly-coloured, matching African-print dresses and elaborate headscarves. They sit under a large tree in the centre of the compound, peeling green beans, cabbages, onions, and carrots. Their hands, which deftly hold sharp knives, are adorned with intricate henna tattoos and rings. I watch them work, while having muted conversations with one another. Some of the women are wearing full make-up, which makes them look like Goddesses. There is an elegant gracefulness about the way they are. They seem to occupy their space in this society with such authority, ease, and dignity.

I yearn to one day be able to embody such confidence and poise while doing the most ordinary things like they are - chopping green beans under a tree. The men are busy at the far-end of the compound, shearing carcasses of goats or sheep. Everything here seems peaceful, with men and women functioning harmoniously in their designated roles. In this compound, the Grand Magal of Touba is a celebration. Although dancing and loud music is strictly forbidden, the people's joy finds expression in other less obvious ways - through the way they dress, and the artwork on their faces and hands including the food that they cook. Amadou introduces me to the leader of the compound as his wife. I ask, as we walk back to our compound, why he had done that.

"What other choice did I have?" he retorts.

"I am a tourist and you are my guide. You could have said that," I responded.

He shrugs. Just then a man approaches us and asks me to step aside. He doesn't say a word to me. Amadou steps in front of me and begins a lengthy discussion with him. It turns out that the man is one of Touba's Police Officers or Police Islamique, tasked with ensuring that Islamic order and modesty prevails in the city especially during the pilgrimage. I have contravened the law.

"He says you're wearing pants and it's not allowed here," Amadou tells me. "He says you should be detained with immediate effect."

Detained? I must be dreaming - I think to myself.

"Amadou, didn't you say that wearing these pants would be allowed here?" I ask, trying to remain calm.

"I know," he says, as if to a child, "but he says it's not allowed. They can't allow you to walk around like this, because they don't want other women to think that dressing like you have is halal. It's okay for men, but not for women."

"Let's go!" The policeman says with agitation.

Amadou tries to negotiate, pleading with him: "She is a foreigner. She is not from here. She's not Muslim. She doesn't understand our ways." But the man does not listen. He points at me and gestures for me to follow him. I feel like a lamb being led to the slaughter.

I can't believe this! I think, shouting at Amadou in my head. You said this would be fine. You said I could wear this, that it would be cool like the Yaye Fall and the Baye Fall.

I am extremely upset and disappointed with Amadou, but my anger will not change anything, so I remain silent and follow the policeman to the holding area.

The detention centre is an old, white tent that is so dirty it looks beige. The policeman directs me inside and instructs me to sit down on one of the wooden benches. There are a handful of other people inside, many look like street traders. I wonder what Islamic laws they have broken.

Some, like me, are inappropriately dressed. I notice a big woman whose clothes are in tatters. It looks as if she's been in some kind of a fight in which her clothes were torn off her body, revealing her bare arms, chest, and parts of her bra-less boobs. She hangs her head. Amadou is standing by the entrance of the detention centre, watching me.

You are the reason I am here... I think angrily. There is another officer who is giving some offenders lashes - after which they are free to go. From where I am sitting, it seems as if it's only men who are getting lashes. But I am not certain that I will be exempt from them, since I don't know what the penalty of my offence will be.

Watching this man take in his lashes with pride makes me laugh at myself inside.

Do I have to be so dramatic about everything? I ask myself.

I begin to reason: I'm not being dramatic. I did ask if what I was wearing would be okay here, and the chief Muslim, my brother leader Amadou, said yes. He prays five times a day! Isn't he a devoted Muslim? How could he not know? Oh my God! The more I try to reason with myself, the worse my situation gets. My mind starts to wonder: He's probably in on it with the police! If he is, how in the world am I going to get out of here? I am going to disappear amongst millions and millions of people and no one except this guy Amadou will know where I am or what happened to me. I am going to rot in prison, to be beaten and punished to death in a Muslim country and for what? For wearing pants, which are ostensibly a skirt with two holes at the bottom for my feet. This is what I am going to prison for, clothes and fashion! How revolutionary! Time moves slowly inside the tent.

I glance back at the entrance, but Amadou is no longer there; he has vanished. I start to panic. How stupid can you be, Jedi! Look now? Where is he? He's gone. Where is he?

This conversation with myself continues unabated. What will I have to do to get out of here?

It is quite something to think of grown people subjecting themselves to lashings as punishment for contravening religious laws. I cannot wrap the idea around my sweltering head. I am also seriously panicking now, as the groans and yelps grow louder and louder in front of me. I am afraid. I am hopelessly allergic to physical pain. It's something I've tried to avoid since childhood.

Today, at the ripe age of 30, I will be punished with lashings. What will I do if they call me next?

I look around at my fellow detainees; we are not many. Most of their facial expressions are vacant. Some are docile, accepting, as if the fact of their detention makes no difference to the overall outcome of their lives. I can't understand this. It's incongruous to me since, in my opinion, my 'arrest' could change the course of my life forever. No one is speaking in the tent. I do not have the language to speak, even if I were so inclined.

As a child I hated hidings, but I was also almost always in trouble, which meant that my parents had to do a lot of running around the house after me if they were intent on punishing me. Before I started school, I even spent an entire day up in the hills of Botlowaka avoiding my grandmother's lashes, after waking up to discover that I had peed in the bed yet again. When I finally returned home at dusk, hoping that the presence of my aunts and uncles would shield me, my grandmother was fuming. I almost lost an eye.

Later, while in Primary School, my father, after lashing my older sister with a special black leather belt he reserved for this very purpose, came after me. But, by then, I had already decided that I was not going to be punished after watching my sister beg for forgiveness: *Ke gopela tshwarelo Papa! Papa! Ke gopela tshwarelo toe!* I ran around the house, while my father chased after me. Eventually, I escaped into the toilet and locked myself in there. My father bellowed loudly at me: "Come out now! Open the door!"

I was not going to open the door while he was that angry. I was petrified of my father. He went away thinking I would get tired eventually. Then, I remembered that the front door was open. If I could get through the passage and lounge area, I would be able to escape. I waited for him to stop pacing up and down the passage. When I thought it was safe, I ran as fast as I could out of the house. By the time my father realised that I was out of the toilet, I was already climbing the fence. He came out with his belt and tried to chase me around the yard, but I would not budge.

"Come back inside!" He shouted, but I was too stubborn. I had decided that this time I would not let him give me a hiding, I would not give in. I stayed there on the fence, thinking about my next move. I didn't want to go back into the house and face the wrath of my father, but I had nowhere else to go. It was too dark to walk to Gogo's house, and I was more petrified of the dark anyway.

Not knowing what to do, I sat on the fence, vowing to sleep on it if that's what it took. I sat there for a while, until my father came out again and demanded I come into the house now. This time, the tone of his voice let me know he meant business. I conceded defeat. I climbed off the fence, while preparing myself for the biggest hiding of my life. But when I got inside the house my father said: "I don't want to see you. Go to your room" - which I did. I never got beaten that night or the next day. However, this also meant that I was constantly anxious and stayed clear of my father whenever I was in the house, because I thought he could turn around at any moment and beat me as soon as he remembered my defiance. Even though he never beat me, the threat that he could give me a hiding when I least expected it, still haunted me for days after the initial incident.

This was something that I had grown used to; it was Mamani's favourite tactic. She had the habit of delaying her punishment, sometimes for days, after you'd done something wrong, waiting for just the moment when you least expected it to make you pay. This was usually around bath time. She would surprise me with hidings with her brown leather skipping rope, after I had taken all my clothes off and splashed my body wet with water. I would most often already be in the bath and would have nowhere to go. She would then remind me of my offence and proceed to beat me until she was satisfied. Sometimes, she used twigs from the apple tree. But the skipping rope was her tool of choice. My wails then would be punctuated with pleas for forgiveness *"Ngicela uxolo! ng'xolele Mama, ng'xolele Mama toe?"*

Beatings did not end there. We also got regular, if not daily, beatings at school for various offences, which included but were not limited to: not covering books properly, not having a clean exercise book, not doing homework, not doing your homework neatly, not wearing a clean uniform, wearing the wrong shoes to school, doing your homework wrong, not finishing your homework, giving wrong answers to the teacher's questions, not answering questions, not sitting in the right place, wearing the wrong shirt on the wrong school day, not polishing your shoes, not cutting or combing your hair, not cleaning your classroom, not cutting your nails, biting your nails, not knowing how to read, talking or laughing in class, and failing a test.

In my primary school, teachers used canes which were hollow, thin, white electrical pipes usually used to install electrical cables in buildings or wooden planks. There was a notorious history teacher who prided himself on using the ominous sjambok - the long, stiff whip originally made from rhinoceros hide, for punishment. Obviously, no one ever wanted to fail his history class. As a result of all this, I was almost always filled with anxiety by the time I was standing in line, in my black and gold school uniform, at assembly singing, *Taru Bawo, Taru, Ibanofefe kuthi... Lord Have Mercy on Us...*

Now here I am, decades later, on the brink of such punishment again and I have no idea how to get myself out of this fix. Amadou left without saying where he was going, or what he was going to do. What if he never comes back? There is nothing tying him to me and nobody would know anything about what had happened. Every second person's name in Touba is Amadou - finding him here would be similar to searching for white salt in sacks of refined white sugar. I start laughing at myself and think: This would make for an interesting story. I could write about this one day.

If I can get out of here, this will be a funny story to tell. Where else could I find material like this? It's not like they would allow me to come and camp here if I declared that I am a journalist coming to see how they treat people who break Islamic laws. It may not have been my intention to end up here, but it would certainly make for an interesting story. Here I am, getting a first-hand account of life in a makeshift Islamic detention centre in Touba. I have not received special treatment for being a journalist. This is the real deal.

Thinking that I will write about this place calms me down, because it means that I will be free. I look around the tent again, to make sure that I take in all the details, to remember everything, even though the light is dull. My stomach is growling.

"Aaiii!!" - a shrill, pained sound escapes from the lips of another detainee who is being punished. His back is bare. I watch as the policeman gives him three more lashes. Oh my God! I think to myself again. I am going to get punished for wearing baggy pants!

I am suffocating. I want to get out of here. Where is Amadou? He must come back! He must tell me what's going on. I will do anything to get out of here. What do I need to do? The answer comes moments later in the form of a 10-metre-long canvas-like piece of fabric.

I can change.

There is a makeshift changing room in the corner of the tent. Inside, there is a stack of clothing left by people who've been here before me. From the mound of clothes on the floor, it seems they have been many.

Amadou throws the fabric over the rail for me. I take off my pants and wrap the fabric around my body in three layers. It is long enough to cover my ankles. When I come out of the changing area, the officer approves of my new look. I am happy to be released but realise, once we are outside walking away, that I have left my pants behind in a rush to get out of there. I persuaded Amadou, who had gone to great lengths to find this fabric for me, to go back to the tent and retrieve them. He says: "Can't we just go?"

"No," I insist.

He has to pay to get them back. Even though I think the fee is exorbitant, I am not complaining. I am exhausted from the day's emotional upheavals. We find a large, silver tray of food waiting for us in an empty tent at our compound. It is so much food I cannot believe that it's meant for just Amadou and me.

"Where are the others?" I ask.

"They have already eaten. This is for us. Eat."

Even though I am intimidated by the amount of food, I take my spoon and dig into rice and large pieces of mutton. From the first bite, it is clear that I am ravenous. I eat heartily and even scrape off the remainder of the food with my hands. The food is delicious. After eating, Amadou suggests we sit outside on the mat with the rest of the compound's pilgrims.

The men are gathered around a tiny brassier, preparing tea. We step outside, since it is too hot in the tent.

After teatime, I relax on the mat and watch two boys wrestle each other on the compound ground. They are imitating their best-loved Senegalese wrestlers. Traditional wrestling is a big sport in Senegal. As I'm watching them, I think: What was I hoping to achieve by coming to Touba? To Senegal? What is this thing that is eating me up inside, What am I searching for here that I cannot find in South Africa? I barely escaped from being lashed for being inappropriately dressed; only God knows what is next.

Senegal is the most conservative, secular country I know. For all its show of freedom, it is a highly-regulated society, with well-defined hierarchies, rules, traditions, and customs which are hidden behind a façade of a modern democratic state.

When I left South Africa, I had imagined that I would be overcome with feelings of joy and great expectation for what the future would hold. But instead, I feel as if I have plunged myself into an infinite abyss. The country seems to laugh at me at every turn, making a mockery of my dreams of adventure, freedom and independence. But more than that I am riddled with guilt. The kind of guilt which keeps me awake most nights, unable to sleep or enjoy anything because, for some reason, I don't think I deserve to be happy. I don't know who to speak to about how torn apart I feel inside. I am broken. How is it possible that I can fundamentally misunderstand the very Being who gave me life?

After my last attempt at suicide in 2010, I didn't want to hear any more about religion or anything associated with spirituality of any kind. Until my last attempt to kill myself, when I thought about death and dying, I often assumed it would be like sleep. A long nap that would never end, but that experience showed me something different - the fact that there is no end to life. My shame made it difficult for me to look my loved ones, especially my sister, in the eye. I couldn't even look at myself in the mirror anymore. I was ashamed of what I had become. I was a disappointment to everyone. I was a selfish, slf-centred person as many of my friends and colleagues who knew about my suicide attempts often let me know. "Who do you think you are trying to kill yourself?", they said. "Don't you think we suffer too? What gives you the right to die?" They asked. I used to be someone who had a bright future ahead of her, but who failed miserably to use all the opportunities that were in front of her.

I wished I was someone else, someone better, who did not have all these issues; someone who was not such a heavy emotional burden on everyone else. The near-death experience revealed something profound to me: there was no escape. Life was the inevitable result of death and death was the inevitable result of life.

I didn't know how to live or die, in peace. My grandmother, Koko Norain tried, in her own way, to help me before she passed on. She called me and asked me to come and see her. She seldom called me directly, so I knew that whatever she wanted to discuss was serious. We arrived at her house on a Sunday afternoon and I found her sitting outside in the shade.

After the standard hellos and introductions, she said, "I called you here because I want to prepare my path, ngilungisa izinto zami."

I had no idea what she was talking about but I was willing to listen to her, to show her respect and understanding while keeping an open mind.

She continued, "I thought maybe it's time you investigate what is going on in your life, find out why you say you don't want to get married, why you sometimes disappear and stay on your own without calling anyone or contacting people. Do you know about your great-grandmother? You and I share the same name with her. Your great-grandmother, my mother, Popane, her middle name was Violet. My middle name is Violet too. You and I have been named after the same person. I'm sure you know that your mother was very close to my mother. She was the apple of my mother's eye. They were inseparable, so much so that before she died, my mother dictated her last will to your mom. She asked her to keep it in a secret place and only produce it after she had passed on, which she did. So, you can see how close they were."

"Yes," I responded. "My mother used to tell me so many stories about my great-grandmother. She adored her."

"She did. Maybe you don't know this about my mother, but she was a gifted woman. She could see; she had visions and dreams. One day, she woke up and told my father that she'd had a dream. They had to go to such and such a place, because they would find treasure buried there. 'But you must go at night,' she told them. My father was scared at the prospect, but gathered my brothers, all five of them and, armed with shovels and a dream, they set out into the night. As they inched closer to the spot where they were meant to dig, they saw that there were people who were sitting around a large fire right where they needed to go. They were all afraid, thinking that those people would attack them somehow, so they went back home. When they arrived, my mother asked, "What did you find?"

My father told her that they had not even started to dig, because they had seen men sitting around a huge fire and had feared that those men would rob or attack them somehow. So, they'd come back. My mother was not impressed. She said, "How else did you expect to see? That fire was meant for you!"

My father and his sons, realising how foolish they had been, replied, "We'll go back tomorrow," but my mother refused, saying, "No. Since none of you were brave enough to start digging, the treasure will be passed on to someone in the future, maybe your children or your grandchildren." She went on: "This episode was forgotten and life continued as normal. Years after my mother died, your mother had a dream. My mother appeared to her, carrying a baby in her arms, and said that she had a gift for her. Soon after she had that dream, your mother discovered that she was pregnant - with you. That's why she named you Lindiwe 'The one we are waiting for', and Popane after my mother. So, you were a gift from her. See? I don't know, maybe you are the one who is meant to find this treasure, because no one else in this family seems to have found it. Maybe it is you. I may be wrong, but I feel compelled to tell you. Maybe you must find out why."

I let the silence fall and settle between us. This had been the last thing I wanted to hear. I knew the story about where my names had come from. My mother had told it to me countless times as a child. Perhaps that is why I always felt I needed to protect her, but the story about the treasure, I had never heard before. While it was a fascinating story, I didn't like it. My mother wouldn't like it either, as she was a born-again Christian.

This conversation scared the living daylights out of me. I didn't want to see the possible relevance it had to my own life. I didn't want to know it. I didn't want to hear it but... Koko Norain was dying.

Koko Norain was one of five girls born to my great-grandmother Mapopane Violet Zulu née Mtshali, who'd had ten children - five boys and five girls. I knew all the girls and one of the boys. The other four boys had died before I was born, or when I was too young to remember them being alive. All of her five remaining children died in my lifetime.

What Koko Norain was telling me opened up a Pandora's Box of emotional issues I felt ill-equipped to deal with or handle with dexterity. However, if this was one of the things that she needed to do before her final journey, I couldn't stand in her way. But how was I supposed to know what gift she was speaking of when she herself had no idea? What did all of this have to do with me? Why did I have to get involved? She was right about one thing. There were things in my life that I needed to deal with. I was haunted by this story, the story behind my name and by the impact of Mamani's death.

After Mamani died, I felt like an orphan - as if I were, for the first time in my life, well and truly alone. There would be no one else who could love me the way Mamani had. That kind of love I could find with no one else, no other living human being. Yet, beneath that love there was also so much pain, so much conflict. I didn't know where love began and where hate ended. In that moment, it seemed all of it was mixed together into one unbearable ball of fire burning inside of me.

Mamani had raised my sister and me.

When I was still a little girl, shortly after I started school, my sister and I were sent to live with her. We moved from Meadowlands, where I was born, to Phefeni Township, in Orlando West. Life in Soweto was good enough for me.

I spent most of my time perched on a branch of the apple tree at the back of the house, watching as trains went in and out of Phefeni Station.

The first time I thought about life and death was after I overheard a conversation in which adults were discussing the death of a man who lived in our neighbourhood. He had been in the army and his wife would now be a widow. I remember everyone being sad. A few days later, I heard someone say a baby had just been born somewhere near the neighbour's house. It was then that I decided that's how life happens: when someone dies, they are born again somewhere else, with a different family.

It was the first independent thought I remember having about life and death as a child. It seemed logical to me that the man who had died had been born again as the new baby.

Apart from the two or three times that I attended the Zion Christian Church - ZCC with my parents, there was no other religious activity in our household. My parents loved music and television. The only time a church service was held in our house was when we watched the crucifixion of Jesus Christ on television, around Easter and Christmas holidays. Otherwise, life happened on the streets. In Meadowlands, we played from morning till dusk, ate dinner, watched television, and fell asleep. Only to wake up and do it all over again.

In Phefeni, there was no television. So, our evenings were spent listening to stories on Radio Zulu, which is now Ukhozi FM, or Mamani would tell us stories. She would beguile us with stories about Onogwaja and Ofudu and other clever wild animals while she did her ironing. My sister and I also took turns to re-tell these stories to each other, using miniature dolls Mamani had brought back for us from work as props. We'd make up songs and spend hours lost in our own world. Sometimes, I would conduct my own story-time with the rocks and bricks in our garden. I would pretend they were school children, tell them to keep quiet, and teach them things I had learnt at school. At school, we prayed every morning during assembly. At home, we would pray before we left the house on long trips. But that's all the religion I had at that time. We spent most weekends, including Sundays, at home or visiting Koko Norain in Meadowlands.

Because religion was never a central factor in my early years, I was curious about it. Next to my school, Thloreng Primary, there was a church. I often wondered what happened inside it, but I'd never had an opportunity to go in. One day, I told my grandmother that I was going to church, she asked me why I wanted to go there.

I said I wanted to see what they did inside.

"Fine," she said. "I'll be right here when you get back."

She gave my sister and me five or ten cents each and we set out. I was so excited, I couldn't wait. We caught the tail end of the Sunday School Service, which was being held outside the churchyard. When the church service started, I wanted to go inside with the rest of the congregation. Most of the adults looked at my sister and me curiously, since we were the only children there without guardians, we were unknown.

The church service was long, but I was stimulated by the newness of everything inside it. When the time for collections arrived, they played the organ, whose strange sounds made the polished brown wooden pew in front of me glisten with rhythm. I had never heard the sound of a real organ before and it was majestic. "Droppings, droppings, droppings, droppings, here the barn is full, everyone for Jesus, he shall bless them all, when the barn is full, he shall bless them all," the congregation sang in unison.

When the collection basket came to my sister and me, I was hesitant to let go of my coin. One of the adults insisted I put it in, and I was very upset by the experience. The rest of the service was forgettable.

When we got home, Mamani was waiting in anticipation.

"I was getting worried about you," she said. "I was preparing to come and fetch you from there myself. What took you so long?"

My elder sister explained: "We went to Sunday School, which was held outside on the lawns. When Sunday School was over, we went into church for the full service."

"How was church then?" Mamani asked me.

"I don't like it," I said. "They looked at us funny and some lady forced me to put my money in the collection basket."

Mamani laughed. "But that's what it's for," she said. "Will you go again?" she asked, still laughing at me.

"No. I'll stay here with you," I said, slipping between her legs and resting my head on her stomach.

Periodically, Mamani would go with us to traditional healers, where she bought herbs and plants. Sometimes we would accompany her to the river nearby, where she collected more plants and stones. I found those trips fascinating. It was like going shopping, but in nature rather than in the busy Maponya Supermarket.

One day, Mamani disappeared for a long time. She left us alone with her husband babuMbatha, who looked after us at night. When she came back, she was different and very distant. There was a hive of activity in the house. There was going to be an umsebenzi ceremony for her. It turns out she had gone to thwasa, the training to become a sangoma and healer.

She had been a sangoma initiate and now she was finished. A graduation ceremony was to be held for her at the weekend. Our room was stuffed full of miscellaneous items that had been removed from her room to make more space for the ceremony. There were chickens, buckets, groceries, suitcases, clothes, and people I didn't know filling up our private space like algae.

Our house didn't feel like home anymore and Mamani had not paid any attention to us since her return that week. I felt like a little mouse that had been rattled out of its hole. Everything had become larger, unfamiliar, with shadows hovering over everything. There were always people with her and around her, and I didn't know how to reach her. I had not spoken to her since she'd returned. Then, on that Saturday night, she was taken by these people from her room to the back of the house. Her head was covered with red and white beads, and she was wearing a white T-shirt and a traditional sangoma fabric around her waist. I strained to see her face, but it was too dark to see it. They went and stood under the laundry fence, near the apple tree. A goat had been tied to the pole hours before and now it was being held up for her to do something with it. Although we were not allowed anywhere near her at this time, I managed to follow her to see what they were going to do to her.

She, unlike the way she'd been every day of our lives, was not in charge this time. Men held the goat up to her, one held its front legs, another held its hind legs, while yet another one held its horns. They said some words to the goat and Mamani, who had a knife in her hand, slit the goat's throat and then quickly bent toward the goat's neck and drank the first blood that came gushing out, until her entire face was covered with blood. By the time she was done drinking it, the goat had died.

They took her away again, and I didn't see her until the next day, when other sangomas came to the house. They all started drumming and singing and Mamani, who was the initiate, was the only one dancing in a way that I had never seen before. As if she were in a trance.

"Ngilandelwa yini, yama bala bala, ngilandelwa yini - What is this colourful thing, which is following me?". These are the words to the song I remember her dancing to. She was so transformed. I missed her, but I didn't know how to reach her. That day I was relieved to see my parents, who often came to see us at weekends or the end of the month. They were the only thing that was normal. Everything else had changed. I didn't know what a sangoma was up until that day. Even then, I didn't understand what had happened. I didn't know what a sangoma was supposed to do. I had only seen sangomas from the street; they were conspicuous with their red dreadlocks and red facemasks, red and white beads and red, white and black kitenges. But I never had any interaction with them. There was a lot of stigma associated with sangomas or traditional healers in townships. Owing to the often mysterious and secretive nature of their rituals, practices, and work, they were often viewed as people who cast evil spells on others through witchcraft, black magic or imithi - medication and herbal-potions.

Although many people in the community consulted them, it was all done behind a veil of darkness and secrecy, so no one was ever clear about what sangomas actually did. Now I had seen what they do - they drank the blood of animals.

I once got into a fight with a classmate in primary school who insisted that I had amadlozi or the spirits of my ancestors who had passed on, hovering around me. My classmate said everyone had them. I insisted that I didn't and since she'd never seen my ancestors, or had a clue about who I was or where I came from, she could not say for certain. She would have to show them to me first, before I could believe her. When I got home that day, I told Mamani. She said nothing in response.

Now, Mamani was a sangoma, but she didn't want to talk to me about her new life. I'd thought that we could talk about everything, but she shut me out.

After the dust of her ceremony had settled, she created a new altar in the corner in her bedroom, where she put her offerings to the ancestors. It was her place of worship, called umsamo in isiZulu. She used a white cloth, with a red cross on it, to cover the corner. My sister and I were not allowed anywhere near that corner. But one day I went in to look, because I wanted to see what was in there. I opened the curtain to find a brown earthen pot or ukhamba, impepho and other things I couldn't identify. Then Mamani saw me and shouted: "Wenzani! Suka lapho. Didn't I tell you not to go there?" I knew then that whatever information I needed to know about traditional healers and their practices, I would have to find out from someone else. The subject was contentious.

I didn't know it at the time, but my mother was vehemently opposed to anything related to African cultural beliefs or traditional healers. I didn't know just how much she hated African traditional practices until years later, when after my sister and I had moved back in with her and my other siblings. We went to visit Mamani for the school holidays, as by then she had also moved from Phefeni and lived in a new area called Snake Park where she'd bought land and was in the process of building a house. While we were holidaying with her, she introduced us to a youth leader who told us about Mamorongwa.

Mamorongwa is a prophet who believed that the second coming of Christ would be in the form of a woman, a black, African woman. She showed us her prophecies, which were written in a black, hardcover notebook. Because it had been written, it was believed to be true.

This woman, like Jesus Christ, was going to save Africa and her people from poverty and oppression. This church was also an African-initiated church, which combined Christianity or Catholicism, in particular, with African beliefs in the ancestors. After the service, believers could consult the prophets, at a nominal fee, who would then write prescriptions directly from the ancestors, which one had to follow without question in order for one's prayers to be answered.

During our visit, she took us to see the prophets. They gave my sister and me a list of things we needed to do before we took baths, or slept, and at different times throughout the day.

When we got home, my mother asked what we were doing with all these things - candles and rocks mostly. We told her that Mamani told us to use them. On hearing this, my mother became very angry. She told us to throw all the things out and never to use them again. Then she asked us for a detailed report of our visit. After that we didn't see Mamani again, until I saw her a few months before her death. We were not allowed to have contact with her, based on those grounds. From my perspective at the time, Mamani was the happiest I'd ever seen her when she joined this church. She was happy in that church, even though my mother detested their practices and beliefs.

Not being able to see Mamani on holidays was heart-wrenching, especially since I knew that my mother loved Mamani as much as I did. This could only mean that Mamani must have done something terrible to hurt my mother, for her to have reacted like that. Although my mother kept contact with Mamani, she shielded us from her.

Some days, my mother would be very sad and depressed and would lie in bed with ulcers. I couldn't stand seeing her like that, so I decided to do something about it.

In our new neighbourhood of Ekangala, I began to search for a church; at first, I went to the ZCC, carrying my younger sister on my back, but I didn't like it there. Eventually we found a church which Gogo attended, where they served food on Sundays after the service, where children who came without their parents were welcomed, where we could wear what we liked and, most of all, where everyone looked free and happy. It was a born-again Christian church. There were coloured people with long hair in ribbons and bright, light faces there as well, which gave it a vibrant, multicultural mix, something I had never seen before. My siblings and I started attending the church, where we accepted Jesus Christ as our personal saviour every Sunday. I prayed for my mom and Mamani to also get saved.

Each morning before heading to church, I would stop by my mother's bedroom and ask if she was coming to church with me. I would tell her that all she needed to do in order to feel better was to accept Jesus Christ as her personal saviour. I believed that he would take away all her pain.

One day that dream came true. My mother came to church and accepted Jesus Christ as her personal saviour. She started attending church regularly. Life improved. When we all became born-again Christians, we knew that the only way we could see Mamani again, the only way she could become a part of our lives again, was if she accepted Jesus Christ as her personal saviour too. To that end, my sister and I prayed fervently. We fasted and read the Bible religiously, believing that our faith could change the course of Mamani's fate. We prayed for all our unsaved relatives in the same way because while we knew that we were mere pilgrims in this life, we hoped to see them all in the afterlife.

Our life outside school was a life of prayer and church. When Koko Norain told me the story of both our names, it was as if she was asking me to undo years of painstaking work. She was asking me to go against my own, as well my mother's faith. Our Christian faith prohibited us from consulting sangomas, or participating in African traditional rituals and ceremonies.

The Bible strictly prohibits the worship of the dead. I would much sooner live a faithless life than embrace African religion; the idea that nothing good could come out of it was drummed deeply into my head. Even so, the story of how

I had been conceived and possibly why I was here, did feel a bit like history repeating itself. I was caught yet again on the fence, in the middle of two worlds which had torn not only my family, but the entire continent of Africa, apart... except that this time the war was happening inside of me. I felt that Koko Norain was forcing me to choose between two worlds - Christianity and African beliefs. A relationship with my mother and Jesus Christ, or a relationship with my relatives and the ancestors. No matter which choice I made, someone would be betrayed. I didn't want to sink in the 'river between' or die from 'nervous conditions'. Things in my life were falling apart and my centre could not hold, as the book titles told. I saw myself as a character in a dramatic saga, which no one before me had been able to resolve. Who was I to even try?

Sometime later, I met a woman who was able to explain things to me. She told me that sangomas or traditional healers also believed in the very same God that Christians worshiped; they simply called him by different names, such as Umvel' Nqangi, or uNkuluNkulu. However, unlike Christians they didn't use his name in vain. They didn't believe that mere human beings could speak directly to God. The ancestors then served as mediators, who interceded and spoke to God on our behalf, just like Moses and the prophets did in the Old Testament.

Just as Jesus Christ is the mediator between born-again Christians and God, or the Prophet Mohammed is a messenger of Allah, traditional healers prayed to God in the name of those who had passed, the ancestors from our family bloodlines. As with every profession or service in life, there were traditional healers who did not heal. They were those who operated on the dark side, with witchcraft, black magic and so forth.

Although some of what she explained to me made sense, I still could not bring myself to believe. I still had so many questions about all the religions I had been exposed to until then. The questions kept flooding my mind: What about the blood sacrifices, the rituals, what about colonialism and the origins of Christianity? Who knew the truth about all of them?

Now, I am sitting on a plastic mat at the Grand Magal of Touba, observing a religion which also goes against my previously born-again Christian beliefs.

I am emotionally and spiritually fatigued. I chose to run away, because I want to free myself of everyone's expectations of me and live a life of my own creation. I listen to what people say, but none of it resonates. Nothing makes sense to me anymore.

Perhaps Cheikh Amadou Bamba and I have a lot in common, even though none of his disciples would agree with my way of interpreting his faith. Like him, I also want to be answerable only to God. It is too easy to pretend to believe in something. I am in Senegal hoping to find myself, my faith, my love, or a reason for being, yet all these things are eluding me.

After taking a nap in the small tent outside, I decide to go for a walk in the late afternoon as the sun is setting, to see what is on the streets, and maybe buy a souvenir.

Outside, the streets have thinned out and there are fewer people on the road. I can see a bit more of what is there. There are stalls, many, many shops lined up on either side of the street selling everything imaginable from fabric, clothes, tea, teapots, tea sets, crockery, religious jewellery, food, religious books and snacks served with Café Touba, the traditional, spicy-flavoured coffee. I decide that I don't want or need anything. I return to the compound feeling a little refreshed and happy, because I managed to go out and find my way back without any anxiety, or drama. Amadou and I decided to return to Dakar that same night, instead of staying one more night as planned. But as we start gathering our things, I discover that my purse, which had all my bank cards and a bit of cash in it, is gone. I tell Amadou that I can't find my purse.

"I had it just now, but now I can't find it," I say.

"You must have lost it during your walk," he replies.

"No," I insist. "It must have been taken."

People in the whole compound emerge from where they were hiding. Everyone begins to search for my purse. I looked in the tent where I had been sleeping. Nothing. On the grounds in the compound. Nothing. I retrace my steps, following where I had been during the walk. Nothing. I am wild with rage. I had managed to hold onto this purse for two years, only to lose it here, on a pilgrimage. My worst nightmare has just come true.

I am lost in a foreign country, without a cent to my name. I am so enraged and naturally begin to think of ways I can simply end my life - because to me this is a disaster.

I can't breathe.

I am suffocating. On the one hand it seems like I am accusing the entire compound of theft, while on the other, I know that I came back with it after paying to get my pants back at the detention centre. Everybody looks at me as if I am crazy.

How can I accuse the whole compound of stealing my purse?

I begin to panic. My God! What am I going to do in this world without money? Determined to find my purse, I decide to retrace my steps, again. This time though, my eyes are clouded with tears and I begin to wail openly when it becomes apparent that I won't find it. I am ashamed to go back into the compound after the drama I have caused. I sit by the entrance and continue to sob. This attracts the attention of passersby and some pilgrims who are leaving the compound. Most people stop to find out what is wrong.

"Ça va? Pourquoi pleurer ? Mademoiselle, can we help you? Nanga def?" A barrage of questions flows at me from every direction.

"Ki kan la? Na'nga def?" Who are you? Where are you from? Where are you going? How can we help you?

"Notodo?" What's your name?

"I'm fine," I answer, between sniffs.

As more and more people come to gaze at the commotion, I pull myself together and go inside to avoid answering more questions.

Excessive emotion is generally frowned upon in Islam, particularly crying, and more especially during the Magal.

Back in the compound, Amadou suggests we stay the night and search for my purse again during the light of day. We need to appease the strained nerves of his Marabout, who wants us to leave the compound in peace.

"You can stay if you want to," I tell him, "but I am leaving tonight."

"What about the bus fare?" he asks.

"It's okay," I tell him, "I have money hidden in my hair. It will be enough to take us both back to Dakar, if you choose to come with me. I've kept some cash on my body, which will be just enough to get us back to Dakar. After which, owing to my lost cards, I will have nothing left."

He is seething with so much anger that I could hold it in my hands and bake some bread with his fire. But I am not daunted. I just want to get out of there.

I walk out of the compound ahead of him and he follows.

"What happened to your shoes?" Amadou asks.

I am too angry to respond. Instead, I stand and just stare at him.

"Let me buy you some shoes," he pleads.

"I'm fine, Amadou. I can walk barefoot until we get to Dakar if I need to. Don't worry about me. I don't want anything from you. I'm a big girl, I can take care of myself," I say.

"Don't be ridiculous!" he responds

"I said I'm fine!" I shout back.

He glares at me, and promptly walks away to find a shoe-shop. I stand there, where he's left me, frozen.

"Sokhnassi, Sokhnaasi. S'asseoir toi, ici, S'asseoir toi."

A man from a shop in front of me is offering me a chair. I have no energy left to fight someone who is being kind. I sit down.

"Jerejef," I say, thanking him.

I'd lost one flip-flop while searching for my purse, after my foot had sunk into a hole full of horseshit. When I'd pulled my foot out, the flip-flop had been left behind. After I'd wiped my foot off on the ground, I'd thrown the other flip-flop away in a fit of anger.

After a while, Amadou returns with cheap looking flip-flops - plain white, with green borders. He puts them on the ground next to my feet and glares at me. We are having a staring contest; and if I don't put my shoes on now, we are both going to be rolling around on the ground, embroiled in a wrestling match.

I put them on, and literally wish I'd had put them on sooner. They are simply the softest flip-flops I have ever worn in my entire life; not even my prized, branded Hang-Tens are this soft. I am so relieved I almost smile at him. But as soon as I stand up, I remember that I am still angry. We don't speak to each other for the entire journey back to the city. Every now and then we throw daggers at each other with our eyes,

When we arrive in Dakar in the early hours of the next morning, I say goodbye to Amadou.

"I am going back to South Africa, tomorrow," I tell him.

It is the 10th of January 2012.

"Please let me take you shopping; at least allow me to buy some souvenirs for your family," he pleads.

"No, thank you," I say. "You have done enough. Thank you for taking me to Touba," I say apologetically. "Please understand that I am not accusing you of anything. This is just the worst thing that could happen to me right now."

We part ways.

When I arrive at Aisha's house, I take a long bath and go to sleep. I wake up later, feeling exhausted. I don't have enough energy to pack, and go to the airport to fly back home to South Africa. In any case, Aisha is due back any day now. I don't want to leave without saying goodbye to her. So, I stay.

Chapter 04
FED UP: THE ART OF PROTEST

A few days later, Aisha returns from her travels to find me reeling from my adventures at the Grand Magal of Touba, which have left me penniless, emotionally drained, have heightened my anxiety and restricted my movements. I feel claustrophobic, as though I am a prisoner in a jail of my own making.

After applying for new bank cards, and asking my younger sister and a friend to wire some money, there is nothing else left to do but wait. I am restless.

I often visit Amadou, who picks me up on his scooter after work. We spend time together with his family until late, but coming home late at night makes me feel guilty, as if I am doing something wrong. Being in Aisha's home now had become extremely uncomfortable. I condemn myself for being a 'lazy person' who does not want to work.

I had hoped relations between Aisha and I would improve when she returned; however, after she arrives, they remain the same. We resume our default position of minimal communication. Despite the silence between Aisha and me, something is abuzz in the city. There are snippets, drops of information I pick up from Aisha's conversations with her colleagues on the phone. The Senegalese Supreme Court is expected to make a decision on whether the incumbent president, President Abdoulaye Wade can run in the upcoming national elections. This will be his third term in office, should he win the vote. If the Supreme Court rules in his favour, his candidacy will be rejected outright because it is in violation of the country's constitution which limits presidential terms to two. I pull the cartoon-decorated duvet over my head. I cannot contemplate going back to work at this point, even though something inside of me is nagging me to.

Aisha nudges me in her own way too.

"Apparently, there will be a protest at Obelisk Square tonight," she says in passing.

I don't know where the square is, or how I will get there since I am penniless and trying to save the little money I still have left. Moreover, nothing in me wants to be out at night, caught up in the midst of angry activists clashing with police.

"Okay," I tell her. "I'll check it out."

But I never do. I just stay in bed, feeling very sorry for myself.

Eventually, the Supreme Court's verdict comes out, validating Abdoulaye Wade's candidacy in the elections. Protests erupt. One afternoon, Aisha comes back from a demonstration singing protest songs. She looks alive and her enthusiasm is beginning to rub off on me. Yet, I am still resistant. I simply don't want to get involved. I am tired and depressed.

One night, while visiting Mathews at his house, I checked my phone to find a message from Aisha warning me to be careful on the way back home.

There had been protests near her house. She had heard gunshots being fired too.

I decided to cut my visit short and go back home. I struggle to find a taxi. Once I do, the taxi driver is forced to meander through fires that are blocking my route home.

The protest is real. It has come right up to my doorstep, begging for my attention. The next day, Senegal is in turmoil. A student leader had been killed by police the previous night during a demonstration at Obelisk Square. The public is inflamed. In the morning, a group of students march to the hospital where the body is being prepared for burial. They are met by police barricades. Clashes ensue between the students and the police. The students run back to Cheikh Anta Diop University, where clashes with the police continue. The university is within walking distance from Aisha's house.

The story which I was hesitant to cover has brought itself to me, leaving me without any excuses. I decided to go and check it out, for real this time.

As I near Avenue Cheikh Anta Diop where the university is, there are rocks, wooden stalls and burning rubbish blocking the entire street. A road, which is normally clogged with traffic including buses, car rapides - Dakar's minibuses - taxis-cabs and private cars, is empty. As I enter the avenue, I meet a few cameramen and journalists, with a crew of medical practitioners from the Red Cross, who are walking up the road. I fall easily into step with them and promptly search for someone who seems open to a conversation, preferably in English. I am immediately drawn to a small-framed photojournalist who later tells me she is from Mauritania. She is works for the Pan African news agency, Panapress. The photojournalist tells me that although she no longer covers the news, she feels compelled by the political situation to go back into the field. She doesn't look out of place in her black T-shirt, olive-green cargo pants and a heavy camera bag. I must have been walking very close to her because she turns to me and asks: "Are you afraid?"

Students who had started a fire up the road, are now fleeing from the police and heading in our direction. There is a lot of smoke billowing in the horizon. I cannot make out what is going on where we are headed.

"No," I answer. "I just want to walk with someone."

"Are you a photojournalist?" she asks, looking at my tiny second-hand camera.

"No," I say. "I just want to keep a record of what is going on."

"So that you can remember?" she asks.

"Yes. I'm a writer actually, an independent journalist from South Africa," I offer.

"Okay," she says and continues to take pictures as we walk.

I follow closely behind her, tracing her movements in the hope that mimicking her will generate better pictures.

When we reach the top of the avenue, we find two buses engulfed in flames. It is not immediately clear if the students had set the buses alight while there were passengers in them, but from the looks of things both buses are empty. The fire that rages through the blue and yellow bus creates a dramatic scene. Plumes of velvet gray-black smoke rise from the driver's seat through to the front windows of the bus. The orange flames make the pictures look haunted against the deserted street.

"Jedi!" I hear someone calling my name.

I look around. The voice is coming from a restaurant on the opposite side of the street. It is Mathews. I wave back and walk over to him.

"How did you know about this?" he asks. "How did you know to come here?" He looks perplexed.

"My housemate told me that there were protests today. Didn't you know?" I ask, also perplexed.

"No," he says. "I was just sitting here enjoying my drink when all this happened."

"What happened?" I ask him. "Did you see anything?"

The restaurant was a few feet away from the burning busses; if he had been sitting outside when the buses were torched, he would have seen it happen.

"No," he answers. "But what are you doing here? It's not safe."

My heart sinks. I am hoping that he will at least be able to give me some information about what took place since he was sitting right next to the action, but he is not interested in my line of questioning. His only concern is my safety. Although sweet, his concerns are not helpful to someone who needs to write a story.

"I am a journalist, remember? I have to be here and write about it."

"Who will you send your story to?" he asks.

"I don't know yet, but I must at least have a story to sell before I approach anyone," I tell him.

"Heh! These kids," he exclaims, looking at the burning bus, his hands resting on his waist in disbelief.

A white police van carrying policemen kitted in riot gear, arrives. The police jump out of the van and some begin to remove the rocks and concrete slabs placed in the middle of the road to block traffic. Others walk down the main avenue towards the main campus, where most of the students responsible for the chaos are hiding. I take a few pictures of the Mauritanian journalist, while we survey the area. She looks so small and fragile in front of the burning bus. The picture is dramatic and I like it. Eventually, the Mauritanian journalist signals that she is heading back. I say goodbye to Mathews.

"I have to go; I'm working."

"Be safe," he says, moving back to his beer.

Despite my earlier fatigue, I am getting energised. I am also slightly disappointed that I missed out on all the key milestones in this story because I hadn't been bothered about it at first.

With the arrival of the police, I am hoping to capture more action pictures. By now, my adrenaline is pumping.

I don't look back as I race down the road to catch up with the police and the other journalists who have gone ahead of me. The smell of tear gas and burning metal perfumes the air. I walk next to the armed policemen, who saunter down the road calmly instead of anxiously panting like I am.

At this moment, I think Senegalese policemen seem much calmer than what I'm used to; in fact, they walk down the road as if they are understanding parents picking up toys forgotten by toddlers after playtime. While I am slightly relieved that the altercation between the police and students has been less violent compared to the previous night, there is still a part of me that yearns for it, for some conflict to take place, so that I can have a story.

By then, I had missed the whole thing: first the announcement by the Supreme Court allowing President Abdoulaye Wade to contest the elections and second, the protests which had led to the death of the university student at the Obelisk Square. I am hard-pressed to find a news angle that has not been covered by news agencies already.

Trying to find someone to interview in this chaos, could put myself and whoever may agree to an interview in danger. As I am thinking about the article, the police begin firing rubber bullets at the students who have been pelting them with rocks behind university walls.

The closer the police get to the student residences, the more the rocks rain down on them. Other journalists, who had been documenting the clashes from the university, joined us in the middle.

Some of them are wearing helmets and flak jackets meant to prevent injuries from airborne shrapnel, or in this case, rocks, and rubber-bullets. Most wear press jackets. As the exchange of rocks for rubber bullets continues, I begin to worry about my own safety. Here I am, yet again in the line of fire, with only my camera and a Mandela Walks Free T-shirt for protection.

In all my years as a journalist, I had never once worn protective gear to a protest. No helmet, bulletproof vest, or flak jacket. Such gear was often worn by the (riot) police, soldiers, and some foreign press. But at this moment, as I hide behind an overturned wooden trading stall for protection, I remember a colleague of mine shaking his head at me for agreeing to go to a war zone without a single piece of protective gear. I'd had no helmet or flak jacket, not even a simple T-shirt that said 'Press' or 'Media'.

"It is irresponsible for you to go on this trip without any protective gear. We are going to a war zone," he'd said. "It's not a game."

We were standing at O.R. Tambo International Airport with a group of other journalists waiting to board our flight to Egypt on our way to Lebanon. While I appreciated his concern, I was also annoyed by him. I was a few hours away from realising my dream of becoming a war correspondent and he was just raining on my parade. I would not let the lack of a flak jacket or helmet stop me from going. I thought this to myself, while listening to him go on and on about how crazy the situation was.

"I can't believe that a whole national broadcaster could be so irresponsible. How can they, in good conscience, send a young journalist to cover a war without a simple vest?" he asked angrily, to no one in particular.

I was worried that his concerns would make the organisers change their minds about taking me on the trip. Even though his concern for my safety was quite touching, I was humiliated by the experience. His fears drew everyone's attention to me. They looked at me with such pity, as if their eyes were saying, "Poor ignorant girl; she's going to die and she doesn't even know it."

"A flak jacket won't protect me from a bomb," I responded stubbornly.

But now, here in Dakar, I wish I was wearing some protection, or at least a piece of clothing to identify me as media. I feel naked and exposed against the rocks that are raining down on us from all directions. Why did I take the side of the police? I ask myself. If things turn really bad, the students will think I am a government agent, an informant, or some type of an undercover police working with the authorities. They may be less inclined to speak to me if I approach them for an interview later. If I am with the students, the police will mistake me as one of them and will shoot at me indiscriminately. I am literally alone. There is no editor calling me for an update; there is no one at the end of the line asking me to file a voice-report, a bulletin copy or to do an interview. In fact, apart from Aisha and Mathews, no one else knows of my whereabouts. I have to be my own assignment editor, copy editor, my own driver, my own gatekeeper, and my own security. Even though having an editor demanding a story at the end of the phone line is not the equivalent of a flak jacket or a helmet, it at least provides some type of psychological insurance. There is a legitimate reason why you are in-the-line-of-fire; it is your job and you are on an assignment. In my case, nobody has given me this assignment, which means that I am the only one responsible for my own safety. I could not have chosen a worse time to have this epiphany. It is an inconvenient light-bulb moment at a time when my head could literally pop. It is too late to do a risk assessment study on the ground. I am already at risk. All I have to consider now is how to minimise the probability of being hit by a rock or rubber bullet.

My behaviour is no different to that of a radio news editor, who'd once asked me if I had recorded the sound of bullets being fired during a protest held by members of the volatile Inkatha Freedom Party - IFP in Johannesburg. Although I had seen a lot of dead bodies during my internship at the SABC in KwaZulu-Natal, I had not been there when the violence or murders had taken place. We often arrived after people had been killed and followed behind police officers as they did the body count and spoke to relatives of the deceased. So, the violence was new to me. For some reason, I thought people preferred to be discreet about breaking the law. I didn't think it was something they would want to do in broad daylight, especially in a situation where they were not being actively provoked. I still believed in the goodness and innocence of people. I believed that people did not mean to do harm, and if they did harm, they would be ashamed and sorry for what they had done, not proud and unrepentant. In the chaos that ensued, I'd been so confused by the gunfire and had run towards the mob of angry IFP hostel dwellers wielding spears and guns, and shooting in the general direction of the media. A photojournalist, seeing that I was running straight into the line of fire, had sped his vehicle next to me and yelled at me to jump in quickly. I hadn't known what had been going on, who had fired a shot or from where. When I'd called the editor to update him on the story, I'd been dumbfounded that all he could think to ask was if I had recorded the sound of the gunfire and this after I'd just told him that they'd been firing at us with live ammunition!

"Did you get the sound on tape?" he'd asked.

I almost dropped the phone on him. I could not believe that the sound of live ammunition was more important to him than my life. He didn't ask if I was okay or in a safe place. I didn't even have my own car at that stage; I had gotten a lift to the story; the car had no longer been there. I understood why I was there. My job was to report on what was going on, including recording the sound of gunfire, but what about me? Would it have been too much for him to ask if I was okay? Safe? How would he have gotten the sound of gunfire if I died or been injured?

Ah, wait a minute, who was I fooling asking myself rhetorical questions. My death or injury would be an even bigger story than broadcasting the sound of gunfire. I could already see the headlines: *An SABC radio news journalist has been killed during a violent protest in Soweto this afternoon.* I would be the top story for at least two hours, which is equivalent to two news bulletins. That story would make the next day's newspaper headlines. I realised that my life was expendable - like a soldiers' life. If a soldier dies or is injured, the army will get another one. Whether I lived or died, the news organisation would survive. If I died, my death would be a story; if I lived, I would write the story. No matter what happened to me, they would still have their story. The news would go on.

My eyes start to sting, as if they have been set on fire, bringing me back to the streets of Dakar. A new batch of policemen has been deployed to the university. They have thrown tear gas canisters a few feet from where I am hiding, so I wrap my scarf around my nose to prevent myself from inhaling more gas. I look for an exit, or a place where I can find water to rinse the sting out of my eyes. I cannot take any more pictures either, as my camera memory is now full. I have to go back home.

My face is itching. I have forgotten how it feels to be tear-gassed. The sting of the tear gas, with its distinctive smell, is so familiar it's as if I've found a piece of home that has been missing in my life up until now.

By the time I was starting school in the early 1980s, the South African apartheid government had declared a State of Emergency throughout the country to suppress anti-apartheid militant groups which were making black townships ungovernable. This meant that our neighbourhood in Meadowlands, Soweto, was replete with protests, army trucks and police. The streets were filled with army patrols in *Mellow Yellows* - township slang for the police's mine-resistant ambush protected vehicles. They were so called because most of them were painted yellow and had a blue stripe, so they looked like a popular soft drink at the time called Mellow Yellow. The provisions of this State of Emergency were broad. They prohibited gatherings at political funerals and certain indoor gatherings; they imposed curfews and banned television cameras from certain unrest areas, preventing local and international coverage of continued protests and police oppression in townships. Being tear-gassed in the middle of Dakar triggered memories of a time in my life when clashes between the police and activists was not the exception, but the rule. I was born into it. I was born into a State of Emergency, into streets perfumed with coal fires, tears-gas, beer, and marijuana. This was my normal as a child. As a result, protest was in my blood. I learnt to walk to its vibration, generated by chants of men and women preparing themselves for battle; toyi-toying for blood, for freedom.

As I walk back to the house, the concrete pavements of Sicap Amitié 1 become the grey soil in Meadowlands covered with black soot from coal, burning tyres and cars.

There was always something happening on Moemise Street. If it was not some stokvel investment or savings society party, often marked by elders sitting outside sipping on Castle or Lion beers while dancing and singing loudly to Stimela's Whispers in the Deep, which drew 'tears like tributaries' from the bloodshot eyes of intoxicated uncles, their tears coming in spurts of halting, hoarse- and smoke-filled voices shouting: "Kawu phinde Mzala, Hololo" into the 'great river of pain', then it was the women playing m'china - the gambling game with numbers and symbols - vaguely remembered from the previous night's dreams. Tsotsis or thieves would run from one corner of the street to another, jumping over fences and walls aptly named 'stop-nonsense' because they were decorated with broken glass at the top, to stab those who attempted to trespass. If it was not the tsotsis; it would be children running away from vicious dogs which had been let loose by bullies from the neighbouring street. Sometimes, it would be the sound of "*amalahle!*" which would send elders running into their matchbox houses to pick coins out of piggy banks and under mattresses to purchase sacks of coal for the winter. At other times the sound of "*Di Botlolo*", which would send us children scurrying to find empty glass cooldrink bottles in exchange for Cheese Curls maize chips, which would be poured into bowls, dishes, plastic bags, T-shirts, dresses, and skirts that would be turned up to form containers as a last resort, from the back of a moving pickup truck. Most times though, it would be the haze of tear-gas which would send everyone running in every direction. Normally, the teargas would be thrown in the mornings or afternoons and we would get caught up in its fumes on our way to or from school.

A life lived under intense police and military surveillance was a normal life for me and quite frankly I never thought there was anything wrong with what I saw or how we lived. I was not aware of the real and serious danger posed to me or any black person walking the streets of Meadowlands, by the white men in brown and blue uniform. My mother often had her hands full with me, because I was always so curious about whatever was happening even when a mob of protesters would toyi-toyi down the street. Their collective fever-pitch energy was so intoxicating; it was more thrilling than playing a game of tins, m'gusha or scotch. I loved the idea of the whole community doing something together. I was yearning to get involved.

For my mother, who had to travel to work every morning, life in the 80s was horrendous. She said: "The smell of death always hovered over the atmosphere, enmeshed with the oxygen vital to sustain life." During those times, there was never a day that went by without someone being killed by the Apartheid government and their agents or freedom fighters. On a morning dash to catch a taxi to work, one would encounter streets littered with smoking carcasses of cars which had been burnt to the bone overnight by activists who were often the ones responsible for riots and general states of unrest and disorder in townships. At times, simple things such as bread would be hard to find, because the activists or students would have looted delivery vans coming into townships from the city. At other times they would put up barricades at various train stations, effectively preventing workers from going to work.

I was not aware of the nuances.

There was a character in the township who stood out for me in the 80s. Someone I thankfully never met, but who undoubtedly dominated the hearts and minds of many people in Meadowlands. His name was S'thupha, a Zulu word for thumb. He was so called because his head was said to be shaped exactly like a thumb. His name came up whenever my relatives would find me sucking my thumb in deep or idle contemplation. They would wag their thumbs at me, threatening that they would call on S'thupha to come and fetch me. This was done to scare me out of sucking my thumb. S'thupha was a criminal, infamous for raping and terrorising women and children, in the community. One day he raped or killed a schoolgirl in Meadowlands, an incident which incensed the community to such an extent that a manhunt was launched for him, until he was found in another township of Tembisa in Johannesburg's East Rand. The students dragged him out of his hiding place and brought him to Meadowlands, where they were going to give him a taste of his own medicine in the cruellest way imaginable.

Word of his capture and imminent death at the hands of activists and student leaders quickly spread throughout the township, pulling mothers, fathers, their sons, daughters, and grandparents out of their homes to see what Sthupha actually looked like. He'd become a legend.

On this occasion, my grandmother Koko Norain and her friends came to fetch my mother, asking her if she didn't want to see S'thupha too? My mother said "No!" She locked the door behind her, as my grandmother walked onto the arena where Sthupha was to be killed.

In the arena, S'thupha was beaten and tortured mercilessly, surrounded by a crowd of spectators, until he was well and truly dead. His head was said to have been decapitated and put on a long stick, which was paraded like a lollipop throughout the township for all to see: S'thupha is dead. My mother says Grandmother Koko Norain and her friends could not sleep for days after witnessing the murder. She was duty-bound to tend to their writhing bodies and wails of terror as they wept, saying they had never seen anything so gruesome in all their lives. It was gratuitous to say that no one, including witnesses and innocent bystanders, was left unscathed by the experience.

As the climate of political activism and unrest escalated, the atmosphere of fear and distrust also increased. Anyone rumoured or perceived to be a sell-out, or working with or for the apartheid government, would be in danger of being necklaced in the streets of Soweto. Even asking innocent questions could get one into trouble. Necklacing was the horrendous act of putting a car's tyre around someone's neck and dousing it with enough petrol or paraffin so that the person caught alight and burnt for hours.

Comrades often used spurious criteria to identify a sell-out, so killings were happening on a daily basis. This is the environment which shaped my perspective on life. This was the norm.

As I push open the heavy iron door into Aisha's compound, I struggle to shake off the nausea. It is hard to accept that a State of Emergency is in fact my normal, the default programming lodged deep into my subconscious. It is hard to admit that this life is exactly what I have been chasing all along. When I was little, I vowed to be where the action was, to find out what was happening on the streets at night and here I was doing it, decades later as a journalist. It is the toe-curling stories of blood being spilled, spirits being taken and lives being snuffed out that got people to pay attention. That's what got many people talking. Death, torture, murder moved people. It got them worried, fearful, angry, and passionate. This is what made the news.

I walk into the house and I am welcomed by Aisha and Nala, who have been at home waiting with anticipation.

"How was it?" they ask.

"I got tear-gassed and my camera needs new batteries and a memory card," I tell them, out of breath. I replace the batteries and download some pictures, which I show them. Then I go out again.

I am determined to find a story to tell about the protests; an angle that has not yet been explored. Back at the university, clashes between students and the police have subsided, traffic is beginning to flow freely and I am clueless about what to do next. The group of journalists who were here earlier have disappeared and I didn't get a chance to exchange numbers with the photojournalist from Panapress. I am beginning to think that my walk back to the university has been a giant waste of time when I notice a young man, holding a camera, standing on the opposite side of the street. He is wearing a navy-blue turban and a wide, bright-eyed smile. I cross over to him to ask if he is part of the protest, or if he knows one of the students from the university.

"Can you speak English?" I ask.

"Yes," he says, with a wide, beaming smile. I introduce myself and tell him I am looking to interview students about the protests. He tells me that he is a university student and is doing some journalism during the protests to document what is going on.

"Everybody feels compelled to do something," he tells me. In fact, he adds, one of his friends had just been to the funeral of the student leader who had been killed the previous night. The student had been good friends with the deceased. "Would you like to meet him?" he asks.

"Yes," I say.

He leads me to the university's drama department, where I meet his friend. He sits quietly in a reclining position in a corner reading the play Les Misérables.

In the room, there are small sponge mattresses that everybody sits on. A small television set is on, broadcasting live news as it happens. Other students are monitoring the unfolding story on the internet and the radio, which they plug into through their mobile phones. They are having 'fire-side' discussions about the implications of the Supreme Court's ruling and reflecting on the day's events.

Many of them tell me they are freelance journalists too.

I introduce myself and begin interviewing everyone in the room.

We speak until sunset and, as everyone begins to leave, the man in the turban invites me to his house.

His house is in a neighbourhood I have not been to before, so I agree to join him out of curiosity. While we are in the car-rapide, he tells me his story: His father is in the military - quite high up in the ranks. Although he is studying at the university for a Masters' in Philosophy, his true passion is music. He is a musician. Soon, he will be moving in with a friend of his from New York, who is also a musician, and they will be working on their first album together. His parents do not approve of his chosen career and this has caused some friction in their relationship, but he loves music and it is worth the risk, he says, smiling.

"I believe in myself and I know that one day I will become a successful musician."
I become an instant believer too. With his smile, charm, and penetrating eyes, I am sure he could do anything he wanted. I admire the passion he has for his craft; even though I haven't heard him sing, I believe he can.

"How about you?" he asks.

I hesitate.

I feel as if my story is changing. I have different thoughts now about who I am, where I've been and where I want to go from here.

I reply: "I'm here because I want to explore what options are available to me in this world. Primarily, I want to be a foreign correspondent. Even though originally, I came here to be on holiday, if I can find work, I will stay on. Maybe one day I could have my own show?" I add, growing more uncertain... "But I'm still trying to figure out what the show will be about."

"Well," he concludes, "anything is possible if you believe. Are you hungry? Let's go eat."

We go to a local restaurant, whose patrons are mainly men, where we eat plates of spaghetti. After we finish, he takes me to the corner to catch a bus and I go back home.

I am anxious to get back to the house before Aisha goes to bed. I also want to start writing the story while it is still fresh on my mind. I spend the rest of the evening and the next morning writing, hoping that my angle is original enough to be published by at least one editor. To my delight, the story is published a few hours after I file it, which is a surprising reward for my efforts.

Motivated by the relative ease of having successfully published a story, I reach out to other contacts that a former colleague has given me. I want to find out if it is possible for me to secure a job in the country. One of the contacts worked at the Radiodiffusion Télévision Sénégalaise broadcaster RTS, Senegal's equivalent of the South African Broadcasting Corporation. It turns out that she is leaving her job as the host of a weekly English television magazine show, showcasing the best of Senegal called, EMag. They are looking for an English-speaking presenter. If I am keen, she can introduce me to the Director of RTS, who will be making the final decision.

I had gone to meet this woman to chat about the industry and now here she is arranging an interview with the director of the organisation.

I am surprised by the turn of events and agree to a connection.

A few days later, I receive a call from the Director of RTS.

"Can you come to my office this afternoon, in about an hour?" he asks.

"Yes, I can," I answer, breathing a sigh of relief since I still have a bit of money to catch a cab, which will be the fastest way to get to the city centre on time.

I fly out of my room, trying to contain my excitement, and ask Aisha if she can lend me a formal jacket for the interview. I want to impress and 'seize the moment', in a Dead Poets Society kind of way.

Aisha rummages through her closet and finds something suitable, a charcoal grey jacket, which I wear with a white shirt. I put on the clothes as fast as possible and jump into the taxicab, heading downtown with my fingers crossed. I am not thinking about what to expect. I arrive on the fourth floor of the RTS building. A soldier stands outside the Director's office. He tells me to wait.

When it is time to go in, a bulletproof door is opened, revealing a reception area where the Director's secretary, sitting behind a large desk, asks me to take a seat.

"The Director is on an important call and will be with you shortly," she says in a sweet but professional tone.

I nod. I am trying not to think too much about anything.

Since the Director is the one who called for this meeting, I decided to follow his cue and answer his questions as best and as honestly as I can. I remind myself to smile; it relaxes me when I am nervous or in difficult situations.

"You may go in now," his secretary tells me softly.

"Thank you," I say out loud, too loudly maybe. Meanwhile, I'm thinking: Here we go! At the very least, I know that I'm safe here. Nothing will happen to me between the armed guard and thick, bulletproof doors.

"Good afternoon," I say to the Director, surprised by his youthful appearance. He is smiling widely.

"Good afternoon, thank you for coming... Lindi, how do you say your name?"

"Lindiwe," I reply, as I sit in one of the two chairs in front of his large desk that is littered with piles of files and pictures of his family.

"What does it mean?" he asks, folding his hands under his chin.

I look at him, and smile sweetly.

"The one you are waiting for," I say, suppressing a sudden urge to laugh.

"Really?" he asks.

"Yes, that's what it means," I respond.

"Okay," he says and dives into the business at hand.

"One of my people told me about you. You know that she is moving on to another place and she says she thinks you will be a good fit for her position. So, tell me a bit about you. What brings you here?"

I give him a summary of my career, up until my visit to Senegal. He is intrigued and asks me questions about the countries I have been to. He tells me about his recent trip to Australia with his son, then reverts to business.

"You are a very brave and courageous young woman," he says. I cannot promise you anything, but we will be having auditions soon for E-Mag and you will be invited. We will let you know the details soon enough. Thank you for coming; it was a pleasure to meet you, Lindiwe."

"Thank you," I say, leaving the room.

My hands are shaking. I am relieved that I was able to hold back the jitters for long enough to get through the interview, which was not typical of any job interview I had ever been to before.

The next day I head to the university to catch up with the students, including the man in the turban to show them the published article that I had written.

I tell the man in the turban about my upcoming audition, which I am extremely nervous about. I can't understand why I am always so nervous. One would think I would be accustomed to live interviews and being in the public eye by now.

Sensing my apprehension, the man in the turban offers to help me practise with his camera. I gingerly write a script on a piece of paper and even though I am in a friendly environment, it feels as if the whole world is watching me.

I start to feel cold and shivery, which means that I have to fish for my voice somewhere in the depths of my stomach.

We do a few takes and the man in the turban decides I need more practise. He doubts that I am ready for the audition.

"Why are you so nervous?" he asks.

I cannot find an answer.

As a child I used to love to entertain older people, especially by mimicking the famed singer Brenda Fassie, who was a huge star until her untimely death in 2004. Because of this, people who saw me perform her, used to say that I would grow up to be a star. I believed them. But since I did not grow up to be a star, I often felt like a failure, regardless of anything else I'd accomplished in other areas of my life. Whenever an opportunity to be on TV was presented to me, I simply froze. The more this happened, the more convinced I became that there was something fundamentally wrong with me. So, this job is important for me because I think it is my last chance to become that star and prove to those people who once believed in me, that they were right.

Eventually, RTS calls me to come in for the audition.

When I arrive at studios, the only other candidate, a young mother of two children, and I are taken to the make-up room. The make-up artist asks if I have my own foundation.

"No," I tell her. "I have no make-up at all." I did not even wear make-up at the time. She peers at me disapprovingly and begins to pile layers of her own foundation on my face. Her foundation is a few shades lighter than my natural skin colour. By the time she is finished with me, I can barely recognise myself. I am yellow. When our make-up is done, we are led into the studio where our auditions will be recorded.

I am trying very hard to contain my nerves.

The mother of two goes first.

I tell myself that I will do two takes and let this dream go once and for all. If it doesn't work out, at least I will know that I had tried.

After our auditions, the contact from RTS tells us that we were not bad.

"It's normal for first-timers to feel nervous," she says.

She invites us to lunch at a popular burger joint, which is near the RTS offices.

After lunch, she tells us that they will be in touch about their selection soon.

As the days move closer to the elections, the protests also increase. The demonstrations, which by now are indistinguishable from the political campaigns run by the 13 presidential candidates, are taking place on an almost daily basis in different parts of the country. All the presidential candidates have dived into the anti-Wade protest river and a vote against Wade has become their main campaign message.

In many ways, I am a virgin to West African politics. The students from the university hold my hand through the political campaigns and demonstrations. The loudest of all the protesters are the "Fed-Up" movement. This is a group of young journalists, activists, students, and rappers who go by the name *Y'en a Marre*, which literally translates as "Fed-up" or "Enough is enough". The Fed-up Youth Movement campaigns vociferously against President Abdoulaye Wade's candidacy, calling it an outright farce. According to them, the octogenarian is a senile old man, who has, by then, accumulated a long record of bad decisions - from erecting the controversial, exorbitantly expensive Renaissance Monument, to engaging in corrupt and nepotistic business deals using his son. What angers many, is the belief that he is grooming his eldest son Karim Wade to take over the leadership of both his political party, Parti Démocratique Sénégalais (PDS) and the state. One of their more popular songs at the time is called, *Gurgi Na Dem*, meaning "Go Old Man". It has an infectious beat that sends everyone jumping in the streets. Violent clashes between young people and the police become the order of the day.

Protestors gather at the Independence Square in downtown Dakar, and proceed through the main streets past Sandaga Market, disrupting trade as police charge after them.

Meanwhile, the Director at RTS calls to inform me that they are offering me the job. He says: "We will let you know when you should come in to complete the necessary paperwork. We want you to start as soon as possible."

By this time I had already been introduced to the team I would be working with, so I had no reason to doubt that it would happen. But the call with further instructions never comes. My follow-up calls and text messages also go unanswered.

I decided to try another contact, who works at a private radio station called West Africa Democracy Radio (WADR). I have been told that they are always looking for English-speaking journalists, who are in short supply in Dakar. I call his numbers, but no one answers.

As days go by, I grow more apprehensive because the story is gaining momentum and I am not filing anything.

There are daily protests, political campaigns, members of Y'en a Marre are being detained for unlawful demonstration, others are appearing in court, press conferences are being held, religious leaders are calling for calm, traders and entrepreneurs are also protesting against the demonstrations that are killing their business, and women are marching for peace. The story is unfolding in front of my eyes and I am not working.

One day, I wake up so frustrated that I decide to personally deliver my CV to the West Africa Democracy Radio office. I look it up on the internet and find an office number. I call the office and ask for directions. It takes me a long time to find them as I am not familiar with the area and I also have to walk. I'm trying to save as much money as possible. I walk for a while, but then realise that I am totally lost. I have no idea where I am or how I got there. None of the locals I ask for directions seem to know the radio station, let alone where it is.

I am beginning to think that this radio station is a figment of my imagination. I continue walking around in circles. I call the office again for directions, but the man behind the phone also doesn't seem to know where I am, so it's difficult for him to give me clear directions to where their offices are. I am on the verge of giving up and going back home when my contact from the station eventually finds me.

Together, we walk back to the WADR offices. As he is showing me around their offices, telling me about the security measures they had put in place in case of violence, a voice inside of me, like a whisper says: "You are going to work here. This is where you are meant to be."

He takes me to the newsroom, where he introduces me to the editor of the English News desk. We shake hands as I introduce myself and hand him my CV. He looks at me with so much suspicion, I don't know how to read his gaze. He places my CV on his desk and says to me: "Okay, thank you."

With that I am dismissed. I can feel my heart sinking to the soles of my feet. I am tired now, hungry, and very disappointed. Based on their reception, I am not hopeful that WADR will call me back.

I go back to writing. I write every day, filling my notebooks with all of my angst and frustrations. When life becomes too claustrophobic in the house, I walk to Amadou's house in the evenings for a change of scene.

On one of those restless days, I decide to walk downtown to catch up with the demonstrations and surprise Amadou with a short visit. In downtown Dakar, it is business as usual. This time though, Amadou is not at his usual post, chewing on his sothiou-stick. I am disappointed. "Maybe he's praying", one of his friends tells me; Amadou is always praying.

Another friend of his finds me sitting on his spot, paging through my notebook. He asks me if I know about the political demonstrations that have been taking place recently. He explains that most journalists converge at the Independence Square and monitor protests from there. I don't know where the square is, so he offers to walk me there and along the way tells me that there have been rumours that a protest will be happening later that day.

"The protests usually start late in the afternoon, after most people finish work," he says.

How considerate, I think.

As we get closer to the square, I can see them - a herd of journalists, with their media jackets and khaki vests with the distinctive 'Press' sign emblazoned at the back. There are a few women among the men, who are identifiable by their flailing wigs and weaves. I begin to feel very self-conscious.

For the first time, I feel like an outsider looking in. I am uneasy. I am now thinking that even though I am one myself, I do not think I like journalists very much.

I loiter around, trying to build up the courage to face my tribe. I don't think I have enough strength to face their suspicious eyes, or stomach their indifference. I am simply not prepared. One can never tell with journalists;

one moment they can be into you, as if you are as essential to their lives as the very air they breathe and the next, you could be as insignificant as a fallen star. I bought some time. I purchased some coffee and Amadou's friend and I shared a cigarette.

I have to think of a strategy. I told the friend that I am going across to join the group of journalists. I asked him to come with me and introduce me in Wolof.

"Wait," I say. "You must introduce me as Amadou's wife. Tell them that I can't speak French and ask if they can help me out."

He agrees. I want to have strictly professional engagements with them. I had made the mistake of giving my number to several well-meaning men, thinking they were genuinely interested in helping me with information, only to discover that their main interest was to take me out on a date. By telling this group that I am already married, I want to take the possibility of dating off the table and just deal with work. I want to erect a boundary.

On the other hand, I also wish that this lie was true.

I have never wished to be married more in my life. It had never occurred to me that my status as a single woman could one day become such a social faux pas. By Senegalese standards, I am way past my prime for eligible bachelors seeking a wife. The fact that I'm not married at 30, can only mean one thing: there is something wrong with me.

Amadou's friend leads the way and I follow him across the street. He greets everyone. I am sure he is following my instructions to the T, as he introduces me to the tribe. As I listen to him, I imagine him saying: "This is Amadou's wife, a stupid journalist who comes from South Africa. She can't speak French or Wolof, but wants to cover the protests. I'm not exactly sure why she is here or if she knows what she's doing, so please take care of her."

They all nod, some smile.

I mean he could have said anything to them; I haven't understood a word. Soon after he leaves, silence befalls the group as if they are meditating on the difficult task ahead. Then one of them begins to laugh.

"You really can't speak French, really?" he asks.

"No," I say.

"You can't speak French, but you want to write about politics in Senegal? Ohhh it's going to be very difficult for you! It's going to be really difficult... I tell you," he concludes in a sing-song voice.

Although he is right, I still want to punch his smug face. He is wearing dark Ray-Ban sunglasses. He is tall and very skinny, with short brush-cut hair. He looks just like everyone else. His only distinctive feature is his smile, which seems to mock me at every turn. Unlike the others, he is not wearing a press jacket.

Who does he think he is? I fume inside.

Then I hear a voice that sounds like mine responding to him with such confidence, I step closer so I can listen to it myself.

It comes out in a hushed whisper: "First of all, you don't know me. You don't know where I'm from. You don't know what I can and cannot do. So, you can't tell me what is going to be difficult and what is not difficult for me okay. It's either you want to help me or you don't. My abilities have nothing to do with you."

After the monologue, I move to the back row and try to find someone who is friendlier. I ask each of them if they can speak English. They all shake their heads no, as if following a cue from him.

This plan to hang-out with journalists is proving to be a disaster. My plan is imploding. They are all so full of themselves. I stand among them for a little, allowing my anger and frustration to simmer. I cannot believe how hostile they are to me, as if I am going to scoop them on a major story.

"How long have you been here, in Senegal?" asks a journalist I hadn't approached.

"Two months."

"Two months?" he queries.

"Yes. I came here in December," I say.

"And you're already married?"

"Yes."

"To a Senegalese guy?"

"Yes."

"Oh, that's so soon, that's too soon," they all chime in agreement.

Oh boy! How do I go back to talking about the real reason we're all here? I think to myself.

"Ah, well, you know one can't be single in Senegal," I retort, losing my resolve.

I suspect they know that I am lying.

Then I noticed a gold ring on the Ray-Ban's left-hand ring finger.

"So, are you married?" I ask, deflecting attention from me. I surprise myself with this question. Where had it come from?

"No. Why do you ask?" he says, smiling again.

"You are wearing a ring on your wedding finger," I say, pointing at it. Either he must have forgotten he had it on, or that he is married. He looks down at his left hand, then turns the ring around with his thumb to reveal a letter on it.

"Oh, that's just a gift I wear. You see it has 'D' on it - for my family name."

"Oh!" I say, feeling stupid and relieved.

Relieved? Why would I be relieved that he is not married?

I decided to change the subject.

"So, what's been going on?" I direct the question to no one in particular.

"What do you mean?" asks Ray-Ban, whom I will refer to as Mr. D.

"The protests - has anything happened today?" I ask again.

"Oh no, nothing yet. Do you even know what the protest is about?" he asks.

"Yes, I think so, but you can tell me from your point of view."

"Okay," he says, "I'll tell you."

I take out my notepad and start writing as fast as I can:

"It all started last year in January. The Constitutional Court of Senegal ruled that President Wade, who was initially elected in 2000, could run for a third term in office. This was a violation of the constitution, which limits presidential terms to two. The new law was introduced by Wade himself shortly after he was elected into office, as a promise to the Senegalese people that he would not exceed his welcome. In court papers however, Wade argued that this rule did not apply to him since that law was changed during his first term in office. This implied that his first term could not be counted within the two term limits set out in the constitution. This made it clear to the public that Wade was not only going back on his word, he was also manipulating the law and the legal system for his own selfish reasons. On the 23rd of June in the same year, Senegalese people took to the streets in opposition to Wade's efforts to retain power. They also challenged his application in court. These protests gave birth to a movement called M23 to commemorate the day. Because of this widespread opposition Wade retreated, hoping that public sentiment would eventually change. But this year, he relaunched his campaign. The Supreme Court agreed with him, saying he was exempt from his own law, and thus qualified to contest for the Presidency for a third time. The court's decision angered the people and led them to take to the streets in protest." he concluded.

I am astonished by his lucidity. He recalls numbers and dates as if they were his brothers and sisters. He paints the picture for me in a clear and crisp way. Even though I knew some of the facts. Listening to him explain them to me feels as if I am reading an English article in the paper.

"If you have any questions, or if there is something you don't understand about the story, you can call me on this number and ask me."

He writes the number down on my notebook and then gets into a car, which appears out of nowhere. He says goodbye to everyone and leaves. Just like that, before I can say anything back. It feels as if I have been hit by a wave from the coolest ocean. I am impressed by him, but my ego is also bruised. I find him so annoying, even though he has been very helpful to me. He has given me background and contextual information in a way that has elevated my understanding of what has been going on. I now have a fuller, clearer picture of the true point of contention. I understand why people are so angry; Abdoulaye Wade was changing the script right in front of the citizen's eyes and with impunity. As I continue to wait, going over my notes in an effort to regain my composure, it becomes obvious that a protest would not be taking place.

The group of journalists starts to disperse. Two of them invite me to lunch with them and I accept the offer, even though I don't have money and cannot afford restaurant food. I have become a street-cuisine aficionado, courtesy of Amadou who regularly shares the food he buys from the streets with me. Left to my own devices though, I live primarily on cigarettes, bananas, and Café Touba; this has been the sum total of my diet of late.

At the restaurant, I sit and listen as they discuss politics in Wolof and French. I have no clue what they are talking about and they do not make any effort to include me in their conversation. I start to get bored and hungry. I am trying to think of a way to politely excuse myself from their company, but I also do not want to seem rude. I want to go with the flow and the flow is grating on my nerves. At intervals, they throw words at me in French. I try my best to follow, but I am too slow for them. I feel flustered and my brain is tired. After lunch, they give me a lift to Amadou's corner and it's a relief.

Even though the day did not work out as I'd planned, at least I now have a better understanding of what is going on. I feel confident that I can provide convincing interviews. Additionally, I have a new contact with a local journalist who can update me on the latest news and events, or with whom I can verify some facts and information. I decided to use his number just for that.

Back at the house, my relationship with Aisha is becoming icy. I am growing more uncomfortable in her house with each passing day, but I don't know how to break the ice since I don't have money to rent my own space elsewhere. I try to spend as much time outside her house as possible, but whether I'm inside or outside it, both are strenuous. I know that the situation is untenable and that it's just a matter of time before something happens to break the stalemate. Not knowing what this something is, only serves to increase my anxiety. At night, I can barely sleep. During the day, I am plagued with hunger and fatigue. I need money to buy food. I cannot ask Amadou, who is already sharing the little he has with me. I cannot ask Aisha, who is already providing me with a place to stay for free. My MasterCard is still en route. My sister is still trying to get some cash together. I have a headache just thinking about the pressure I have put on myself and everyone else around me. I don't want to even think about what Aisha must be thinking of me, since I do not have an answer for her question: "What's your plan?"

At this point, it is already too late to regret my decision to stay longer; I have to live with it. I have been out of the news loop for a while and so I decide to call Mr. D to find out if there is anything of significance happening on their news diary. In my mind, I imagine that his office works like the South African Broadcasting Corporation, a newsroom where I spent many years as a radio reporter.

We worked on a system where the most important item in it was the Diary. Everyone in the news departments lived according to what was on the diary. The central news department had three national editorial diary meetings a day, which were attended by all regional offices responsible for reporting the news in the country's nine provinces. Each province or region would present its news items for the day, listing all the top stories or the important news stories that they planned to cover. Each item on the list was discussed and/or debated by the Assignment Editors and Executive and Senior Producers of current affairs shows. From there, a national diary would be compiled that listed all the top stories from the provinces that made up the top news stories for the country on that day. Each journalist had access to both their regional diary, where they worked, and the national diary, which comprised other stories that were happening in other regions of the country; including the International diary. When I call Mr. D, I assume that his office, or whoever it is he works for, will be using a similar system. In addition, journalists also had access to News Wire Diaries from corporate news agencies which sell news to subscribers such as national, private, and international news broadcasters and newspapers. Their diaries covered news of international or global importance. If a local story was on the newswire diaries like Reuters or Associated Press, it was considered to be a big story.

While pre-election violence in Senegal was a big story it was not an exclusive one.

I have very limited resources, so I figure I need to be a bit more strategic about how I use them. I ask him if there are any updates to the political story or any new information.

"Not really," he says, "but I will be at the same place where we met today; you can meet me there."

Later that day, I went downtown to meet him and stop to greet Amadou at his stall, as usual.

"Be safe," Amadou says.

I had gone downtown much later than usual. As I arrive, I see journalists getting into their cars to leave. I'm walking around the square aimlessly when one of the journalists, the one I'd gone to lunch with a few days previously, recognises me. He calls out and asks me to come join them in their car. I don't want to appear rude or absent-minded, which I am, so I go along with him.

The worst thing is that I can't recall what Mr. D looks like anymore. I am concerned I won't be able to tell him apart from everyone else.

I settle in the back seat of the minivan and the journalist introduces me to the driver, cameramen and other journalists sitting inside. They are going back to the office, because there is no story. Another cameraman gets into the van and offers me a banana, which I take and eat ravenously. I am always hungry these days and bananas are my favourite. When I was little, I used to eat bananas along with their peels, a habit that caused my grandmother Mamani to tease: "One day a banana tree will grow in your stomach."

Eventually, Mr. D comes around and gets into the front seat of the car. He confirms that there has been no protest and none is likely to take place so late in the day, so they are all going back to the office. I start to get out of the car, but he says they'll drop me off wherever I want.

"Please drop me off at the corner, near the Sandaga Market," I ask.

"Where do you live?" he asks. "We can drop you right at home."

"Amitie Deux," I tell him.

I am grateful that I don't have to worry about getting back home and suddenly feel relaxed. I wasn't aware of how tense I've been. It's a relief to know that I can stretch out the money I have, by saving it with this free ride. The van makes stops at various points along the way, dropping people off. We pass the neighbourhood where I live and I start to get nervous, especially as it's already dusk. I ask where they're going, since they are passing my neighbourhood. I don't want to yell like a lunatic, but I am doing just that inside.

"Don't you want to see where I work?" Mr. D asks.

Not necessarily, I think.

"I want to go home," I tell him.

"Well, if I were you, I would want to see what other newsrooms look like," he retorts.

"I guess," I replied. "As long as you'll take me straight home after I've seen where you work."

By the time we arrive at his offices, it is already evening. I want a cigarette. He makes me some coffee and then disappears, leaving me in the newsroom with two or three of his colleagues who are still working.

He works for a private media company called TFM or Télé Futurs Médias. TFM is owned by the Grammy award-winning musician and singer-songwriter Youssou N'Dour, and has three components: Radio, which was called Radio Futurs Medias - RFM; a TV station; and a newspaper, L'Observateur, which has the widest circulation in Dakar. I sit and watch as video editors chop pictures from the day's news. The newsroom is very modern and clean. The walls are plain white, with a colourful painting of the media groups' proprietor, Youssou N'Dour. When Mr. D is finished at the office, he comes back out into the newsroom and says: "Let's go."

"Have you been on a motorbike before?" he asks.

"Yes," I fib confidently, like an old pro.

Meanwhile, the truth is I am petrified of motorbikes. Amadou regularly drives me home on his scooter, which was initially frightening, but I have gotten used to it. A motorbike on the other hand, I consider a no-go zone.

When I was in high school, a classmate's friend was killed in a motorbike accident while they were on it together. I often thought about him and the look on his face when he told me in his Polish accent that his friend had been killed in a motorbike accident. He had been badly bruised - physically and emotionally. Men who ride motorbikes are largely notorious for their reckless love for speed and taking unnecessary risks. I didn't want to become a casualty in their game of Russian roulette.

The first and only time I had been on a motorbike, I did it to overcome the fear of death and possible injury. It was a harrowing experience. Once, while on a work trip in Kampala, Uganda, I decided to take the infamous Boda-Boda motorbike transport because it got passengers to their destinations faster than any other mode of transport. Although a friend was showing me around the city in his very safe SUV, I decided to take a Boda-Boda just for the experience. The motorbike meandered through the streets of Kampala like a water-snake. I remember holding on so tightly to the driver, hugging and squeezing him as if he were my long-lost husband. The driver eventually had to pry my hands off his chest, which was embarrassing to say the least. So, when Mr. D asked if I had ridden a motorbike before, I said, "Of course!" I did not want to appear like a sissy, even though the stereotype fit me perfectly; I was very scared.

As we ride, I try to focus on the horizon. He glides his machine down the highway and I discover that the view of Dakar at night on a motorbike is spectacular. I let the evening air brush up against my face and for a brief moment I begin to understand the charm of motorbikes; the sense of power and freedom is addictive. The rush of having to fully pay attention to the present moment because a second of distraction could be fatal, is enlivening. As we ride, I notice that Mr. D is taking a different turn. We are not going in the direction of where I live.

"This is not the way to my house," I shout over the traffic.

"Yes, I know," he replies. "I'm taking you to my house. Don't you want to know where I live?"

Not really, I think to myself.

"I want to go home!" I shout.

It is difficult to have a conversation in moving traffic.

His house is located in a very obscure corner, in a place where one would never think to look for a house, but as I glance around a little more, I realise that he lives in a part of town I am very familiar with. I recognise, by a few landmarks, that he lives in a suburb called Mermoz, not far actually, from where Mathews lives. I have driven down this way a few times before.

Discovering that I know exactly where I am. and that I can find my way home from there, helps to calm me down. In another context, this could be considered a kidnapping, but that isn't the case here because I'm a willing participant. I had consented to this take-over out of curiosity to see where things could go. Also, I'm avoiding going back to Aisha's apartment, so this mystery man is a perfect detour.

"There's no one home," he tells me.

His brother and his brother's wife who live with him are out of town and won't be back for a few days.

After he opens the door, he pulls a blue curtain open to reveal two double-bed mattresses placed on the floor top of each other on the left-hand side of the room. The beds are neatly made. There is a brown wardrobe at the foot of the mattresses. On the other side is a very low coffee table, with a computer and a big radio on it. He turns on the radio.

I am surprised by his modest living conditions. He starts to play reggae music. By then I have become familiar with reggae and the ragga music scene, after having spent half of the year dancing and listening to it at the infamous House of Tandoor in the inner-city suburb of Yeoville in Johannesburg, during 2011. I have a tricky relationship with music. I like its philosophy of 'one love' and 'black power', but there are other elements about the culture attached to it that I find problematic, patriarchy and misogyny being amongst the most prominent.

"I only listen to reggae music," Mr. D tells me. "Luciano is my favourite artist amongst all of them."

I tell him that I enjoy reggae music too and used to listen to a lot of it with my brother.

He lights indigenous incense called thiouraye. Most households burn this incense as a way of creating a warm atmosphere and pleasant scent in the house, but Mr. D is using it to mask the smell of weed.

"You're about to smoke, aren't you?" I ask.

"Yes, how do you know?" he asks, reaching into his wardrobe and pulling out a crumpled-up piece of newspaper. "This is my medicine," he says, as he opens it and starts to crush the herb inside with his fingers. "Do you know what it is?" he asks.

"I wasn't born yesterday," I answer.

I shake my head and smile at him.

I would never have pegged him to be a closet Rasta. I was fooled by his appearance. He looks so prim, so suave, like a real 'corporate' suit. Is he a true believer in love, or is he in it for the herb and the women, like most people? Anyway, who am I to judge? After all, why did his motives matter? Enough people in the world smoke this weed considered to be a gateway drug to the deep underworld of narcotics, for recreational reasons. Many of them do not believe in the philosophy behind it, or in anything in particular. He could be one of them. After smoking, he tells me he's hungry. We have to find something to eat. We go out and he buys two huge burgers.

On our way back I ask, "I thought you were taking me home?"

"Let's go to my house and eat first, then I'll take you home afterwards."

We go back to his apartment. I don't know what it is about him, but I find him both intriguing and annoying. At the same time, it is easy to talk to him. I can speak my mind without editing my thoughts. It is refreshing to be able to talk to someone so openly without feeling judged. While munching on the ridiculously huge burgers in his room, with Luciano playing in the background, we chat about our respective careers, where we have been before and where we hope to go. We also speak in general about African politics and subjects related to the socio-economic development of Africa and Africans. We talk until it is nearly 2:00 in the morning.

"I have to go home," I tell him.

"I'm tired," he says, plonking himself on the mattress and preparing to go to sleep. "I won't be able to drive you back now; it's very late. You can sleep here. It's fine. I won't touch you," he says, closing his eyes.

I sit on the edge of the bed for a while, staring at him. He takes my breath away. I cannot believe him. My heart starts beating out of my chest. It's the only sound I can hear now.

What do you think you're doing? I ask myself. Sleeping in a strange man's house? What if something happens to you? What would you do then? How will you explain this? If anything happens, you'll be the only one to blame because you put yourself in this situation. The voices inside my head are so loud, they pound through my ears.

Even though I think it is a very bad idea to sleep out, there is not much I can remedy at this point. Aisha is already in bed sleeping. It is 2 a.m. after all. I don't have the keys to her house, so if I insist on going home now, I will have to wake her up so that she can let me in. I don't want to do that. My decision to get into the TFM car in the afternoon and every concession I made afterwards has led me here, to this mattress, sleeping next to a man I barely know. This moment right here is the consequence of my decision; no matter how bad it is or whatever happens as a result of it, I must accept it.

I lie down on the mattress, as close to the edge as possible and as far away from Mr. D as I can be, without sleeping on the floor. I can't sleep. I am quite frankly freaked out by my own brazen risk-taking propensities.

At this point, it is clear to me that I have no fear. These are certainly not the actions of someone who is afraid. I listen to the incessant accusations I hurl with abandon against myself. I keep checking for the time on my cell phone which is in my hand, willing and praying for the sun to come up, before this man I am sleeping next to can get any ideas. I become more and more restless when it nears 5 and 6 a.m. in the morning. I don't want to wake Mr. D, but my entire body is itching to go. I want to flee out of his house. I am almost sleeping on the floor, ready to run, by the time it is about 7 a.m. Sensing my apprehension, Mr. D says, "You are not my prisoner, you know? You can go if you want to!"

I jumped up to leave, curious about how he knew I was not sleeping. But I don't ask any questions. I am out his door in two minutes, without even looking back. Both the door to his bedroom and the main house aren't locked, which means that I could have left at any time. I think that I am literally lucky to be alive, lucky not to have had nothing happen to me. He didn't even try to touch me.

As soon as I get home, I put down my belongings to get ready for bed, only to discover that my camera is missing. After repeatedly searching for it in my bag, I realised that I must have left it at Mr. D's house! Where is your head, woman! the voice inside my head shouts. This is what you get for sleeping in strange people's homes. You lose your head and your belongings.

On the way home, and after my unceremonious exit, I promised myself that I will not have anything to do with Mr. D after spending a night at his house, which I had not intended to do in the first place. I had told myself that I'd never call him nor see him again, but now that I've left my camera at his house, I have no choice. I am going to have to call him and see him again. What a nightmare!

Eventually, after I stop berating myself and have quietened the judge and jury in my head, I pick up the phone and call him. Yes, so soon.

"Hi, I'm sorry to call back so soon but I think I left my camera in your bedroom this morning. Are you going to The Square today? Oh, good, then can you please bring it with you? Thank you very much."

After this is done, I go to bed, feeling relieved that at least my decision to stay at his house did not cause any permanent damage. I still have my camera and my dignity. I woke up in the late afternoon.

I quickly get dressed and head downtown. When I arrive, the main street is filled with people. There is a demonstration happening - finally. Several Presidential candidates have come out into the street, including the most popular candidate, Youssou N'Dour, who has joined a coalition movement under the slogan, I Am A Witness. It is part of the M23 Movement against Wade's 3rd term campaign. Tensions are high on the streets whenever protests or demonstrations take place. The police often use force, claiming protesters have not received official permission to assemble publicly on the street. Journalists are everywhere, which means a big story is expected to come out of the protests. I am eager to start working, now that something is happening. I text Mr. D to arrange the meeting point. I am bewildered by his tepid tone on the phone, but decide not to dwell too much on it. After all, it doesn't matter whether he is happy to see me or not; he just has to give me back my camera.

He tells me where he is and I start to run towards his location. When I finally meet him, he looks dejected, which alerts me to the fact that something is wrong.

"I'm sorry. I forgot your camera at home," he says.

I am speechless. So, this is the problem. I started to have a mental conversation with him: But I called to remind you. I've been sending you text messages. You could have told me at any point during this time. Why wait until this very moment, right in the middle of a protest, to tell me this? You could have told me earlier! But I don't articulate a single word of what I am thinking because even if I did, it would not bring my camera into my hands.

I look at him and say okay, and then sit down on the nearest street-pot-plant. This is the other shoe falling off. This is what you get for sleeping in stranger's homes. Now you don't even have the tools of your trade on a day that a story is actually happening. I try to think of my options. I have no money to catch a taxi back to his place to fetch it; even if I did, I might as well walk to Mermoz as the traffic is so jammed. By the time I came back, everything would be finished, so I would have missed the story altogether anyway. I will just have to forget about my camera now and get it from him some other time. As I am getting up to walk away, he calls out to me.

"Here, take a taxi and go fetch it. Here is the money."

I look at him and dig my hands further into my jean pockets.

"It's your work," he says. "You know where I live?"

"Yes," I replied.

"My cousin will be there to give it to you. I can't leave here."

I am reluctant to take his money at first, but then decide that it's fair and take it.

"Okay, thank you," I say and leave without looking back. I get into a cab and go straight to his house, as if I'd driven there many times before. His cousin is already waiting at the door with the camera when I knock.

After I pick up the camera, I decide that the further away I am from Mr. D, the better. If I want to make it as a foreign correspondent in Senegal, I will have to be more focused than I have been up to this point.

The next day, I go back to the streets. The protests have turned violent. Tear gas, rubber bullets and stones cause the protesters to seek shelter in shops, under trees and behind high walls. The police charge ahead mercilessly, while activists, who cover their faces in black scarves and bandannas, throw stones and makeshift petrol bombs at police. At some point, while hiding behind a tree, seeking shelter from flying rubber bullets, I hear a rather distinct voice recording a voice report. It is the voice of Ofeibea Quist-Arcton, one of the veteran African radio journalists of our time. While I knew of her, and had heard many stories told about her within the SABC newsroom, we had never met. She had been working for the British Broadcasting Corporation - BBC, when she was seconded to assist the SABC transition from a state-owned-controlled broadcaster into a national public broadcaster. She is widely respected for her work ethic, accuracy, and precision. People who know her describe her as an eccentric character, who has a deep distaste for people who mispronounce her name: Quist-A-rc-Ton. She has travelled widely and has lived in several African countries. She speaks multiple languages, wears colourful scarves and African-print clothes. She is now based in Dakar, as the West African correspondent for NPR. Hearing her voice, especially amid the cacophony of violence and watching her duck rubber bullets and proceed to report fearlessly, fills my heart with pride. She is my senior by decades and even though she is not at all aware of me at that moment, her presence and voice inspire me and give me strength. Whenever I hear her voice on the radio I think, If God were a woman, He'd sound like her.

The first time I met or rather saw Ofeibea Quist-Arcton was in 2004, in a boardroom at the Sunninghill Hospital in Bryanston, Johannesburg. EMI Records was having a press conference to officially announce that my childhood icon, the Queen of African Pop, The Madonna of the Townships, singer Brenda Fassie, had died. Her family had pulled the plug on her life support after she had suffered a coma induced by a drug overdose. I arrived late, just as they were about to make the announcement. Ofeibea Quist-Arcton interrupted the proceedings and asked the EMI spokesperson at the time, Advocate Leslie Sedibe, to wait for me to set up my recorder. When he hesitated, Ofeibia added, "She is a reporter for the South African public broadcaster. The people deserve to know."

Quist-Arcton hadn't had to defend me or speak on my behalf at the press conference; she'd had nothing to gain by asking him to wait. This simple act of kindness stayed with me and made me respect her even more. Even though we had never met officially, I regarded Ofeibea as a kindred spirit and I looked up to her. Her work was another reason I aspired to become a foreign correspondent. I thought there was a lot of psychological freedom in writing and reporting about events happening in a country other than your own. Abroad, one was unlikely to be affected by nostalgia and historical baggage, and there were not as many inborn biases. One could see things from a different perspective - which hopefully leaned heavily on truth, accuracy, fairness, and justice.

Being in her vicinity again now gives me the courage I need to push through and get as much out of the protests as possible. Soon after I hear her voice, she disappears into the large crowd of journalists and protesters. At that moment, I resolve to stay focused on being a journalist and to tell the story as best as I can.

I follow the protests and eventually meet up with the photo-journalist from Mauritania amongst the crowd. I fall in step with her, as she photographs the mayhem that is unfolding in the streets of Dakar.

Because of the protests, some civic services like waste management have been interrupted. Residents take the opportunity to burn most of their refuse in the middle of the streets. As a result, in some areas like the Medina, streets become open-air incinerators for garbage.

I do the best I can to follow the unfolding uproar, running after students who are running away from police. Despite all these actions though, the truth is I still do not have a news story.

I decided to focus on the youth movement Y'en a Marre, which is becoming increasingly popular with the general public, especially young people. They are the ones who are driving the most violent protests and they are the most vocal against Wade's presidential campaign. Their songs and their slogan Y'en a Marre are passed along in the streets of Dakar like a secret password to an invisible revolution. They change their location and numbers often, which makes them difficult to locate.

One day, I hear that they'll be holding a press conference at their headquarters in a part of Dakar I've never been to. I decide to go and find them, hoping that my efforts will yield an in-depth feature story. I spend the whole day walking around the neighbourhood, with Amadou and I getting completely lost in a maze of sandy streets. When we eventually find their headquarters, the press briefing has ended and everyone and their friends are moving to another location for another event. Some of them are responding to interviews on their phones, while others are eating. The house where the press conference is held is a hive of indefinable activity.

Someone tosses me a press release, but no one has time to stop and talk. They have said all they've needed to say. If I want to do proper interviews with one of the leaders, I will have to ask one of them for their personal number. Although I manage to get a phone number for one of them who speaks better English than the rest, he also refuses to do an interview then. He tells me that we'd have to arrange a time at a later date. I feel completely defeated. I lost a lot of time getting lost and now I have nothing to show for it.

Y' en a Marre's headquarters is just the way I imagine a house of a revolution to be like inside: Each room is full of good-looking young men and women, who have fire in their eyes. They are also clothed in hip, trendy and militant-style outfits, which give them an air of mystery and intrigue. The atmosphere is imbued with a potent mix of fear, passion, excitement, and moral indignation. It makes me nostalgic for a place and time that didn't actually exist in my life: a time when I would have been part of a group of brave young men and women who were driven by a purpose bigger than themselves - liberty, freedom, and equal rights.

In my nostalgia, I have forgotten about a time when, out of sheer frustration, I had started something. It had been an online group, which aptly described my feelings: Fed-Up!! With Tax Plunder!! I started the group in response to increasing reports of corruption within President Jacob Zuma's government, coupled with a failing public sector which I'd borne witness to when my mother had been admitted to a public hospital. Although fairly new, the group had gained momentum and I had been interviewed about it in a front-page story about corruption in The Sunday Times newspaper.

A few weeks after the story was published, I discovered that I was being followed and that my house was under surveillance. Whoever they were, they now had pictures of my entire family, my mom, dad, sisters, and brothers, and I had no power to protect them. The price had been too great.

However, I had no memory of that brief moment of activism in my life. In Senegal, no matter how many times I heard the words "Fed-up!" it didn't ring any bells or connect to my own activism.

Unfortunately, I do not succeed in securing an interview with Y'en a Marre and, even if I had, there is no media house interested in a story from me, at least not yet.

I stay home more and keep on the matter by calling Mr. D, asking him if he's had any interesting updates. Each time I call him, he is either not in the office, at home, or on the way to the office; he is never in the office. I realise that I am wasting my time with him. At home, Aisha tells me that she will be moving to a new place at the end of the month. She has already signed a contract for occupation for the 1st of February in the new house. She will have to pay double or triple rent, unless I can take over her payments. Will I be able to take over the lease from her? I think this would be a convenient arrangement - if I had the money. But, I don't, and neither do I have a secure job. I am still waiting for my bank cards. I don't know how long it will be before they arrive. I want to help, but I can't. It becomes weird for me to continue to stay with her rent-free. My stress levels are shooting through the roof. I cannot sleep anymore. I hardly eat and I don't know how to communicate. The panic attacks come back.

They have me shivering and shaking at times to a point where I think I am sick. I start to feel like I am going to die at any moment, that each day is my last. I stay out later and later and later, until one day I come home and find the house locked. I had already said goodbye to Amadou, whom I had been visiting that night. So I start to wander the streets of Dakar, looking for a place to hang out safely until morning. First, I go and sit with two security guards nearby, then sit outside a petrol station near my home until a security guard comes and chases me away like a fly! Eventually, I end up at a shop that sells barbecued meat all night. There, I meet young men who share stories of their discontent. One has a Master's Degree in Communication, but tells me he cannot find a job anywhere. We speak about politics until they leave and I am left alone in the restaurant. I sit inside in a corner crocheting, until a group of women led by a big imposing man come in and order a pile of meat. A television set is blasting the latest pop club-house music on a loop. I am cold, tired, sleepy, and hungry. The man and the women look like they're nightshift workers; the women are sex workers, and the man is their pimp. He is big, wears a dark suit and seems to be in control of everyone he is with. I must have looked pitifully at them or their food, because one of the women throws money at me on their way out - one mille CFA, which is enough for me to buy a small cup of coffee, a piece of bread and a bit of airtime in the morning. I stay up all night. When the sun eventually comes up, I rush out of the shop and go home. No matter what, I need to find a new place to stay, but I am also out of options. I ask Amadou if he can find me a place, but he knows of nowhere with a spare room. I go to a woman who teaches at a local international primary school, whom I was referred to by a dancer friend who did not have a spare room in his house. She does the interview with me at the school after her last class. After I tell her my story, she tells me that she cannot allow me to come and stay with her. She says:

"I definitely have a room in my house, but I am sceptical of you. You seem like someone who habitually takes risks and makes bad choices. You are frankly too irresponsible and unpredictable for me. I simply cannot have someone like you living under my roof. I am sorry, but I cannot help you. I don't trust you."

It is painful to hear this, but I agree with her concerns.

After the interview, I continue my search for a place. I have no time to feel sorry for myself. I am disturbed by the experience of having been locked out of Aisha's house and don't want to end up spending another night on the streets of Dakar. Out of desperation, I even ask Amadou to marry me. He laughs and says, no-way! When the end of the month comes, I pack my bags without knowing where I'm going next. While Aisha and Nala eat supper, I tell them that I'm leaving. The atmosphere is tense. As I hug her goodbye, my blood is racing and tears are threatening to cloud my vision, but I cannot let them fall. I drag my suitcase behind me and walk out without looking back; I cannot afford to.

Chapter 5
LINDIWE: THE MISSING STORYTELLER

"Why did you come back? We thought you were doing so well in Dakar? We were reading your stories in the paper and hearing your reports on the radio. "Did you find love?"

"Yes."

"Did you find work?"

"Yes."

"So why did you come back? Don't get me wrong, it's good to see you but I was hoping you would at least spend five years in Dakar so that you could experience life in a foreign country. I mean, what do you have here? What are you going to do now?"

I don't know how to answer these questions from curious friends. The more I search for reasons why I am back in South Africa, the less they make sense. I begin to feel as if I have made a gigantic error in judgement.

Since returning from Senegal, I feel different. I am no longer the same hopeful girl who boarded the *Kenya Airways* flight in December 2011. At the same time, I am not certain who this new person is. I left South Africa intending to create a new life and possibly a new identity for myself. I wanted to build something solid; get married, have children, and host my own radio show, but when all those things were offered, I panicked and flew back home.

How could I have been so stupid?

After leaving Aisha's house, I ended up renting a room in the apartment Mr. D. shared with his family. Shortly after moving in with them, WADR called and offered me a job as a Producer and Anchor at the radio station from where I covered the elections. As time went on, Mr. D. and I became close friends until one day he proposed, sort of.

"What would you say if I asked you to marry me?" he asked one starry night while we were strolling around the island of Gorée.

"*Are* you asking me to marry you?" I asked.

"I just want to know what you would say?"

"Well, you have to ask me first," I said, laughing.

"But I can't ask if I don't know what your answer will be," he persisted.

"Well, you won't know what the answer is until you ask," I concluded.

After this impasse, we began to discuss marriage and a potential future life together.

Back in South Africa, I told an acquaintance about Mr. D's "non-proposal, proposal."

"Really?" she asks, her brows arching.

"Yeah."

"There was someone who wanted you, exactly as you are with all your problems and your baggage... someone who said they loved you for you; they wanted to spend the rest of their life with you and you said no?"

"No, I didn't say no."

"So? What are you doing here then? Why aren't you engaged or with him right now? Why did you come back?"

My answer is: "Because he never asked," but instead of saying this I am plunged into an ocean of despair. *Was my mother the real reason I came back? Or did I just use her as an excuse because I was too terrified to receive love, or commit to someone, or to anything for that matter?*

A few weeks before leaving Senegal, I had a dream that my mom was in bed weeping while surrounded by all her children. When I called to check if she was okay, I also told her about my new relationship with Mr. D which was becoming serious. She told me that she was fine, but advised that I should come back home first before making any rash decisions. So, I packed my bags and left everything.

I keep asking myself: *What is wrong with you Jedi? Why do you keep making decisions that don't make sense? Why can't you be normal like other people? What kind of life is this? How long will you live like this; moving from couch to couch, floor to floor and bed to bed? Living out of a suitcase? When will you stop running and settle down? Where is your home? Who are your people? What is going on with you? What do you want?*

The regret, guilt and confusion are so overwhelming; they seep into every area of my life and infuse every fibre of my being. If I'm sitting with a married couple, thoughts will come rushing in, like: *This could be you. You could be engaged. You could be sitting here talking about your future husband, but you're not.*

After I stopped drinking alcohol in 2011, I thought things would become much better or clearer for me, but I discovered that I was even more confused, impulsive, and hypersensitive in my sober state and less able to withstand any pressure or consistent probing and interrogation. I was always on edge and everything seemed like an intense emergency. I was irritable, short-tempered, uncommunicative, hyper-defensive and very raw emotionally. Tears flowed at the drop of a hat. The tiniest problem became a life-threatening situation. Moreover, I was not eating.

My friendships also began to disintegrate. I was no longer on the same page with many of my peers. My social life shrank remarkably. There was very little about my life that I was willing to discuss. I didn't even know where or how to begin. I was so confused. Since I had no one to talk to, I turned to books to help me figure out what was tormenting me.

In one of my suitcases, I pull out a self-help book by American author Julia Cameron titled: *The Artist's Way: A Spiritual Path to Higher Creativity*. The book teaches techniques and exercises to assist people gain self-confidence by harnessing their creative talents and skills. Cameron's book emphasises a connection between artistic creativity and a spiritual connection with God.

I had bought the book in 2009 after a friend recommended it, but I'd never read it. This time, it is my only option. Reading *The Artist's Way* was the most cost-effective, discreet way of investigating what was going on with me.

Going to a new country hadn't solved my problems; it had only made them more pronounced. I was aware of all the ways in which I was failing, all the ways in which I was not functioning properly as an adult human being in the world, but I did not know how to fix any of it especially since I could not identify the source of the problem.

The Artist's Way places a lot of emphasis on doing things you enjoy. It encourages users to explore childhood dreams, desires, and fantasies in a safe way. So, most of the time I felt like I was playing and having fun, even though I was confronted with what seemed to me to be insurmountable emotional obstacles. The course required a lot of writing and executing solo activities throughout the week, which I relished since I had a lot of free time after work. I had just started work as a producer for *SAfm's* current affairs show *Midday Live*.

Doing something also kept me from ruminating over Senegal, and everything else that was wrong with my life. Since I still suffered from intense insomnia, it also gave me something constructive to do when I couldn't sleep. I spent a lot of time on my own, mostly wandering through the streets of Johannesburg in the afternoons.

The 16th August 2012 finds me doing just that, wandering around my childhood neighbourhood of Phefeni, Soweto, looking for a friend's house. I am supposed to be attending his father's funeral but, as so often happens with me, I am lost. Even though I grew up in Phefeni, and I know the streets, at some point I become completely disoriented and lose all sense of direction.

As I walk past the landmarks of my childhood, tears begin welling up again. I have so many memories here. I am overcome with grief. There is *Phefeni Secondary High School*, commonly known by the acronym *Pesesco*. It is the secondary school my mother and cousin Nana attended and which I hoped I would also attend once I finished primary school. Next to *Pesesco* is *Matseke High*, whose students were notorious for causing trouble and being rebellious during the 80's. Then there is the original *Mandela Home*, which has been turned into a museum. I had taken friends from America and India there on a tour once. Then I walk past my own school, *Thloreng Primary*, which has been turned into the studio for a production company that produces Soweto TV. As I walk past the school, I see myself sitting in the second row in my Sub-A or Grade One class, listening to the fearsome old teacher telling me to keep quiet and sit down, or she will hit me with the shiny wooden stick she always carries in her hand.

I had been so thrilled to see my cousin Nana walk into my class that I'd jumped off my chair and screamed her name out loud, causing the entire class to laugh at me.

My Grade One class felt a bit like home, since my teacher had also taught my mother when she was around my age. She would often say, "I know your mother *wena* Poppy", whenever I was disruptive in class.

Nana had come to fetch me. My family was fighting again and sometimes those fights spilled out onto the street. I was somehow included in the commotion, even though I had not been there when the conflict happened.

My eyes move from the school grounds to the side of the road where there is a large 'June 1976' - Soweto Uprisings mural on one of the walls, fencing in several houses. It hadn't been there when I was young.

Nana had also been the reason I became the laughing-stock of my entire Grade Two class in *Thloreng*. One day, my classmates discovered that I had no panties on. I had forgotten to put them on while getting ready in the morning, because I was in a rush to walk with Nana to school. It was a

Monday and some of the girls were showing off their brand-new underwear that had been bought over the weekend. One of them dared me to show mine. When I definitely said go ahead, she lifted my pinafore... and exposed my nakedness underneath.

The road leading to my great-grandmother's house reminds me of the day we returned from a school trip to the Johannesburg Zoo. My sister and I were so excited as we boarded the blue Putco bus in the morning. All the way to the zoo, we sang: *Irobe Joe asiyagago Joe, keyamagoa Joe!* urging the driver to move faster. When we returned in the afternoon, we bumped into my cousin Nana, who was also still in school uniform, strolling languidly with a boy along our street. I remember threatening her, saying I will tell Mamani that *uyajola* - you are seeing boys.

I start to feel dizzy. I am in the most famous township in Africa and I am lost. I left my life and a love in Senegal for this? I am hot, cold, thirsty, hungry, tired, frustrated, and sad. When I start to feel too tired to continue walking, I call my friend:

"Dude, I can't find your house. I am standing at a corner shop not far from *Uncle Tom's Hall* on Kumalo Street, can you fetch me?"

"But how did you manage to get lost?" he asks, laughing. I love hearing his cheerful voice, considering that he has just buried his father.

"I don't know," I answer.

"Okay, wait there, I'm coming," he says.

As I stand there waiting for him, I realise that I've been in a similar situation before - almost at the exact spot, many moons ago.

That Saturday, everything had been glorious. My sister and I had woken up early in the morning, eager to be part of the school choir that was competing in the *Inter-School Choir Competitions*, which were being held at *Uncle Tom's Hall*.

Our black *Toughees*-brand shoes were sparkling, our black, two-pleated pinafores were pressed flat and our bright yellow shirt collars ironed stiff.

Our hair had been twisted and brushed into place and our faces had a sheen from Vaseline. We were left with nothing else to do but to sing at the top of our voices. To get to *Uncle Tom's Hall*, we walked hand-in-hand in a long chain-like formation, with two teachers walking on either side of us to help us cross the roads that separated the school from the hall. Soon, it was our school's turn to sing. I felt proud of myself and happy to be in the front row, when our principal signalled with her hands that we should start. I sang soprano, but our school's harmonious voices blended together was the best thing about singing in a choir.

I scanned the audience for a familiar face, but there was none. I wished everyone I loved was there in the audience to watch us, because in my heart I was singing for them.

After the singing competition, I got caught up playing with new friends, I lost all sense of time. I emerged from my playtime to find that it was already late in the afternoon and I could not find my sister or any of my schoolmates; all of them had gone home.

I was in big trouble. While I knew how to get home from *Uncle Tom's Hall*, I was afraid to cross the busy road on my own. It was getting late. The sun was setting and the road was gridlocked with fast moving traffic. Frustrated, afraid and distraught, I stood on the edge of the road wailing until eventually, as if by a miracle, I saw a familiar face emerging through my cloud of tears. It was him! My great uncle Bhut' Vusi, standing on the other side of the road, waving and smiling at me. He signalled for me to stop and wait, because at the sight of him I immediately felt confident enough to start crossing the road on my own without even checking to see if there were any cars coming from either direction.

He came over to my side, took my hand and we crossed the road together. I will never forget how relieved, safe, and comforted I felt when he took my hand in his. I felt so loved. Wanted. However, even though I felt good about myself, Bhut'Vusi reminded me that I was still in trouble.

"*Aye ye Poppy, u mama uzok'shaya, ub'ukuphi sonke les'khathi,why ungabuyanga noNhlanhla?*" He was warning me that my grandmother

Mamani was beside herself with worry; I would be getting a hiding when we got home.

Although I was scared, I felt secure in the knowledge that as long as Bhut' Vusi was around, no matter how angry Mamani was she would not punish me with the leather skipping rope she favoured so much while he was there. I saw him as my protector. Bhut' Vusi, Mamani's brother, was our favourite great uncle because he was the only one who interacted with us often. He was strict, but kind. He also used to appear and disappear just like his oldest son Thente.

When he disappeared for long periods of time, it was usually because he had been arrested for one crime or another. But I did not know this as a child. I assumed he just went to work or lived somewhere very far. When he was released, he usually came home to Phefeni first, before going anywhere else. I would spot him coming through the gate while sitting on the apple tree, from where I enjoyed watching the world go by.

From the apple tree I could see *Phefeni Station*, and each time a train stopped on the platform I would wonder if it was bringing any visitors to our home. I was also familiar with the loud noise our gate would make whenever someone opened or closed it. The screeching sound of the latch being pulled from the concrete fence when our gate was being opened was so distinct that it felt as if someone was pulling ice-cold, steel rods from my earlobes, which scraped against grains of sand inside my head. The sound pulled at my heart-strings. When I heard the sound, I would run to the gate or go into the kitchen to see who was coming in.

I often ran to Bhut' Vusi when he came home, but instead of greeting me, he would stop me dead in my tracks, signalling sternly and silently that I should not come near him or even attempt to touch him. I would lurk behind him as he went into the outside toilet and wait until he was done bathing with the cold water and aloe leaves left in a bucket for him. As soon as he was finished, I would run to him again and he would pick me up and swing me around, kiss me and tell me how much he missed me. Then my questions would start pouring in: *ung'phatheleni, ubuyaphi?; uzolala la? uzohlalanathi? 'be u kuphi; 'be wenzani etoilet? Why ungafuni ngibone? Why ungafuni ngikugijimele?* I had so many questions and he had a way of responding to me as if everything

I was asking made him the happiest man in the world. He had a great laugh and the most brilliant smile that always made my heart glow.

During one of his visits, he gave me a whole, pink R50 note and sent me to buy beers from a house which sold them on our street. I was in awe because I had never seen a R50 note before in my life, let alone held one in my hands. He trusted me with his money.

Bhut' Vusi had interesting habits, such as eating raw potato skins. I would mimic him. *"Imnandi"* he'd say mischievously, while chewing vigorously. This would annoy Mamani immensely, delighting Bhut' Vusi who would laugh heartily at having successfully irritated his sister. After the incident at *Uncle Tom's Hall,* my grandmother bought me a Casio digital watch we called *"panya-panya"* to help me keep time.

Eventually, my friend's maroon Fiat stops at the shop to pick me up. The memory of Bhut' Vusi has calmed me down. We go to the house, where I pay my respects and condolences to the family and we eat lunch. On our way back to Johannesburg, we turn the car radio on and listen to a news report announcing that police have killed at least 30 striking mine workers in an area called Marikana, near Rustenburg, in the North West Province.

The report says the police acted in self-defence against an armed group of striking men who were demanding a wage increase to net 12,000 Rands a month about US$1,200 at the time. The workers had, they said, refused to disperse from their protest area, a *koppie*, after the police ordered them to leave.

We are all mortified. I start to think that perhaps the incident took place around the same time I was walking around Phefeni, lost. I am struck by the seemingly coincidental nature of events in my internal life, which seem to mirror events in larger life. *Marikana,* as it becomes known, feels like a personal incident to me, as if I have personally lost a close relative in the massacre.

The next day at work, I am struck by my colleagues' reactions to the event in the newsroom. Most of them believe the police had done the right thing.

During editorial meetings and corridor-conversations, some of them utter statements such as: *I would also shoot them, if I were the police. I mean these guys put muthi on themselves to make them bullet-proof and invincible. If the police had not shot those miners first, they would have been attacked.*

I am astonished at the tone of the conversations. It is strange for me to see colleagues choosing to ignore the evidence which makes it clear that it was the police who shot at the miners. It was not a shoot-out. It was a one-sided attack. The suggestion that the police - who were supposedly trained to deal with conflict and mobs - could be frightened by rumours that workers had consulted traditional healers and *inyangas* who had endowed them with supernatural powers, including 'invisible spiritual armour' and 'bulletproof vests', was a little more than preposterous. Despite this, many people seemed to believe wholeheartedly that the police had done the right thing; that they had been defending the nation.

What would you have done if you were faced with a mob of armed men?
Although the conversations around the Marikana shootings are uncomfortable, I am also intrigued by the language used to describe and define what happened. How we speak about it within the newsroom seems very biased in favour of the police and *Lonmin*, the platinum mining company which employed the striking miners.

Initially, editors and journalists of most news organisations are gripped by the events that happened on the *koppie*. For a few hours on that day, they broadcast the news as it happened. But as more information comes through, and the more the footage is re-played, it becomes apparent that what happened was not an accident; it was a direct and deliberate attack on the workers.

At some point, we are given *Editorial Guidelines* on how to speak about Marikana. The SABC and the news station eNCA stop showing footage from that day. The footage, they say, will be used as part of evidence in a Commission of Inquiry hastily set up by then President Jacob Zuma to investigate events leading up to the bloodshed on the 16 August 2012. My initial instinct is to get in the car and drive out to the mines to collate interviews with workers on location, just to get the feel of the story, so to speak. But as a Producer for *Midday Live* I am desk-bound. I can only do telephonic interviews with newsmakers and conduct research online or via the telephone. In addition, there are enough journalists from the SABC newsrooms in Pretoria, Rustenburg and Johannesburg who have been assigned to the story. Under those circumstances, if I want to cover the story, I have to find another way of doing it. I dig for possible angles, until I find the contacts details of some of the widows whose husbands had been killed at the mine. I notice that the voices of the miners are missing from most reports. Since I cannot get a hold of the miners, I surmise that my best bet is to speak to their families, especially their wives.

I keep calling, until about two or three of the widows agree to speak to me.

The story of *Marikana* has multiple angles. There is the Legal story of the *Farlam Commission*, the Labour unions, *Lonmin*, there is a police investigation and a Political angle. All these stories are being reported on a daily basis. I have to think of fresher angles to pursue. By the time I find people willing to do interviews with me, I am working double shifts just to get them on tape. For instance, I have to get to the office two hours earlier in order to make phone calls, set-up interviews, conduct them, transcribe them, edit the sound, and write the scripts before the editorial meeting at 8:30am, after which I'll be assigned other stories to chase on the day's line-up for a show that starts at midday.

One morning, while editing an interview with one of the widows, two Executive Producers at *SAfm* walk into my booth and ask what I am working on. I explain my story to them.

"Can we listen to your package please?" they ask.

"I'm still working on it. Is there something wrong?" I ask.

I'm surprised, because it is unusual for Executive Producer's to check on stories directly; this job is often left to the Senior Producers.

"It's fine. Just play what you have so far."

"Okay," I say, and play the package. There is a sound-clip from one of the widows who says: *"I blame the police, I blame Lonmin, I blame the unions, and I blame the government for what happened..."*

"Stop! Stop! Go back. Yes, that part. Take that part out," one of the Executive Producers instructs me abruptly.

"Which part?" I ask.

At this point, I am not even aware of what is going on.

"That part, the part where she says she blames the government and the mine, take it out."

"This part?" I am confused. The sound is fine. There is nothing wrong with it and her voice is clear.

"What do you mean? Why?" I ask again.

"We actually don't know who is to blame for *Marikana*, so we can't be apportioning blame on anyone at this point," one of them answers.

"I understand that, but she's not singling anyone out. She is including everyone involved. Also, it is her opinion. Why is this not acceptable?"

"*Sisi we! Wesisi! Into e ngiyibonile! Angikaze ngiy'bone into eso empilweni yam', amaphoyisa bewabulala nje, ngibonile kulama video bebangi sendela wona, wesisi! Awazi!*"

I keep hearing the woman's voice replaying in the background, as I try to understand what is actually going on in the booth. It has taken a lot of time for me to convince the widows to speak to me. Our conversation had been long in which she had told me of cell phone footage she had received, clearly showing the policemen attacking and killing the miners. She had also confessed to thoughts of suicide after the loss of her husband, and I'd tried to dissuade her and encourage her to seek help. She'd told me that she was broken by what she'd seen. That's why she was blaming everyone involved.

The Executive Producers just stand there, watching me silently. I concede. I drag the cursor over the clip and I press delete.

"Play it again," One demands.

I do, and they listen to the whole story again.

"It's fine like that," they conclude, and walk out of the booth.

Up until that very moment, I had never experienced anything like this in my career at the SABC. Was my mind playing tricks on me?

The way that censure and political interference at the SABC was spoken of, made it seem like a big deal would be made out of it, if it were to happen to anyone there. I never thought it would be like this; so close, personal, intimate, and private. I expected to receive an email or something to notify me, not to be given a word-of-mouth instruction which cannot be traced or easily corroborated. If I decide to say or do anything, it will be their word against mine.

I am one person.

They could potentially argue that this occurrence had never taken place, except in my mind. Even though many prominent journalists had left the SABC citing 'political interference', lack of independence and editorial censorship, I had never before experienced it.

Those of us who worked in general news, unless our stories were political, never experienced editorial interference. The most prominent case of censorship that happened during my time, was the banning of anti-Mbeki political commentators on SABC news bulletins and current affairs programmes. The 'blacklist saga' eventually led to the resignation of SABC's veteran journalist and anchor of the *SAfm Morning Live Show*, John Perlman, in January of 2007. John Perlman had challenged then SABC spokesperson Kaizer Kganyago about the existence of the 'blacklist', live on air. Newspaper reports claimed that Perlman resigned because the public broadcaster was unwilling to address the commission findings set up by then SABC CEO Dali Mpofu, which found that there was an atmosphere of fear and distrust at the broadcaster. Political interference and/or censorship at the SABC was an open secret, discussed in bars and restaurants of trendy suburbs like Melville after work, but no one was willing to be quoted. The reports in the newspapers and from other news organisations made carrying an *SABC News* business card and microphone in the field very difficult. We were not always welcome, and depending on who you were, or who knew you, you'd generally be viewed as an incompetent, nepotistic appointee, a government mouthpiece or a spokesperson for the ruling party. Many people felt justified in hurling insults at you, because you worked for the SABC.

I survived by reminding myself of the reasons I had become a journalist. My desire was to be *'a voice for the voiceless'* majority of South African black people, whose stories had not been told or heard. For as long as I was able to continue to do that, I would stay on at the SABC. In my mind, I was always serving the people's right to know the truth and to have the experiences they had lived through, reflected in the political discourse. Until that moment in the booth, all the editorial input that had been made or suggested on my stories was to either improve the quality, or to make it fit into a particular time slot. It was never political and even if it was, I never noticed. My personal mandate was to *give voice to people* who would otherwise have none.

This incident, which forced me to cut off that voice, meant that I also effectively cut off my own. Not only was I cutting off my voice, I was also eviscerating my raison d'être. If ordinary people's voices and opinions were no longer allowed on air, or if a widow who had lost her husband in one of the most tragic events in South African history since the 1960 *Sharpeville Massacre* could not voice her opinion about what was going on in the country anymore, this meant that not only had I failed to do my job but I also had no job left to do.

Before they leave the booth, the Executive Producers tell me that I should probably discontinue my interviews with any more widows - 'Just in case,' they warn and walk out.

It takes a while for me to process what happened and to understand that I was complicit in the gagging of the public's voice.

Because I was working through *The Artist's Way*, I tried to find creative ways to deal with my frustrations at work. I journaled a lot, because I found myself socially and professionally alienated. There was no one I could speak to about the incident at work. I didn't trust anyone in the office. I also didn't want to make my issues theirs. I had been so broke by the time I got employed at the SABC that I'd had to ask one of the Executive Producer's in the booth to loan me money for transport for the first month of my contract.

I didn't know who to turn to, because it was the very people whom I had admired as journalists of integrity who'd asked me to look the other way and who'd given me guidelines on how to speak about Marikana, portraying it as a 'tragedy' and not a massacre. They were the ones who had opined in the newsroom that all things considered, the police had been reasonable in their approach to the striking mine workers.

I also have to tell myself the truth: mine is not a 'stellar' name. I am not a well-known news anchor like John Perlman, Karima Brown or Nikiwe Bikitsha. I don't have political connections or access to friends in high places. I will not have editors lining up to offer me employment, if defying their orders leaves me without a job.

Everything I had gotten in my life had been through hard work, persistence, and perseverance. I had no magic formula for getting lucky. Because even a broken clock is right twice a day, I also had breakthroughs in life. At that point in my life, I felt completely alone. I, like the widows of Marikana, had no voice and no agency, no one was willing to listen.

If I went against the orders of the Executive Producers, I would be left out in the cold without a job. So, I decide, I must continue to work, earn some money, and tell authentic, newsworthy stories of ordinary South Africans. *But how do I do that?* I ask myself. How else can I tell the Marikana story without personally going out to the field, speaking to relatives or anyone who could somehow be a potential witness in the commission of inquiry? How do I tell the story differently?

Then an idea comes to mind.

Some weeks after my return from Senegal, a journalist friend who was an Arts and Culture critic and writer, invited me to join him to watch a play he was reviewing for a local newspaper. The play was called *The Line*, but he didn't know what it was about. He didn't seem enthused by it either, but it was his job to watch it. I chose not to probe and focused instead on the stage, which shimmered with Console glass bottles. I had seen a few plays at *The Market Theatre*, in downtown Johannesburg, but this was the first time I was going to see a play 'blind', without knowing the subject matter. Naturally, I was curious.

However, I was deeply moved by the play - tears from start to finish. I was still crying when my friend and I went out for coffee afterwards.

"I didn't know. I'm sorry," he said, looking concerned.

"You couldn't have known," I assured him, while willing the tears to stop flowing. "I didn't know that I would react like this myself."

The Line is a play which sprang from actor and Director, Gina Shmukler's Master's thesis. Gina Shmukler was attempting to answer several questions: How does a victim become a perpetrator? What happens when a government becomes complacent and fails to achieve the most basic of its people's aspirations as set out in the *South African Freedom Charter* of 1955? What happens when a lack of education, employment, housing, and dire poverty leave a population looking for scapegoats on which to take out their anger?

The play is based on a series of real-life interviews with victims and perpetrators of the 2008 xenophobic attacks on African foreign nationals in South Africa. The interviews are presented in a patchwork of chilling testimonies, characterised in performances by two actors on stage. As I watch and listen, my mind is flooded with memories. I start to remember some things I had forgotten, particularly the days I spent following closely on the heels of armed, special force policemen, who kicked down corrugated iron doors in actions reminiscent of images of apartheid-era policing of black townships, demanding to see all the receipts of payment for the electronic items in a foreign national's home.

The image of the *'burning man'* - the man who had been set alight by angry mobs remained impressed on my mind, even though I had not been there when the Mozambican national had been burnt to death. Images of his body engulfed in flames on the front page of most newspapers, shook me to the core. I couldn't get them out of my mind. The fact that photojournalists had stood by and watched the man burn long enough to take the picture before dousing his body with water, made me physically ill. I ended up in the doctor's room after my back broke out in hives from stress.

"Black Bags Meant for Garbage, Are Prized Possessions Here."

This is the opening line to a radio feature story on the aftermath of the xenophobic attacks, which I was co-producing with a colleague who was training for a new posting as the new *United Nations* correspondent for SABC

News in New York. It was a bittersweet partnership. His posting outside the country had been my dream job, the one I'd hoped I would one day get. I had shared this dream with a cameraman named Akash Bramdeo, while still an intern at the SABC. One day, on a drive back from a story, I told Akash that I wanted to become a foreign correspondent. He had always encouraged me to dream big and have a clear vision and focus for my career.

When I told him my plan, he asked, "Do you have a passport?"

"No," I replied.

"You should get a passport, so that when the opportunity arrives, you'll be ready for it. In fact," he paused, "Let's go… Let's get you a passport right now!"

On that very afternoon, Akash Bramdeo took me to an agency where I applied for my passport. He paid for everything.

"It's a gift," he said.

However, despite all my travels and assignments abroad on that very same passport, including a month-long assignment in Lebanon, I am still not ready or fit enough for the job.

While we are interviewing displaced African immigrants, who are boarding buses to return to their homes in Mozambique, my colleague is perplexed at my reluctance and hesitancy to interview them.

"What's wrong with you? Why do you hesitate to ask questions?" He asks, snatching the mic from my hand, showing me how it's done. *How to ask direct questions to aid workers helping victims of xenophobia in 2008* - 101.

The story leaves me numb. I envy his ability to be so disaffected by the plight of these people. By the time he is shadowing me, I have spent days on the story, visiting displaced foreign nationals in the suburb of Lenasia, the *Central Methodist Church* in Johannesburg, *Jeppe Police Station* and various other hot spots. I have been interviewing displaced foreign nationals fleeing for their lives, or interviewing their South African neighbours in townships like *Ramaphosa Township* in the East Rand who were high-jacking and moving into the newly-vacated plots of land, shacks and homes abandoned by the fleeing, previous owners.

Where should we go? Men with glazed, bewildered eyes wonder at me and at no one in particular. *We have nowhere to go.* Mothers and fathers with children become children themselves. These are the helpless victims of hate. How do you tell the same story again and again? Their voices will not stop asking: *Where are we supposed to go? What did we do wrong? What are we supposed to do now?*

I have even broken my own protocol and attended a march against the xenophobic attacks held in Johannesburg. My friends and I, some of whom are foreign nationals themselves, wear printed T-shirts with slogans such as, *More Zen, Less Phobia*, or *Ubuntu Died May 12*. We hand out these T-shirts at the march. I also spend time interviewing filmmakers, who produce several documentaries on the attacks under the banner of *Filmmakers Against Racism* - FAR.

The story of South African photojournalist's Dean Hutton, featured prominently in the play, resonates with me. The xenophobic attacks have shaken him to the core.

The experience had led him to question his beliefs and core values. This idea of *Ubuntu*: "I am because you are". He had associated *ubuntu* with Nelson Mandela, a man who represented the forgiving heart of black people. But now he was left to wonder; how could black South Africans turn around and do the same thing to other black people that the apartheid government had done to them? The xenophobic attacks had left him without an anchor. He was shattered. He found himself getting involved in toxic relationships, which had caused his personal life to spiral out of control.

Even though my situation was not the same as Dean Hutton's, I could relate to his story.

I was still thinking about alternative ways to tell the story of Marikana. Speaking to the journalists who had covered the story became an obvious angle.

I began a series of interviews, which I named *Between the Lines*, with the *Star Newspaper* journalist Poloko Tau, whose front-page story of the man in the green blanket became the iconic image of the *Marikana Massacre*. I wanted him to tell the story as it had happened from his perspective.

Poloko explained: "I was very shaken by the experience. I had been standing amongst the striking miners when the police opened fire on the men. The 16th of August began with a press conference hosted by the *South African Police Service - SAPS*, *Lonmin* representatives, and the *North-West Provincial Commissioner*. The commissioner emphasised that the strike was going to end on that very day. At the press conference, the authorities also warned journalists to stay within the safety zone that was behind the fences separating the striking miners from the police. After the press conference, I went back to the *koppie* to join the miners who had gathered there. From the statements uttered at the press conference, it was obvious that the police were going to use force. They had brought in a large contingent of officers from five provinces, who had brought all the required tools to deal with large crowds, such as rubber bullets, stun grenades and water cannons. No one expected them to use live ammunition. The police also warned us not to go to the *koppie* where the miners had gathered. Despite the warnings, we persisted. We had spent days speaking to the miners, building trust. It was a risk, but readers needed to hear the worker's side of the story."

Poloko continued: "When the shooting started, I was busy tweeting. I assumed that the police were using rubber bullets; then, all of a sudden, there was dust everywhere. A lot of it blurred my vision within the enclosure. I couldn't see anything, but once the dust settled, I saw a number of people lying on the ground. That's when I spotted one of the workers I'd been speaking to earlier, the one wearing a green blanket. He was face down. He had been shot. Because everything had happened so quickly, I was confused. I went to one of my colleagues who had been photographing everything. There was the man in the green blanket, lying in a pool of blood, a bullet wound in his head. Thirty minutes went past and I noticed the man was not moving. In fact, none of the men I saw lying down were moving. I took it as confirmation that they had been killed. We were angry. One journalist started shouting at the cops, but he was a lone voice. The police were shouting and screaming profanities at us: *Voetsek you Journalists! Go Away*."

Poloko told me that although covering the story was strenuous for him, he had wanted to see it through to the very end. After the shootings, he went to the Eastern Cape where Mgcineni Noki - the man in the green blanket - was buried. Attending the funeral gave him a bit of closure.

Despite numerous suggestions from friends and family who advised him to seek counselling after the incident, Poloko didn't think he was ready for it. He was still dealing with the aftermath of the events in his own way. One of the side-effects included an inability to take a shower because as the water hit his face, it felt like bullets on his skin.

The more I pursued this storyline, the more it proved difficult to find more journalists who had been reporting on the day that *Marikana* happened, willing to speak. Some, like Dean Hutton, declined to speak to me; some needed to consult their bosses, while others were still on the story, as a result of which none of them could find the time for an interview.

Despite these difficulties, I decide that the idea of speaking to journalists who report on violent conflicts, is still a good angle. I contacted a former colleague, who was the Director of the *Institute for the Advancement of Journalism* (IAJ) at the time to ask him if journalists were fully prepared for what happened in Marikana.

Michael Schmidt is a passionate advocate for journalists to receive conflict reporting training which, according to him; is not given nearly enough in the industry. He began to reflect quite seriously on the impact that conflict reporting had had on his life after he had visited a friend and mentor in Cape Town who was suffering from an extreme case of *Post-Traumatic Stress Disorder* - PTSD. Not wanting to end up like his mentor, he had decided to seek counselling. During his reflections, he discovered that he'd seen more than a 1000 dead bodies in his career as a journalist, which was, according to him, much more than combat soldiers ever saw. He also found that he was exploding at times, and becoming irrationally violent. Realising that this was a problem, he had sought counselling, not only to deal with his own issues, but also to educate his colleagues whom he found had not had either conflict-reporting training or any kind of proper psychological debriefing after traumatic events.

Schmidt explained: "Seeing a dead body is one thing, but watching someone die in front of you is an extremely difficult thing to bear. When it happened to me, I was still a young reporter. I had been covering a motorbike accident, in which a woman had died at my feet. After the incident, I wrote a poem to try and exorcise the memory of it, but it continued to play on my mind quite significantly afterwards."

During the interview, I ask him to share significant moments in his conflict-reporting career that he could not forget. Michael shares two stories:

"The first happened after I'd been to the scene of a massacre to commemorate the *36 Year Civil War* in Guatemala, which took place between 1960 and 1996. A month later, while watching an underground film about death squads in that country, I suddenly started to smell human corpses all around me; it was a distinct nauseating scent which I will never forget."

Schmidt went on: "The second one involved reporting on the Hezbollah-Israeli war of 2006. You were also there, when we went down south to Saidon, fairly close to the front lines, to the funeral of a family that was being buried after having been killed the previous day at a funeral. This family was being buried in the same cemetery where they had been the previous day. It was a terrible *Kafkaesque* moment. As I stood in 37-degree heat, with sweat trickling down my neck, doing my best to remain respectful but also get the right shots of men in agony burying young children who were wrapped in winding sheets, I felt trapped. I couldn't leave. The Hezbollah security wouldn't allow anyone to go anywhere until the whole ceremony was over. While there, I heard the first drone overhead. I knew that somewhere in the frontline or in Tel Aviv there was someone, a youngster perhaps, with a joystick, who was deciding - much like a Roman Emperor - whether it was thumbs up or thumbs down. There was no escape, absolutely no escape. It was as if I was already in my grave. I felt stuck in this narrow little trench, with nowhere to go."

These two very different incidents were defining moments for him personally.

He stressed: "It is important for journalists to talk about the trauma with other people and to be explicit about experiencing it, so the public also knows what journalists go through to get them the news," he concluded.

The interview with Michael sends alarm bells ringing in my ears. I am numb. It leaves me feeling very uneasy, because I couldn't remember theis particular scene in Saidon that Michael described with such impeccable detail. At some point during the interview, I stopped listening to him and searched my mind's archives for something familiar - but I was completely blank. I couldn't remember standing at the gravesite, nor what happened after my colleague had given me the scarf to wear at the funeral.

Nothing.

The fact that I cannot retrieve this scene from my memory scares me.

The only thing I remember is walking into the home of one of the families who refused to leave Saidon. We waited outside their iron-wire-meshed gate and after numerous calls, a man appeared from the house and agreed to do an interview with us. He was with his wife, his brother, and two children. My TV colleague and I decided to split the interviews to save time. I spoke to his brother, who had been smoking the *hookah* outside the yard. As we are conducting the interviews, we start hearing drones above us. I looked back at my TV colleagues, who were still asking questions, while the children were playing around their parents. Then *Bang!* The first bomb went down. The man with the *hookah* pipe said: "Don't afraid, don't afraid," holding my arm. *Bang! Bang!* A few more strikes. Eventually, the man of the house tells his children to go into the bunker. Since the man I was speaking to seemed calm, I thought I'd continue the interview for as long as he was comfortable, in a valiant effort to demonstrate a lack of fear - even though I was panicking internally.

Bang! Bang! Eventually, my interviewee pulls me into the family's bunker, where we all sit and wait, while listening to more airstrikes raining down outside. After the airstrikes subside, we continued with the interviews outside, since it was too loud to continue while the shelling took place inside the bunker. The family tells us that they are used to such a life. Every day, in the afternoons, they have to go into a bunker and wait out the bombings, but they won't leave their home because of war.

They would rather die defending it.

I know I was there at the refugee camp. But I don't remember. Getting interviews with journalists from other news agencies proves challenging. I decided to search internally for journalists within our newsroom who had experience with conflict reporting. Although PTSD is not the main subject of the series, I decide to pursue it nonetheless since it seems to be a recurring theme.

I asked my former assignment editor at SABC Radio News, Zola Ntutu who had been part of a team of journalists who reported on the *Truth and Reconciliation Commission* - TRC hearings between 1996 and 1999 - for an interview. Zola had been mentioned briefly in Antjie Krog's book, *Country of My Skull* published in 1998, which is a non-fiction account of the findings of the TRC. After having read her book, I wondered why the black journalists that she'd been working with had never written their own accounts of the TRC experience.

I had listened to Zola Ntutu's TRC reports. I ask if he had found any closure or healing after having covered those testimonies.

He had not.

This is what Zola Ntutu said: "You see, the problem with listening to gruesome testimonies, is that journalists become emotionally attached to them. There is nothing more painful than listening to a parent relaying a story of what happened to their children, or how their children were killed. While hearing someone weep makes for good radio sound effects, journalists are often not aware that replaying those soundbites or clips does actually inflict more pain on the person involved."

Zola had witnessed many cases of peers trying to erase images or information they had received in the course of their reporting. However, this technique of hiding was not helpful because no matter how much one tried to suppress it, at some stage all journalists that were involved in conflict-reporting would suffer from Post-Traumatic Stress Disorder. He explained that PTSD affects people in different ways: Some become delusional, some have difficulty sleeping, while others can be affected physically by overeating or eating less.

Zola admitted that because there were no: 'Do's and Don'ts kit' for journalists who covered conflict; it was difficult to help them to mitigate the impact of PTSD. He went on: "Many journalists return from conflict zones and request more stories, thinking that doing another story will erase the trauma from the previous one. This behaviour makes it extremely hard for editors to assess how individual journalists are coping..."

Slowly, the lights begin to come on in my mind like spotlights in a dark cinema. There was a name for it. Could I be suffering from PTSD too?

His words echoed in my mind.

No matter how much you try to suppress the effects of what you experienced at one stage, you will suffer from PTSD because there is one incident that will trigger everything.

Zola Ntutu, known by fellow journalists as "The General", had been my editor since I'd joined the SABC Johannesburg newsroom in 2002. We met during the *United Nations World Racism Conference* in Durban in 2001. I had been taken to his hotel room by Phil Molefe, who was the head of the *SABC Africa Channel* at the time. I often hovered around the *SABC Africa Channel* studios and desks, watching its two anchors, Lerato Mbele and Xolani Gwala, prepare for their shows. Phil Molefe used to periodically come in to check on them and that's when he saw me and invited me for a walk through the park, which ended up in the hotel room where he introduced me to a room full of SABC Radio news editors and journalists.

While I was intrigued by the world of journalism, I was also equally intimidated by its practitioners who seemed to be rather brash, harsh, and completely blunt with just about everything and everyone.

A born-again Christian at the time, I didn't quite know how to relate to this calibre of people who were drinking and smoking freely, while having loud debates about everything, especially politics and the latest American power tactics, while throwing profanities at each other - words like 'shit' and 'fuck' - as if they were sacrificial offerings to God.

It was a different world to mine. This world resembled the one that I read about in my journalism class. Even though we were in a hotel room in a 5-Star Hotel, it felt like I had entered into a scene from the *Drum Magazine* era of the 1950s in South Africa. The hotel room became '*a shebeen in Sophiatown*'. I imagined myself as a narrator, like *Drum* journalist Nat Nakasa who observed colleagues, artists, hustlers, writers and friends as they drank their blues away. I wanted to be a part of the chaos.

In my journalism class, I was surprised at how easily my classmates decided to nickname me "*Nat Nakasa*". Although, I was initially offended by the nickname - because it was meant to mock me - I accepted it. So what? The real-life tragedy, though, was that Nat Nakasa ultimately killed himself in New York, while on a journalism fellowship at *Harvard University*.

My classmates' belief that I had an 'identity crisis' as a black person was nothing new. It had been the bane of my existence throughout my school career. Even though only 30% of the latter part of my school education had been in mixed-race or former Model C schools, while 70% of my schooling had been in black township schools, it did nothing to change their perceptions of me.

It was normal for me to over hear black friends speak of me in disparaging ways or allude to the fact that I either didn't belong, or that I was a black person trying to be white; or a black person who looked down on others by attempting to make herself better by speaking English: *uzenza ngcono* they'd whisper. *Who do you think you are?*

The thought processes that those who accused me of being a '*sell-out*', a coconut, intrigued me. Was speaking good English an attempt to be white? Was interacting with people of different races evidence that I hated black people?

Personally, I understood myself to be a black person in every way possible. There was no distinction, in my mind, between black people who were considered coconuts (white on the inside and black on the outside) or black people who were *black*. We were all black. Only black people could evolve into '*coconuts*'; their personal and political aspirations did not change this fundamental fact.

Finally, even the derogatory words used to belittle me only served to reinforce my blackness. Race, however interesting a subject, did not fascinate me as much as people assumed. I reached out to people who were different from me in race, cultural backgrounds, or religion because I was fascinated by the *difference*.

I saw an opportunity to learn more, and expand my knowledge beyond my own cultural background and racial proclivities. Meeting people from different countries and cultures was another way for me to travel. I got to live in different worlds from mine, without spending a cent. I was not confused about my blackness.

The next time I saw The General - Zola Ntutu - was when I started to work in the SABC Johannesburg newsroom a year later. One day, reporting for work on my afternoon shift, I noticed him lying on the floor under his work desk sleeping. I was concerned by this because I thought he was sick. When I asked what was wrong with him, people said: "Ah! That's just Zola."

Back then, I didn't know what being hung-over was because I did not drink alcohol or hang out with people who did. I was intrigued by him. Despite his notoriety, Zola Ntutu was well-respected by many journalists in the newsroom. He was certainly not a pushover and could debate anyone on any subject, or defend journalists and their stories. Moreover, he was not plagued by the fear of authority as I was, a trait I admired most about him. He was irreverent. If I aimed to please, Zola aimed to piss people off or to simply speak his mind which would then piss people off. Whenever we were both on duty, he'd call me into his office without fail while editing my work. He would ask what I meant by this sentence or that word or what I was actually trying to say: "But Jedi, your story doesn't make sense, this sentence is too long. What are you trying to say here? Just write this story again, I can't edit this."

I always looked forward to the day when he would check my script without asking me a long list of questions. This hardly ever happened. He challenged me. Even though he was a colleague, he was still an elder in my mind, someone who could ostensibly be my father, so I chose not to ask him about the personal details of his experience with PTSD, a question that most colleagues expected me to ask. I could not bring myself to probe any further.

At the *Racism Conference*, I also met journalist Angie Kapelianis. Angie and Zola Ntutu were in the same team of reporters working on the TRC reports. They both went on to collectively win several awards for their work. One day during the conference, Angie pulled me from my desk and asked: "What are you doing?" Since I was not assigned to any story at the time, she said, "Come with me. I have a story for you."

She sent me to the *NGO Forum*, which was populated by approximately 8,000 people representing non-governmental organisations from all over the world. Everyone who was there represented world groups who were oppressed, ostracised, alienated and segregated or people whose Human Rights were being violated. There were academics, social scientists, anthropologists, lawyers, advocates, human rights activists, researchers, traditional healers, indigenous queens, and kings, all there campaigning against a myriad of human rights abuses.

My job was to find compelling, sound-rich stories in the midst of it all.

It was a dizzying experience. There was so much diversity, so many interesting people to speak to, I didn't know where to look or how to start.

Until then, I had not realised the infinite nature of people's problems. Each person at the *Racism Conference* represented a particular problem which affected millions of people in the world.

The *World Conference Against Racism*, including the *NGO Forum*, ended in discord, with the main world power brokers - the United States of America and Israel walking out of discussions due to disagreement on the language used which equated Zionism with apartheid racism.

Journalist Rachel Swarms wrote in the New York Times at the time that, "Secretary Powell said negotiators here had failed to persuade Arab delegates to remove criticism of Israel from proposed conference documents that assail "the racist practices of Zionism" and describe Israel's treatment of Palestinians as a "new kind of apartheid." Questions about whether Israel should be condemned for its treatment of Palestinians and whether the West should pay reparations for slavery and colonialism have roiled conference preparations for months. Washington has said repeatedly that it would not consider language that criticized Israel or legitimized reparations for descendants of slaves."

Overall, the outcomes of the conference were eclipsed eight days later by the September 11 terrorist attacks at the *World Trade Centre* in the United States, which killed a recorded 2,977 people.

Angie Kapelianis took me under her wing at the *Racism Conference*. We developed a mentor-mentee relationship. I enjoyed sneaking into the *SABC Archives* to listen to some of her radio feature stories for inspiration.

I was blown away by her use of sound, writing and her storytelling abilities. Her radio features took me to places I had never been before - from sitting in the middle of traders selling fruit in Bali to inside the memorial service of Beyers Naudé's funeral, watching his wife and daughter holding each other's hands as black voices sang hymns. I admired and respected Angie, both as a person and a professional. When I moved to Johannesburg she donated her old mattress to me after I moved into my own place for the first time. I also visited her at her home once and noticed that she had a basket full of crocheted squares.

"You crochet?" I asked, thinking that she was so full of surprises.

"Yes, sometimes when I'm stressed, I just make these squares. They help me relax and not think too much about things. You should probably have something too, an extramural activity that you do to de-stress."

I nodded my head in agreement, but without understanding.

"What are you going to do with these?" I continued with my inquisition.

"I'll probably make a blanket out of them, or my mom will," she said laughing. "I don't know. I think the point is to make them; what happens afterwards is not so important."

I felt nervous looking at the squares; they reminded me of my primary school home economics class where we were taught to knit, crochet, and sew. My home-economics teacher Mrs. Mbatha was very strict, much like Angie, and emphasised cleanliness. My hands were always sweaty from nervousness and general clumsiness. I always feared being punished because I felt I couldn't get anything right. Either I had lost my pins, didn't have enough wool, forgot my needlework at home or my work was dirty, skew, or wrong. I was always stressed out as a child, but I was also good at hiding and deflecting.

When I spoke to Angie about the effect that conflict reporting had had on her life, I remembered those multi-coloured crocheted squares that I had easily dismissed many years ago. Until this interview, I had always perceived her as someone who was strong, bold, and direct. I never once recognised that she, like me, could be vulnerable too.

Angie said, continuing her explanation: "What I find difficult - and it doesn't matter that I've done this for many years - is when somebody has passed away and I have to phone the family and confirm a death. I have to muster up the courage to do that. Two incidents I will never forget come to mind: I was in the thick of things with colleagues, when the *Shell House Massacre* on 28th March 1994 happened. We'd had a very traumatic day, right from the start at the hostels with the IFP march and all the way to downtown Johannesburg, where we literally stumbled on eight dead bodies outside the old ANC's headquarters. I was at the corner of De Villiers Street and King George, near the ANC office in Plein Street, where there'd been a blood bath and several bodies were scattered all over the place... I was shaking. I don't think I'd ever had a day like that before. Much later, when I was covering the *Truth Commission*, we were having a session with a psychologist for the TRC staff. The psychologist asked everyone to just stop and very quickly draw a traumatic incident. Without realising it, I drew eight stick men. Two years later, I realised that I had never dealt with the trauma and the experience of witnessing and having to report on the *Shell House Massacre* when downtown Johannesburg had been turned into a frenzy, with bullets going off, ricocheting off the skyscrapers, not knowing where those shots were coming from but having to report on it and then just carry on as usual the next day. It made me realise the fragility of who we are as human beings and journalists."

Angie went on: "Secondly, in 2004, on the 14th of August, I lost my dad to leukaemia. It really turned my world upside down, especially because I am the eldest child and the only girl in my family. Parallel to my story was the fact that the anti-apartheid activist Beyers Naudé was not well. When I phoned Oom Bey's older son Johann, I said to him: "I need to tell you that I have actually just lost my father. This has hit me in a very big way but, at the same time, I have been asked to cover the death of your father." In many ways I say the death of Beyers Naude was a blessing to me, because it brought me out of my shell. I didn't want to face the world again after experiencing such a loss, but I went to the memorial service. As I was walking around with my microphone interviewing people, the tears were running down my cheeks. People would give me hugs. They thought I was strange, but I don't think it mattered to me, though it might have disarmed them. I was just dealing with my emotions to the best of my ability. Life is quite strange in those instances where the personal mixes with the professional and it's often very hard to separate the two. I think that, as journalists, we are told to put our emotions aside, that we must be really strong and have a spine of steel. In reality, it doesn't quite work out like that. I think the first thing is to speak about it, to let the others, especially the younger journalists, know that it is okay."

The interviews opened up a new vista for me. I had no conception or understanding of trauma or how it manifests itself. Until then, I had assumed that if I was able to get through difficult assignments, death, shoot-outs, war and suffering without breaking down at the scene, then that would be the end of it. I did not imagine there being any residual effects after the story happened. I had never considered the possibility that these traumatic events, which happened by and large to other people, who were ostensibly the subjects of my reports, could affect me negatively. The two things never mixed in my mind because, as I understood it, only those who were directly affected by tragedy could claim to suffer trauma, not witnesses.

Around the same time, as I am producing Between The Lines, internationally-acclaimed photojournalist Alf Khumalo passes away. I feel compelled to attend his memorial service, even though we hadn't been particularly close. I had seen him several times while on Nelson Mandela assignments, either at the *Nelson Mandela Children's Foundation* in Rosebank or the *Nelson Mandela Foundation* in Houghton. I respected him and his work and, even though I was not a photojournalist per se, I admired him.

At the memorial service, I met the two remaining members of the famed *Bang-Bang Club*, a group of photojournalists who had documented violence in black townships of South Africa during the apartheid period, particularly between 1990 and 1994, and who had co-authored a book about their experiences. Greg Marinovich was sitting with his wife Leona, and João Silva looked at ease there. I asked him how he was doing.

"Pretty good," he said. Then he proceeded to explain in great detail all the operations and medical procedures he'd had and those he was still meant to have.

João Silva had lost his left leg below the knee, and his right leg from just above after stepping on a mine while on assignment in Afghanistan in 2010. I remember being utterly distraught by the news of his injury. I had spent almost an entire day interviewing him and Greg Marinovich about their lives being turned into a movie based on the book they had written. I conducted the interview with the two of them and the main actor in the film, American Ryan Phillipe, during the filming of the movie in the artsy suburb of Melville, in Johannesburg. I remembered specifically asking João, who had been working for the *New York Times* and various international media organisations at the time, why he kept going back to war zones after having reported on so much conflict in his life.

"Don't you think it is enough? What about your wife and children?"

His answer was pretty definitive: "I love it. I can't stop."

Now the job that he loved so much had cost him his legs, yet he was still very hopeful, saying: "I can't wait to go back!"

I couldn't believe it. I looked at Greg and he shrugged his shoulders the same way he had done when we'd stood under a tree during my interview with them all those years ago.

Now, I fully understood him. On assignment is where João came alive. That's why he had to keep doing it again and again. It was the only environment where he felt completely alive.

Parallel to his story, I also met up with the Bureau Chief of an international news organisation that had offices in Johannesburg. We had met through mutual friends and had developed a good friendship.

A few years earlier, she had invited me for dinner at her house for an intervention. She told me that I was drinking too much and she feared that this could affect my future prospects as a journalist.

This time, when we met, I had stopped drinking, but she was not well. She had taken ill. What had started off as a dizzy spell had ended up becoming a problem that the best doctors in Europe and South Africa had been unable to identify. She kept falling, and at times became motionless, unable to move a muscle in her body. She went through countless MRI scans, tests, and more tests. The doctors couldn't figure out what was wrong with her. I listened to her recounting the details of her medical procedures until it dawned on me that maybe she could be suffering from Post-Traumatic Stress Disorder.

"Have you thought about what you went through?" I asked her.

"What do you mean?" she asked.

"Have you thought about what you went through during your time in Croatia, Kosovo, Afghanistan, Lebanon and those places? Don't you think that maybe your condition is related to…?"

"No. No. No," she interrupted, shaking her head vehemently from side to side. "No!" she said emphatically.

"You don't want to go there?"

"No!" she said; and that was the end of the conversation.

I began to realise that maybe admitting to having psychological trauma as a direct result of your work, was more debilitating than never having the use of your legs. It was, in a way, career suicide.

João Silva intimated as much in a speech he gave at the *Bronx Documentary Centre* on 2nd August 2011, a year before Bra Alf Khumalo's memorial service. His words: *"I'm going to go back to photography, without a doubt. I'll continue working for The New York Times. It's just a matter of time. If I can go back to combat, I will. If I can go back to war zones to cover what I like doing, I most certainly will. There's no doubt in my mind. Mentally, I've always been strong. I was pragmatic from the get-go. I got injured. I've seen it happen to people around me, so it's okay. My number came up. Bad numbers come up, so now we move on, you know? I'm hopeful..."*

I realised that I was asking too much of my fellow journalists.

PTSD was very serious and extremely personal. It was not something people could easily admit to, let alone speak about. I was still trying to wrap my head around it. I was still unable to fully connect the dots, or to even admit to myself that this new information I had received was true.

After six episodes of the *Between the Lines* series, the senior editor let me know that if I wanted to continue with the interviews, I had to write a proposal that would have to be approved by the Executive Producers. They didn't want to hear, on air, something they had not listened to before.

With the series canned, I decided to reach out to a publisher to ask if they would be interested in publishing an anthology of Post Traumatic-Stress Disorder stories from South African journalists. The publisher asked: Who is the audience? How many people are you targeting? How much money is it going to make?

I had no answers to any of her questions.

"Call me back when you've done your homework," she said.

While I understood where she was coming from, her response still stung.

I put the phone down and bit my lip. *There must be something I can do to take the story further. But what?*

One day, as I am visiting my brother, I start to read out loud a passage from a short story book I've been carrying around with me. An anthology of works by South African born, author and activist Bessie Head. The stories, published posthumously, are called *Tales of Tenderness and Power,* published in 1989. The short story I am reading to him is called *The Dreamer and Storyteller.* As I read on, my brother suggests that we record it.

I agree enthusiastically. I read the story again, as if I am reading a news bulletin. After the recording, my brother adds some background music to my voice and suddenly the story comes alive. I fall in love with Bessie Head's writing. I find myself thinking how much of a genius she is, not only because she uses such resplendent imagery in her prose, but also because what she's written resonates with me in a powerful way.

Even in her time, nobody welcomed the dreamers or storytellers. One night, failing to sleep, I get out of bed and start writing. At first, I am not sure what I am writing, but it turns out to be a radio-script.

The script is a combination of facts about my life and facts about news and current affairs events of the time, woven together to create a fictional story. I title it: - *Lindiwe: A tale of a missing storyteller.* Lindiwe, in this play, represents both journalists and the public, ordinary South Africans whose voices are largely missing in the news and political discussions, with particular reference to *Marikana*.

When I approach an actor or actress with the play, they tell me that it is my story to tell and therefore I should be the one to act in it. I think they are being ridiculous. Even though I had longed to act in the past, when no opportunities to do so ever came up, I gave up on that dream. It was a closed door and I was content to never open.

I reach out to a French filmmaker I know, who runs community film and acting workshops with young people in Kliptown, Soweto. She has confessed during one of her film-screening events that local professionals are unwilling to take part in community projects without pay. I make her an offer to

collaborate: to have her children practice their acting skills using my script, which she can then record and make into a film.
I invite her for lunch and over bites of food she tells me the same thing.
"I think you should do it yourself," she says, "especially since you don't have a budget to pay the actors, or even provide food and transport."
Left with no other option, other than to wait for better days when I may have the money to hire professional actors, I decide to take on the roles myself. I scout around for places that can offer a performance space for free.
I have been frequenting *The African Freedom Station* - a gallery and Jazz music space in the suburb of Westdene, west of Johannesburg. I know the filmmaker, Bra Steve Mokwena, who owns and runs the venue. We had tried to form a collective with like-minded people a few years earlier, without much notable success. He allows me to use his space. After we confirm the date and time, I begin to rehearse everyday like a maniac. I direct all my energy towards my acting.

I reserve and manifest all my nerves, anxiety, frustration, anger, and everything I haven't been able to express, for all the seven characters that I will portray in the play. I use my own clothes as costumes, and newspaper headlines that I pull off from street poles on my walks back from work as set dressing. God will take care of the rest, I say. I am very concerned about remembering my lines because, given that it's a play, there is no second take. I can't afford to lose my focus.

I have to become one with my characters, the dialogue, and the story, so that everything is natural and unforced. I invite all my friends and colleagues to come and watch my solo performance. After 30 minutes, one evening in November 2012, it is all over. I have no pictures or records of the event. I think my friends, who came out in support, clap for me out of sheer solidarity. The silence that comes over me after that is too loud. Since, I have no record of it, I don't know if the play is good or bad, mediocre, average, or forgettable. My friends say I did well. My family praises me, but I am not sure about what took place that night or what to make of it. All I know is that I did something and the room fell silent. Why was there so much silence?

I go back to work a day later, feeling emptier than before. It seems as if everything I try to do is in vain. Towards the end of my work contract with

SABC's *Midday Live*, the Executive Producer of the show calls me into her office and offers me an extension of my terms. While she speaks, I can't block out her face in the editing booth:

Did I imagine the 'delete the Marikana widows' booth incident? Were you not in the booth with me, telling me to cut parts of the story out? My mind races over her moving lips, and time slows down.

"You have the right of first refusal," she says, bringing me back in time.

"What is that?" I ask.

She explains what it is, then says with surprise: "Oh, I thought you were one of us, a fellow exile?"

"No, I'm not," I tell her. "I have lived in South Africa all my life."

"Well?" she asks. "What's your answer?"

"I will exercise my right and decline the offer… but thank you," I say.

When the contract with SABC ends, I pack my suitcases, board a plane and jump out of the country… hoping that one day a net will appear.

EPILOGUE

Since the writing of this book, the SABC made headlines in 2016 after eight of its journalists dissented against censorship at the broadcaster. This was following a directive from then Chief Operations Officer, Hlaudi Motswaneng, banning the broadcast of service delivery protests across all SABC News channels, claiming that the broadcasts would invoke more violence and encourage other disaffected youth to do the same.

The protests against censorship led to the intimidation and harassment of the journalists. Threats which ultimately led to the death of one of the 'SABC 8' as the group became known. *Radio Sonder Grense* (RSG) Journalist Suna Venter, died from *"broken-heart syndrome"*, a heart condition caused by excessive stress. The Executive Producer of the current affairs programme RSG, Foeta Krige, who was one of the SABC 8, subsequently published a book with the same name, detailing the events that took place behind the scenes during that time. Zola Ntutu, veteran journalist and radio news assignment editor also passed on, a year later in 2017. He died alone in his flat in Kenilworth north of Johannesburg. He was 51 years old.

In his 2003 book, *Dangerous Lives: War and The Men and Women Who Report It*, Dr Anthony Feinstein, Professor of Psychiatry at the University of Toronto, conducted a study with close on 200 war or conflict reporters from around the world, and explained that Post-Traumatic Stress Disorder has a myriad of symptoms which include:

- *Intrusion symptoms* - which are recurrent and involuntary distressing images, including thoughts, dreams, and flashbacks of the traumatic event.
- *Arousal symptoms* - which include difficulty with sleep, anger control, concentration, heightened emotions, and hyper-vigilance.
- *Avoidance symptoms* - which is a tendency to ward off thoughts and/or conversations associated with the trauma, including feelings of detachment or estrangement from others, and an inability to recall important aspects of the trauma.
- *Conversion disorder* - which is rerouting emotional distress into physical ailments or the unconscious process of converting emotional dysfunction into neurological abnormalities causing as

examples - inability to speak, move one's limbs or to experience sensations such as pain.

However, despite the numerous psychological injuries they suffered, he found that very few of his respondents were willing to connect their symptoms to their work, with one respondent stating: *"There is an unspoken view within the profession that you either cut it or you get out - there are no half-measures. Reporting on war is all about the right stuff; sure, we know that we drink too much and at times our emotions are all screwed up, but that comes with the turf. If you find that hard to deal with, there is always the royal family to follow or a Wimbledon to report on..."* What makes Post-Traumatic-Stress Disorder hard to detect or treat among journalists is the fact that everyone is different, and has a different set of unconscious value structures which direct the content of their perceptions, morality, and ethics. In the spectrum of human psychology, there is an emotional core that produces a whole range of associated ideas, which is called a *complex*. It has a life of its own or a micro-personality. This core often has a negative tinge such as anger or resentment, because negative-tinged emotions are still problems and they will emerge automatically as the human body's threat-detection system forces these emotions into the consciousness, causing what we generally refer to as *triggers*.

After my second attempt at suicide, the SABC offered me free counselling services which I skipped after two sessions because the councillor was asking about my grandmother and my family which I wasn't ready to talk about. There was no time for a diagnosis or any reference made about my work being part of my emotional distress. Between 2008 and 9 I saw a life coach who was also trained as a psychologist. I stopped seeing her when she brought my mother up as a subject of discussion.

The book I started writing in 2011 was not about trauma even though it was because of it that I found myself with no other option but to write. The quick successive deaths of my uncle and my grandmother Mamani within three months of each other in 2006/7 were the events which triggered my trauma. It was only in the process of writing this book, that it also became clearer to me what my trip to Senegal represented. Senegal was a trigger point for me. Because of its similarity in culture and language to Lebanon. While I was in Senegal physically, my mind was back in Beirut. Being there brought-up all the trauma I had experienced private and professional life. This further heightened my already aroused state, including symptoms of intrusion that went far into events in my childhood and private life, which were not at all connected to my work in journalism. In the past ten years or more, I have seen episodic manifestations of all the above symptoms of PTSD in my own life; and in the stories of my interlocutors; that I never connected to my line of work, until much later. Some of these symptoms still persist.

In my case, it was not until I took some time to pay attention to my own psychological patterns of behaviour that I was able to recognise some links and traumatic incidents, some of which, particularly with regard to Lebanon, I still don't have full recollection of.

However, I was not aware of the link between my work and the emotional turmoil in my private life until they were made explicit through conversations with other journalists.

While numerous international studies published on *the impact of trauma on journalists* have found that journalists are largely a resilient group, and apart from only a handful of extreme cases in which journalists are either killed or become dysfunctional alcoholics or drug addicts, they are no more affected than ordinary citizens reading some of their reports.

It has been my own experience, including that of many other journalists that I have worked with at the SABC and more recently in Juba, South Sudan, that Post-Traumatic-Stress Disorder is not as inconsequential as some of these studies would have us believe. PTSD remains a real, unattended challenge in African newsrooms and society in general. Not only is it imperative for journalists entering the field to be made aware of it, and its symptoms, which can lie dormant until much later in life when they are triggered by seemingly unrelated events, it is also a moral duty for media agencies and organisations who employ them to not only provide support and training, but to be explicit about the sometimes fatal, consequences of PTSD. Not only will a flak jacket and a helmet not protect journalists against psychological bullets; but PTSD is a guaranteed award for courageous reporting of war, conflict, and violence. *When* it will manifest itself, however, is just a matter of time.

Jedi Ramalapa
2021

ABOUT THE AUTHOR

Jedi Ramalapa's experience and knowledge is rooted in Broadcast Journalism. She began her career as a Radio and Television reporter at the South African Broadcasting Corporation (SABC) in 2001 where she assumed several roles including being a radio journalist, news anchor for radio news bulletin on SAfm and Radio 2000, a current affairs producer, voice-over artist and producer for SABC's flagship investigative program Special Assignment. During her tenure at the SABC, she was sent on a number of international assignments to cover the opening up of China's Economy (2006), the war in Lebanon (2006), and the ratification of the Kyoto Protocol in Canada (2005) among others. In 2009, she joined Inter-press News Service as a Multimedia editor, responsible for creating the agency's african radio podcasts platform. She is also the recipient of the United Nations Reham Al-Farra Memorial Journalism Fellowship (2008). Recently she worked in South Sudan as a Media Trainer for Canada's largest international media development organization; Journalists for Human Rights (JHR). She is currently editor in chief of Sound Africa, a non-profit, non-fiction audio documentary organization with a mission to produce African stories which advance social justice and amplify the voices of everyday people.

www.ingramcontent.com/pod-product-compliance
Lightning Source LLC
Chambersburg PA
CBHW060352110426
42743CB00036B/2816

Praise for Loving Hard

"Anyone who has felt the agony of desire will discover a piece of their heart in this collection. The author throws back the sheets to expose the naked essence, with all its beautiful flaws, of love, loss and longing. So, kick off your shoes, toss that bra on the floor, pour a glass of wine and embrace the journey that waits for you. Don't forget the chocolates."

Lania Rocha, Staff Writer
VIEW Newspaper Group

"Finally, someone else feels what I have felt in relationships and put it into words! The illustrations only enhance the power of the word. This book has become my favorite birthday gift for all my sisterhood of girlfriends."

Elaine Gorbut-Lemiere
Housewife and Mother

"The only thing better than this book would be hearing it in the author's voice. Can't wait for the audio to come out.
Splendid!! Heart touching!! Two thumbs up!!"

Stephanie K., Morning Drive Host
CK105.5

"From author to author-Congrats! Wordsmithing at its best. You bring tears to my eyes with your story of love and loss. Your insight into police officers is astounding. Well done!"

Steve LeBel
Award-winning Author